AF361355

QUESTIONING THE CHINESE MODEL

Oppositional Political Novels in Early Twenty-First Century China

Questioning the Chinese Model

Oppositional Political Novels in Early Twenty-First Century China

ZHANSUI YU

UNIVERSITY OF TORONTO PRESS
Toronto Buffalo London

ISBN 978-1-4875-4434-8 (cloth)   ISBN 978-1-4875-4436-2 (EPUB)
                                   ISBN 978-1-4875-4437-9 (PDF)

Library and Archives Canada Cataloguing in Publication

Title: Questioning the Chinese model : oppositional political novels in
    early twenty-first century China / Zhansui Yu.
Names: Yu, Zhansui, author.
Description: Includes bibliographical references and index.
Identifiers: Canadiana (print) 2022026693X | Canadiana (ebook) 20220266999 |
    ISBN 9781487544348 (cloth) | ISBN 9781487544362 (EPUB) |
    ISBN 9781487544379 (PDF)
Subjects: LCSH: Chinese fiction – 21st century – History and criticism. |
    LCSH: Political fiction, Chinese – History and criticism. |
    LCSH: Opposition (Political science) in literature. |
    LCSH: Politics and literature – China.
Classification: LCC PL2443 .Y9 2023 | DDC 895.1/35209358 – dc23

We wish to acknowledge the land on which the University of Toronto Press operates. This land is the traditional territory of the Wendat, the Anishnaabeg, the Haudenosaunee, the Métis, and the Mississaugas of the Credit First Nation.

This book has been published with the assistance of a grant from Nazareth College.

University of Toronto Press acknowledges the financial support of the Government of Canada, the Canada Council for the Arts, and the Ontario Arts Council, an agency of the Government of Ontario, for its publishing activities.

**Canada Council   Conseil des Arts
for the Arts   du Canada**

**Funded by the   Financé par le
Government   gouvernement
of Canada   du Canada**

Contents

Acknowledgments

It has been a long journey, since I started the project a decade ago. In the process, I have received inspiration, support, and help from many people, to whom I feel deeply indebted. First, I would like to express my heartfelt thanks to Jeffrey Kinkley for reading the entire manuscript and providing many invaluable comments and suggestions, which helped elevate the quality of the book enormously. Thanks also go to Richard King (University of Victoria, Canada), who also read the entire manuscript and offered many insightful comments and suggestions, from which I benefited greatly. I am grateful to my two advisors and mentors at UBC, Michael S. Duke and Timothy Cheek, who read part of the manuscript and helped me tremendously with their highly inspiring comments and advice. Andrew E. Clark (Ragged Banner Press) also read part of the manuscript and provided valuable opinions, and my thanks go to him too. I would also like to thank Jeffrey Wasserstrom for publishing a previous version of the chapter on *The Fat Years* on the website of *The China Beat* (23 August 2010). I am also indebted to Ban Wang for his support and help during the past few years.

I thank our provost at Nazareth College, Dr. Andrea Talentino, and our dean of the Division of Liberal Arts and Sciences in the College of Arts and Sciences, Dr. Thomas Lappas, for their support of the publication of the book. I thank Nazareth College for awarding me grants for this book. I would also like to thank my students at Nazareth College, whose views and arguments expressed in class discussions and essays have inspired me in many ways.

I am especially indebted to my colleague Harry Murray, a distinguished professor of sociology, who edited the entire manuscript for me and whose expertise, insight, and wisdom helped improve both the style and content of the book tremendously. The generosity, kindness, and collegial support from Harry endow the book with special meaning. My thanks, of course, go to my editors at UTP, Mark Thompson and Carolyn Zapf, who showed their expertise, judgment, and high degree of professionalism in every step of the publication process of my book. I also thank the two readers at UTP for their highly insightful comments and suggestions, which helped improve the book greatly.

I would like to thank my parents and brothers for their unfailing care, support, and love during all these years. My deep thanks and love go to my wife and my son. The many heated debates on literature, arts, and social issues between my son and me have continuously refreshed my mind, preventing my thought from being outmoded. My wife has always been a driving force for my academic pursuits, for which I feel grateful and fortunate.

QUESTIONING THE CHINESE MODEL

Rise of Oppositional Chinese Political Novels

The emergence of a cluster of fictional works, which might be collectively dubbed "oppositional political novels," is a conspicuous phenomenon in the otherwise rather quiet Chinese literary world of the early twenty-first century. These works can be considered "political novels" because all of them take political articulation as their major purpose. According to Irving Howe, a political novel is "a novel in which political ideas play a dominant role or in which the political milieu is the dominant setting."[1] They are "oppositional" because all of them question the fundamental principles and intrinsic logic of the Chinese model in certain ways. Radically differing from previous political fiction in the post-Mao era, as exemplified by anticorruption fiction (*fanfu xiaoshuo* 反腐小说) of the 1990s, which only targets specific flaws or symptoms of the Chinese one-Party system while affirming its fundamental principles, these oppositional political novels produced in the early twenty-first century transgress the "prohibited zones" prescribed by the Party, challenge the fundamental principles of the Chinese system, and question the morality and political legitimacy of the Chinese model, though they have to do so in highly subtle and artistic ways under strict censorship in the Chinese context.

Rooted in the soil of present-day Chinese politics and society, these novels and their reception reflect the political milieu, intellectual trends, and social ethos of early twenty-first century China. These novels display a discursive incisiveness and audacity rarely seen before in Chinese political fiction in probing contemporary Chinese politics and society. The insight expressed in these novels is especially thought-provoking and valuable today, given that the Chinese Party-state is making full use of its propaganda machine or its "soft power" to sell the Chinese model everywhere and that many people all over the world, not only Chinese, are avidly and blindly willing to buy it.

Based on close readings of five representative oppositional Chinese political novels, this book examines the sociopolitical connotations and epistemological values of these novels in the broad context of modern Chinese intellectual history and contemporary Chinese politics and society. Through the examination of these works, I attempt to create a sketch of the social, political, and intellectual landscape of present-day China and to investigate the dialectic relationship between art and politics in the Chinese context, the mechanisms and dynamics of censorship, self-censorship, and counter-censorship in the age of the internet and commercialization, and the ideological limitations of oppositional Chinese political novels.

This introductory chapter discusses the intrinsic dynamics and the external social and political milieu for the emergence of oppositional political novels in early twenty-first century China. It first provides a sketch of the development of Chinese political fiction in the twentieth century, and then moves on to explain how the increasingly intensified sense of social, political, and moral crisis of the Chinese people, the re-politicization of Chinese society, and the favourable external environment created by commercialization, globalization, and the spread of the internet in the early twenty-first century provided necessary conditions for the birth of oppositional political novels. The chapter also introduces the purposes, main themes, methodology, values, and structure of the book.

Chinese Political Fiction in the Twentieth Century

Jeffrey Kinkley and Catherine Vance Yeh, two accomplished pioneer researchers of Chinese political fiction, both conclude that the political novel emerged in China with the advent of the modern age. Whereas Kinkley traces the "roots" of the Chinese political novel to late Qing fiction of condemnation (*qianze xiaoshuo* 谴责小说),[2] Yeh's study of late Qing political novels in the context of the worldwide "migration" of the genre indicates that the political novel was introduced by Liang Qichao from Europe and Japan to China at the turn of the twentieth century and adapted to fit in with the Chinese sociopolitical reality and reflect the political agenda of the Chinese reformers.[3] Both scholars also emphasize that, although the political novel as a literary genre emerged in China quite late, there has been a long, strong, and influential tradition of socio-politically engaged literature in China,[4] which provides favourable soil for the birth of political fiction. Their argument proves highly convincing because obsession with history is arguably the most prominent feature of classic Chinese fiction,[5] which endows fiction with a political consciousness, as politics is an integral part and a crucial dimension of history.[6]

In her exhaustive and inspiring exploration of the emergence of the Chinese political novel in the late Qing, Catharine Vance Yeh identifies two factors – "sociopolitical crisis with its perception and a public sphere conducive to political articulation" – as the two "necessary conditions" for the birth of the political novel.[7] By the former, Yeh means that the political novel always emerges during a time when a nation faces a sociopolitical crisis and the entire society, especially the intellectuals, is seized by the sense of crisis and motivated by the idea of reform. By the latter, she means a favourable intellectual and media environment for the publication, distribution, and promotion of political novels. Yeh's perception that the political novel arises from sociopolitical crisis and the people's sense of the crisis is supported by Irving Howe's study of the political novel in the West. As Howe points out, the political novel always comes into being in a time when "the fate of society itself" becomes a question, and consequently the "profoundly problematic aspects" of society and "social contradictions" are a preoccupation of the people at that time.[8] In other words, Howe also insists that social instability and the consciousness of sociopolitical crisis are a necessary condition for the emergence of the political novel. Yeh's and Howe's insight into the origin of the political novel provides a useful perspective for the present research to elucidate the rise of oppositional political novels in early twenty-first century China.

Indeed, as Yeh's study convincingly demonstrates, the birth of the political novel in the late Qing is a synthetic result of the grave sociopolitical crisis at that time, a strong sense of crisis on the part of the intellectuals, a relaxing political environment, and a booming publishing industry due to the development of modern technology. The late Qing period marks the collapse of the over-two-thousand-year-long Chinese imperial system and the affiliated Confucian belief and value system.[9] During that period, ceaseless domestic uprisings and uninterrupted foreign invasions brought enormous, grave sociopolitical crises to the nation.[10] In the face of the unprecedented crises, people from all walks of life in the late Qing, though for different reasons, unanimously appealed to the political approach for national salvation. Whereas the Qing imperial court launched a wide range of institutional and political reforms, collectively dubbed the New Policy (*xinzheng* 新政),[11] in an attempt to overcome the crises and save its rule, the oppositional force regarded toppling the Qing dynasty as the sole solution to China's calamities. The late Qing intellectuals as represented by Yan Fu and Liang Qichao also took the pursuit of national wealth and power and modern governance in China as the ultimate goal for the nation.[12] Moreover, the dominant intellectual trends in the late Qing, such as social Darwinism,[13] anarchism,[14] and nationalism, were all more or less sociopolitically oriented. All these factors gave birth to a highly politicized mindset at that time,[15] which is quite understandable, given that politics, after all, is the quickest and most effective way to change the status quo of a country in the short term.

The birth of political fiction in the late Qing also benefited from the favourable intellectual and media environment at that time. As just mentioned, in the last few decades of its rule, the Qing imperial court was confronted with an unprecedented, all-round crisis caused by uninterrupted foreign invasions and domestic uprisings. As a consequence, its control over society and its suppression of rebellious thought had weakened tremendously. The large influx of modern Western ideas and values, brought to China by returned overseas students, foreign missionaries, and businessmen, became an unstoppable torrent beyond the Qing ruler's capacity to control. Moreover, with the emergence and development of modern consumer society and the rise and growth of the middle class in China, especially in the big cities, the late Qing witnessed a boom in the modern press and publishing industry.[16] The press boom not only made the circulation of ideas much easier and faster but also created a rapidly growing readership. All these factors formed a favourable soil for the birth of political fiction in the late Qing.

After enjoying prosperity for two decades in the late Qing period, Chinese political fiction gradually faded away when China entered the May Fourth era, and was replaced by May Fourth "enlightenment critical realism," characterized by a basically cultural-intellectualistic approach.[17] Whereas May Fourth literature inherited the critical stance of the late Qing fiction of condemnation, it levels criticism at the illness in traditional Chinese culture and the "Chinese national character" rather than at the incompetence and corruption of the government and politics. The sociopolitical reality of China after the downfall of the Qing dynasty made Chinese intellectuals realize that political change was far too short and superficial a means to transform China fundamentally and that a far more important and effective way for social reform was to change people's minds. This insight explains the shift in the Chinese intelligentsia from the politicized mode of thinking in the late Qing to the cultural-intellectual paradigm in the May Fourth era.[18]

Though the May Fourth literature ebbed in the mid-1920s, its legacy of critical realism and its cultural approach to social problems nevertheless did not come to end; instead, it has survived and developed into the most influential literary tradition in modern China, due mainly to the enormous effort and incomparable influence of Lu Xun, who has since become the most powerful icon of the May Fourth legacy. Not only did he inspire a "brood of imitators,"[19] but he also personally sponsored the literary works that inherit the May Fourth tradition.[20] Due to the profound influence of the May Fourth legacy and Lu Xun, the cultural-intellectual approach still maintained a strong hold in Chinese literary circles during the second half of the 1920s and the 1930s, which constituted an obstacle to the return of political fiction in China.

The Chinese literary landscape remained largely unchanged until the advent of Communist domination, first in Yan'an and later over all of mainland China. From a retrospective point of view, it should be no exaggeration to say that Mao's famous Yan'an talks on literature and art in 1942 completely changed the direction of Chinese literature.[21] Mao's theoretical formulation that literature must serve the people, the Party, and politics not only pushed the political dimension in literature to an extreme;[22] his demand that literature must affirm and eulogize the Communist cause and the Party, and the execution of Wang Shiwei and the persecution of other outspoken writers for their exposure of the corruption of the Communist leadership in Yan'an, declared the doom of the May Fourth–style critical realism.[23] In accordance with the Maoist formula, Chinese literature displayed a paradoxical character. On the one hand, because of literature's submission to politics, all literary works in Mao's China possessed a strong political consciousness. During the Cultural Revolution, almost all Chinese literary works were simply reduced to a kind of melodrama and allegory of class struggle. On the other hand, these politically charged Maoist literary works did not fall into the category of political fiction in a strict sense, because literature in the Maoist formulation was supposed to honestly reflect the social reality in Communist China, and the political overtone in literature simply mirrors the political nature of life and people's mentality. As such, they are social fiction rather than political fiction, at least in theory.

Following Mao's death, along with the adoption of the Dengist policy of reform and opening up, China witnessed the loosening of political control over literature and the gradual de-politicization of literature and society. As a consequence, Chinese literature in the 1980s, from scar literature (*shanghen wenxue* 伤痕文学),[24] root-seeking literature (*xungen wenxue* 寻根文学),[25] to Chinese avant-garde fiction,[26] moved further and further away from Communist ideology and the Maoist formulation of literature. For the purpose of the present study, neorealistic fiction (*xin xieshi xiaoshuo* 新写实小说), a literary genre that emerged in the late 1980s and flourished in the 1990s, which aims at a naturalistic picture of the grey life of ordinary people in contemporary China,[27] deserves special attention. Thematically, neorealistic fiction develops in two different directions. Whereas some writers like Chi Li and Fang Fang focus on the mundaneness and triviality of the life of petty urbanites,[28] Liu Zhenyun, the representative writer of fiction of officialdom (*guanchang xiaoshuo* 官场小说), depicts the mechanism of contemporary Chinese officialdom and the life and mentality of the lower- and middle-ranking officials with naturalistic accuracy and nuance. Liu Zhenyun's fiction of officialdom harbingers the anticorruption fiction of the late 1990s and early 2000s, a literary genre regarded as political fiction by Jeffrey Kinkley.[29]

The Chinese literary and intellectual landscape underwent a drastic and profound transformation in many aspects in the 1990s, mainly caused by the Tiananmen crackdown and the ensuing surge of commercialization and consumerism. One of the most conspicuous and significant changes is the retreat of avant-garde fiction and its underlying idealistic and utopian mode of thinking from the Chinese literary world and the return of the realistic paradigm to Chinese literature.[30] Chinese realism in the 1990s bifurcated and moved in two different directions. One trend is the popular tendency of "privatized writing" (*sirenhua xiezuo* 私人化写作), which can be regarded as a continuum of neorealism, focusing on the private realm of the individual. The other is realism as defined in the conventional sense, which is divided into two branches thematically. One strain might be dubbed "historical realism," represented mainly by those well-established writers of "serious" literature, aiming at realistic presentation of and critical reflection on Chinese history and society. The other strain might be dubbed "Party-sanctioned critical realism," mainly referring to anticorruption novels, a literary genre that emerged in 1995 and enjoyed high popularity in the second half of the 1990s and the first few years in the 2000s.[31] As indicated by its name, the anticorruption novel possesses a dual theme: exposing the rampant corruption of Chinese officials on the one hand and portraying how the upright Communist heroes fight and defeat the corruption under the Party's leadership on the other. Jeffrey Kinkley refers to them as political novels. One century after the emergence of the political novel and fiction of exposure in the late Qing, China once again witnessed the return of the political novel.

Like late Qing political fiction, the rise of anticorruption fiction in the late 1990s, as Jeffrey Kinkley's study demonstrates, is also a result of the combination of sociopolitical crisis and favourable environment for political articulation. By the late 1990s, the implementation of the Chinese-style market economy for nearly two decades not only brought an economic boom but also produced a wide range of serious problems, among which official corruption as a result of unchecked and unrestrained power was the gravest.[32] Corruption and other serious social problems once again made politics the focal point of people's attention. Parallel to the intensive political consciousness on the part of the Chinese people and the heavy political atmosphere in the nation is the relatively relaxed, tolerant, and free social environment in the second half of the 1990s, resulting from China's adoption of a market economy, the strengthening of reform in many social aspects since Deng's "tour of the south," and the individualization of Chinese society.[33] As renowned sociologist Yunxiang Yan argues, the decade of the 1990s "was the most liberal in China in terms of the phenomenal growth of the private sector, the retreat of the party-state from its previous control over social life, the replacement of the dominance of the Communist ideology by neoliberalism, and the re-structuration of life chances and mobility channels that set hundreds of millions of Chinese on the move."[34]

Despite the audacity of anticorruption fiction in exposing the corruption and darkness of Chinese officialdom, ideologically this kind of "Party-sanctioned critical realism" places stress on "anti" rather than on "corruption." The core message that anticorruption fiction conveys is that, however rampant and grave the corruption is, the Party has the ability, wisdom, and resources to control and defeat it. In other words, the gravity of corruption presented in anticorruption fiction mainly serves to highlight the greatness of the Party's leadership and ability. In fact, anticorruption fiction just criticizes some flaws in the Chinese officialdom; it is never intended to challenge the ideology and fundamental principles of the Chinese Party-state.[35] Serving as a vent for ordinary people to release their resentment and frustration with the system, "Party-sanctioned critical realism" works to consolidate the repressive system rather than to undermine it by filling people with illusory hopes and confidence in the Party-state.[36] This standpoint makes it an inheritor of the political rhetoric and mode of thinking of the highly politicized Maoist fiction but essentially different from both political fiction as defined in the Western context and late Qing fiction of condemnation.[37]

Sociopolitical Crisis and the Re-politicization of Society in the New Century

China did not witness drastic and fundamental changes in society and the intelligentsia after entering the new century, but some noticeable and meaningful new tendencies did emerge. One conspicuous phenomenon is the increasingly intensified consciousness of sociopolitical crisis among Chinese intellectuals and the general public. As discussed earlier, along with the further development of the Chinese model and the grave problems it brought about, politics since the mid-1990s once again returned to the centre of Chinese social life, becoming a focal point of people's attention. This tendency has not slowed down but rather has speeded up since the advent of the new century for various reasons.

First of all, in the early twenty-first century, after the implementation of the Chinese-style market economy coupled with political dictatorship for nearly three decades, the predatory nature of the Chinese model of development and its disastrous consequences had become even more conspicuous than in the 1990s.[38] This model, with pursuit of the gross domestic product (GDP) as its sole goal and its unsustainable mode of development, hijacked by varied interest groups and local governments, has not only produced perhaps the heaviest pollution in human history[39] but has also created within only three short decades probably the largest gap ever seen between rich and poor, between rural and urban areas, and among different regions. Due to the lack of democracy and freedom of speech, the corruption of the Chinese bureaucracy had reached an unbelievably crazy degree. The Chinese regime, however, intoxicated with the so-called Chinese economic "miracle," is growing more and more confident in the Chinese model; as a result, it has become increasingly unrestrained in violating human rights, trampling on universal human values, and suppressing the dissidents and people it regards as threats to its rule. Consequently, the confrontation and hostility between the regime and dissidents, and between officials and underprivileged people, have escalated drastically after the Tiananmen crackdown. Since the 1990s, each year a huge number of collective protests and social riots have broken out in China,[40] and consequently "maintaining stability" (*weiwen* 维稳) – a euphemism for "social control with state violence" in the Chinese Communist terminology – has become the paramount task for the Party-state.

Along with the sociopolitical crisis came the nationwide moral and spiritual crisis on every level of the society: the Party-state, the intelligentsia, and the general public alike.[41] As far as the Party-state is concerned, the June Fourth Massacre not only shattered the Party-state's former source of political legitimacy based on the Maoist claim of "people's sovereignty"; its cold-blooded suppression of unarmed people, as it "resorted to ruthless power without even a pretense of principle,"[42] also destroyed the Party-state's self-proclaimed moral superiority. As David Apter incisively points out, the Tiananmen Massacre is not only a political event but also a "moral moment" with tremendous symbolic implications.[43] In some sense, it can be said that the massacre completely destroyed the political and moral myth of the Communist Party and Communist rule in China, which had been painstakingly constructed by the state propaganda machine over the decades. The massacre created probably the gravest political and moral crisis for the Chinese Communist Party-state thus far. Chinese intellectuals, widely regarded as the social conscience in traditional Chinese society, who launched the "second enlightenment movement" in the 1980s, gave up their role as critics of power and spokesmen for the people after the Tiananmen crackdown. Terrified by the incredible cruelty displayed by the regime during the massacre, the overwhelming majority of Chinese intellectuals have been bought off by the regime under the Party's policy of carrot plus stick; many have even become mouthpieces for the Party and part of the oppressive dictatorship machine since the mid-1990s. The lure of material gains under the commercialization of society and the nationwide tide of hedonism only worked to push the moral degradation of Chinese intellectuals even further in the twenty-first century. Chinese society has also gone through a process of moral depravity and spiritual bankruptcy in the post-Mao era. After the death of Mao, with Maoist revolutionary ideology being replaced by Dengist economic determinism, the Party-state completely abandoned the Communist ideal of socioeconomic equality – though still paying lip service to it – and the Maoist voluntarist belief in the superiority of spiritual power over material pleasure;[44] instead, it quickly turned to vulgar materialism and stark utilitarianism. As a result, the whole nation has rapidly fallen into the abyss of sensuous revelry, money fetishism, and moral nihilism. This situation explains why in the post-Mao era so many extreme cases of moral violations and crimes have occurred in China. Even worse, the inculcation of extreme nationalism, education of castrated history, and brainwashing propaganda since the mid-1990s serve only to reinforce people's consciousness of political conformity, but fail to re-establish a strongly rationalized moral system in China after the death of Mao.

As a result and a manifestation of the increasingly intensified sense of social, political, and moral crisis prevailing over the entire nation, China has also witnessed a re-politicization of society after Tiananmen, though this process is obviously different from the one seen in the Mao era, not only in scope and magnitude but also in origin and expressive form. Whereas in the Mao era, the politicization of society was carried out in a way that politics and ideology predominated all other dimensions in society, in post-Mao China the process mainly takes the form of politicization of the economy. As mentioned earlier, after the bloodshed in Tiananmen Square shattered the former source of the Party-state's political legitimacy based on the Maoist claim of "people's sovereignty," the Party-state began to identify the economy as the new source of its political legitimacy. As such, in post-Mao China, economic growth is used by the Party-state not only to justify its dictatorial rule but also to reward the people's acquiescence to its rule.[45] Moreover, the enormous wealth accumulated through economic growth in the post-Mao era also provides the Party-state more material resources to co-opt the intellectuals, especially the elite members, into the system.[46] As a consequence, there has never been a historical period in the history of Communist China when the political significance of the economy is so pronounced as it is after Tiananmen. The shift in the interaction among the Party-state, the people, and the intellectuals – the transformation of the "political triangle" in China after Tiananmen – has created an intertwined and symbiotic relationship between politics and the economy, which largely accounts for the paradoxical parallel and coexistence of the all-round commercialization of society and its gradual re-politicization in twenty-first century China.

Along with the re-politicization of society after Tiananmen is the politicization of the Chinese intelligentsia since the 1990s onwards. When looking at the development of the Chinese intelligentsia, a fundamental difference can be seen between the 1980s and the 1990s and beyond: whereas the Chinese intelligentsia of the 1980s took a basically cultural and intellectual approach to the Chinese reality, its diagnosis of and solution to China's problems since the 1990s are essentially sociopolitically oriented. Unlike the Chinese intellectuals in the 1980s, who, following in their May Fourth forefathers' footsteps, targeted the supposed ills in traditional Chinese culture and attempted to rejuvenate the nation with modern Western values and ideas, Chinese intellectuals since the 1990s onwards have been preoccupied with contemporary Chinese politics and China's future. The highly politicized mindset of the Chinese intellectuals is explicitly demonstrated by the nature of the issues covered by the decade-long debate between liberals and the New Left – the two major contending intellectual groups separated along political and ideological lines – from the mid-1990s to the mid-2000s. Those issues, including the assessment of the Maoist legacy, the nature of the Chinese model, the causes of the Chinese sociopolitical crisis, and the path that China should take in the future, are clearly of political nature.[47]

Propitious Circumstances for Political Articulation

As made manifest by Yeh's and Kinkley's studies, a favourable intellectual and media milieu for political articulation is as crucial as the existence of a sociopolitical crisis for the birth of the political novel.

In the following pages, I will discuss the social, political, and intellectual circumstances conducive to the emergence of oppositional political novels in the new century. To begin with, it is worth noting that the Chinese censorship system does not work, as some would imagine, by the Party imposing censorship at will while the intellectuals passively accept it without counteraction; nor is it a stagnant and enclosed structure with fixed criteria of censorship and boundaries. Instead, the system functions more like a political arena in the Foucauldian sense, where control and resistance, the censor and the censored, are in dynamic interaction, though under the Chinese one-Party system, the former is always in a more active and advantageous position. As Guobin Yang's insightful study of online activism in China convincingly demonstrates, the Chinese people, subject to Communist dictatorship for decades, have acquired and accumulated plenty of wisdom and strategies to "creatively negotiate political power" to resist oppression.[48] As he points out, in contemporary China under Communist rule, "the simple truth is domination is always met with resistance"; "as the forms of domination change, so do forms of resistance."[49] As a consequence of the dynamic interaction between control and resistance, the criteria of Chinese censorship and the boundaries of the "prohibited zones" drawn by the Party are constantly shifting, depending on the policy of an administration, the intellectuals' attitude and counteraction to oppression and censorship, and the domestic and international political atmosphere.

As mentioned earlier, the 1990s was a decade of openness and political relaxation for China; it is even acclaimed by some as "the most liberal decade" in contemporary Chinese history.[50] The social milieu of openness and political tolerance, along with the rampant official corruption at that time, according to Jeffrey Kinkley's study, brought into being anticorruption novels, the first group of political fiction that emerged in post-Mao China. Much credit should be given to Jiang Zemin, who ruled for the entire decade, for the highly open and dynamic social and political milieu. After taking over power in 2002, Hu Jintao largely inherited Jiang's ruling principle and policies. Consequently, China's politics and society in the first decade of the twenty-first century displayed a substantial continuity with that of the 1990s, which is clearly expressed in the most famous buzzword in the Hu era: *bu zheteng* 不折腾, a phrase with no proper English word to translate it, which means "do not make any ridiculous policy or movement on the part of the government that would cause nothing but troubles for ordinary people."[51]

In the early twenty-first century, the political control and censorship in China over thought and the media under Hu Jintao's administration to a certain extent turned tighter than in the Jiang Zemin era. Nevertheless, because of the rather rational and eclectic style of governance under Hu's leadership, political control and censorship during his rule were quite moderate, which makes a sharp contrast with what is going on today under Xi Jinping's reign, where the political dictatorship goes to extremes not seen since Mao.[52] Moreover, due to the fundamental continuity in guiding principle between Jiang's and Hu's administrations, a "propitious" atmosphere for political articulation and for the rise of political fiction[53] continued into the Hu Jintao era (2002–12), during which all the novels discussed here were published. Most importantly, new circumstances that emerged in the new century – the impact of globalization after China joined the World Trade Organization (WTO) in 2001, the accelerated process of marketization, and the wide spread of the internet – helped mitigate to some extent the negative effect of tightened control on political articulation.

Above all, the integration of China into the international community after it joined the WTO has greatly accelerated and strengthened China's process of marketization and commercialization, which has brought about many fundamental and far-reaching changes in society. The change in the Chinese intelligentsia caused by commercialization is remarkable. Richard Curt Kraus, based on his study of the relationship between politics and the arts since the 1990s, concludes that the commercialization of literature and arts in China – the shift from state patronage of the arts to a mixed system of private and public sponsorship – is "intellectually liberating," because it has tremendously undermined the state's institutions and capacities of control over the arts and, consequently, brought more autonomy and opportunities to writers and artists.[54] Shuyu Kong, in a well-received book, provides an exhaustive and insightful analysis of the transformation that commercialization has brought to all stages in the process of literary production – from creation and publication to distribution – since the 1990s. As Kong argues, "in the Chinese context, the positive results of commercialization have outweighed the negative ones, since they have led to a much more vibrant and open literary production scene than existed under the socialist system."[55] She believes that the marketization of literary production in China, especially the emergence of "the second channel" – the financially independent publishers and book dealers – provided writers with more means and opportunities to broadcast their "politically incorrect" ideas.[56] Indeed, the process of commercialization in China has liberated writers, artists, and media practitioners from the Maoist totalitarian control and provided them with a bit more autonomy and incentives to overstep the boundaries set by the Party-state.

Moreover, since the advent of the new century, international markets have provided alternative channels and sources of income to those rebellious mainland Chinese writers, especially the well-known ones, which in turn reinforces their courage and determination for political opposition. Yan Lianke, widely acclaimed to be the most defiant writer in contemporary China, is an exemplar of this phenomenon. Since the advent of the new century, Yan Lianke's novels have become more and more politically offensive and audacious, and all his recent novels have been banned in mainland China as a result. This suppression nevertheless has not destroyed his writing career. He not only survives but also thrives, which would have been unimaginable in the Mao era. According to Lynda Ng's study, Yan Lianke is actually among the most highly paid writers in contemporary China, due mainly to global markets, because his fame as an audacious dissident writer in China opens new markets for his books in Hong Kong, Taiwan, and overseas.[57] Yu Hua, another conscientious and rebellious writer in contemporary China, also benefits greatly from global markets. According to his own account, up to September 2017, his works have been translated into thirty-five languages and circulated in thirty-eight countries. Given his fame and popularity in the anglophone world as well as in other parts of the world, it is not reckless to infer that the royalties he has received from international markets are considerable.[58]

The wide spread of the internet in China in the new century has also made substantial contributions to the construction of a public sphere conducive to political articulation. As Guobin Yang points out, "of all the aspects of Chinese Internet culture, the most important yet least understood is its contentious character."[59] Yang believes that the internet has greatly transformed China in many positive ways, as it provides channels and tools for Chinese people to voice their anger and resentment towards repression and to act against injustice. He argues that the online activism that has taken place in China since the mid-1990s marks "the palpable revival of the revolutionary spirit" passed down from the 1989 Tiananmen democratic movement.[60] Min Jiang suggests that the use of internet technologies gives the Chinese people limited freedom and space to talk and negotiate with the essentially authoritarian regime, and allows some sort of political "deliberation" to exist in present-day China. He coins the term "authoritarian deliberation" to refer to this phenomenon.[61] In comparison with Yang and Jiang, Margaret E. Roberts seems more pessimistic about the impact of the internet upon Chinese society. Roberts argues that the internet provides an authoritarian regime like China more mechanisms to create "porous censorship" and "customized oppression." The porousness of the censorship, according to Roberts, is deliberately created by an authoritarian regime to divide the elite and the common populace, and to allow "the government to avoid widespread use of observable repression, which is well-known to spark backlash."[62] The porousness, nevertheless, also provides loopholes and opportunities to be used by people for political resistance. Clearly, the internet has played a significant role in fostering political opposition in China.

The publication of some of the novels discussed here is a direct result of the synthetic function of commercialization and the internet. Hu Fayun's *Such Is This World*, for example, was first posted online and gradually gained fame there. Later on, printed copies of the text came out and were circulated underground among readers. Encouraged by the popularity of the novel and seeing a potential business opportunity, a Hangzhou–based literary magazine took political risks and published a slightly "sanitized" version of the novel, which immediately improved the sales volume of the lesser-known magazine from about 2,000 copies per month to 11,000 copies for that issue.[63] The magazine's venture eventually resulted in the book's publication by a state press.[64] Clearly, the publication of the novel is a positive result of the combination of commercialization and the internet, plus the courage and determination of both the novelist and the editors.

The circulation of Chan Koonchung's *The Fat Years* on the mainland was largely ascribed to the internet. After its publication in Hong Kong, the novel was immediately banned in mainland China. In order to make it accessible to mainland readers, the novelist "pirated" his rights from his own publisher and posted the novel online to let Chinese mainlanders read it for free. Afterwards, numerous digital versions of the novel have circulated and sparked heated discussion on the Chinese internet,[65] and it has also created a huge sensation among Chinese intellectuals. Less than two years later, an English translation of the novel came out and made a wave in the anglophone intellectual world as well. The novel won Chan Koonchung fame as an important writer in contemporary China, and he used the fame to create more novels that tackle contemporary Chinese politics.[66] Hu Fayun also took advantage of the fame earned from *Such Is This World* and continues to critically reflect on the politics of contemporary China.[67] In both cases, the label of "dissident writer" served as a powerful catalyst to help elevate the novelists' fame and encourage them to go further on the path of political opposition.

In the Chinese context, intriguingly, even certain negative consequences of commercialization and the internet – the marginalization of "serious" literature caused by the all-round commercialization of society and the rapid rise of internet literature[68] and other entertainment literature and arts since the 1990s – have produced some positive effects for the rise of oppositional political novels. The decline of the influence of "serious" literature and of intellectuals upon the general public serves to slacken the Party's vigilance, oppression, and censorship of writers and intellectuals, which in turn provides them with more freedom and autonomy to conduct critical reflection on the system and society.

The rise of oppositional political novels, of course, cannot be separated from the overall development of Chinese literature in the early twenty-first century. Along with the re-politicization of society and the intelligentsia, Chinese literature has also retrieved its political character since the mid-1990s, which is most evidently indicated by the rise of anticorruption fiction and subaltern literature (*diceng wenxue* 底层文学).[69] Subaltern literature concentrates on the miserable life of the people who struggle at the bottom of the society, especially the enormous inequality and injustice they suffer, and their desperate and hopeless rebellion in present-day China.[70] Because of its strong political implications and its breadth and depth in exposing the darkness of post-Mao Chinese society, subaltern literature is acclaimed the "most significant literary genre that China has produced in the twenty-first century thus far" by some mainland Chinese critics, and is also linked to "the leftist literature and the democratic and liberal literary traditions of the twenty century."[71] The revival and flourishing of politically charged literature since the mid-1990s lay the foundation for the rise and development of oppositional political novels.

Scope, Themes, Methodology, and Structure of the Book

In this book, I adopt the term "oppositional political novels" to designate a cluster of politically charged novels produced in early twenty-first century China, which are considered "oppositional" because of their shared theme of challenging the fundamental principles of the Chinese Party-state, questioning the Chinese model, and breaking the political red lines drawn by the Party-state.[72] Due to great differences in style of these novels, I do not assume that they make up a unified subgenre within the broader category of "political fiction." In this book, I will elaborate on five of them: Jiang Rong's *Wolf Totem* (*Lang tuteng* 狼图腾, 2004), Yan Lianke's *Lenin's Kisses* (*Shouhuo* 受活, 2004), Hu Fayun's *Such Is This World@sars.come* (*Ruyan@sars.come* 如焉@sars.come, 2006, hereafter referred to as *Such Is This World*), Chan Koonchung's *The Fat Years* (*Shengshi: Zhongguo 2013* 盛世: 中国2013, 2009), and Yu Hua's *The Seventh Day* (*Diqi tian* 第七天, 2012).

I am aware that it might be disputable to dub some of the works discussed here "political novels" if the term "political novel" is defined in a strict sense. This appellation, however, can be justified on the ground that the main concern of the present book is not with the definition of political novel but with the political ideas and the underlying implications conveyed in these novels. Moreover, as Irving Howe points out, a novel can be regarded as a political novel as long as political ideas are its dominant theme or the political milieu is its dominant setting, and a political reading thus does not lead to "radical distortion" of its connotations but instead to "analytical profits."[73] For all of the novels discussed here, political ideas are the dominant theme. By focusing on the political ideas in them, the present book not only does not distort the connotations of the novels; on the contrary, it sheds light on some profound implications embedded in the deep narrative structure of these novels. Most importantly, the political reality in contemporary China under its one-Party system helps justify a broadly defined notion of political novel. Because talking about politics in an explicit way is too dangerous under strict censorship in China, the writers have to use varied literary devices to camouflage the political messages, and as a result, the work may not seem to be a "political novel" on the surface.

The present research represents the first effort in the English-speaking academic world to study oppositional Chinese political novels produced in the early twenty-first century; it will fill a gap in the studies of Chinese political fiction. The book benefits greatly from previous studies on Chinese political fiction. To the best of my knowledge, up to now only a few books can be found in the anglophone world that deal directly with this subject. Jeffrey Kinkley's book *Corruption and Realism in Late Socialist China: The Return of the Political Novel* studies anticorruption novels of the late 1990s and early 2000s. His book not only provides profound and incisive analyses of several representative anticorruption novels but also sheds light on the discourse of corruption in the Chinese context as well as on the relationship between realism and Chinese political fiction. Kinkley's book lays a solid theoretical foundation for studies of Chinese political fiction, from which the present study benefits greatly. Catherine Vance Yeh's book *The Chinese Political Novel: Migration of a World Genre* examines the late Qing political novels from a global, comparative perspective. Her book offers insightful observations on political novels in different areas of the world and on the unique features and accomplishments of the Chinese brand of political novels in the late Qing. The analyses of the motifs in these books and their implications for the late Qing political novels are especially perceptive and inspiring. David Der-wei Wang's book *Fin-de-siècle*

Splendor: Repressed Modernities of Late Qing Fiction, 1849–1911 dedicates a chapter to the late Qing "grotesque exposés" – widely regarded as the first cluster of political novels produced in modern China. Wang demonstrates that this literary genre, along with three other neglected late Qing fiction genres, represents a literary modernity long repressed by the dominant May Fourth discourse. It also explores the influence of these late Qing fiction genres upon Chinese literature in the twenty-first century. Wang's book focuses on the social and aesthetic values of late Qing "fiction of condemnation" and leaves behind some highly valuable analytical terms and strategies for reading Chinese political novels. The book *China and New Left Visions: Political and Cultural Interventions*, edited by Ban Wang and Jie Lu, focuses on the interaction of the New Leftist political-intellectual trend and Chinese literature since the mid-1990s from multiple perspectives. It also includes insightful studies of politically charged literary genres in post-Mao China, such as "subaltern literature," "poetry of migrant workers," the "short-short genre," the "red" classics, and others.

Some other books, though not directly dealing with political fiction, also offer inspirational insights into the relationship between literature and politics in post-Mao China. Perry Link's book *The Uses of Literature: Life in the Socialist Chinese Literary System*, for instance, explores how literature was still used by the Chinese Party-state as an institution for political purposes in the early 1980s. Geremie Barmé's book *In the Red: On Contemporary Chinese Culture* demonstrates the continuities and changes in the relationship between politics and culture under the new conditions of commercialization in post-Mao China. Another book edited by Ban Wang, *Words and Their Stories: Essays on the Language of the Chinese Revolution*, investigates political catchphrases and their history and function in the Chinese Communist revolution, shedding light on the power of language in politics. Jeffrey Kinkley's two other books, which deal with crime fiction in Chinese literature and visions of dystopia in China's new historical novels, respectively,[74] provide valuable perspectives and analytical terms to probe the political edge in Chinese fiction.

Taking previous studies as a point of departure, the present research attempts to contribute to the scholarship of Chinese political fiction by examining a special group of political novels that have never before been under close scrutiny. This study focuses on the content or the discursive strength of the novels rather than on their form or their stylistic and aesthetic value, though in any literary criticism the study of the two cannot be completely separated. Based on close readings of the five aforementioned representative oppositional Chinese political novels, this research aims at four goals.

The first and foremost goal is to explore how these novels, through their presentation of and reflection on the "political triangle" in China – the relationship of the Party, the intellectuals, and the people – and other serious sociopolitical problems facing today's China, subvert some fundamental myths created by the Party-state and its propaganda machine, and question the morality and political legitimacy of the so-called Chinese model. By closely examining the motifs, main themes, and political and intellectual implications of these novels in the broad context of modern Chinese history, I shall demonstrate their tremendous historical and epistemological value. By linking these literary works closely with the social reality in which they are rooted, I also aim to create a sketch of the rapidly changing social, political, and intellectual landscape in post-Mao China, especially the impact of commercialization and the internet on the relationship and interaction between state power and writers. This goal is the foremost goal of the present research, the foundation of the book, and the starting point for all the other goals.

The second goal is to explore, through readings of these novels and observation of their reception, the structure and dynamics of the contemporary Chinese intellectual realm as well as the extremely complicated relationship – conflicted yet interdependent – between knowledge and state power. The third goal is to shed light on the ideological limitations of oppositional Chinese political novels caused by censorship and self-censorship, the relationship between politics and art in Chinese political fiction, and the channels and narrative strategies employed by oppositional Chinese political novelists to circumvent censorship. The fourth goal of this research is to briefly explore the development of political fiction in China, thereby to explain the internal and external reasons for the emergence of oppositional political novels in the twenty-first century.

In selecting the novels elaborated in the research, I take into consideration the following factors. The first concerns the discursive significance and social impact of a novel. All five novels are highly influential among readers, and all of them have made substantial contributions to Chinese literature and thought in some way. Moreover, almost all of these novels have not before been subjected to intensive scholarly scrutiny in English-speaking academia. The second factor relates to the motifs and main themes of a novel. Because the major concern of the present research is the Chinese model, all the selected novels focus on sociopolitical issues or discourses of the post-Mao era. This focus explains why *Wolf Totem*, despite its setting during the Cultural Revolution, is included: because it deals with the state ideology of post-Mao

China – nationalism and social Darwinism. The third consideration is related to the discursive diversity of oppositional Chinese political novels, as each of the selected novels focuses on a particular aspect of the Chinese model. The fourth factor is associated with the methodology and the approach of the research. The relatively small number of novels elaborated in the book, five in total, makes it possible for me to read each novel "closely" and thus be able to appreciate the nuance of the thematic import of each novel. The last factor concerns the availability and potential reception of a novel in the anglophone world. All these novels discussed here are available in English translation, which allows English readers to access them easily.

Here I feel it necessary to explain why *The Fat Years* is included, even though its author, Chan Koonchung, is legally a Hong Kong resident and the novel was published in Hong Kong rather than in mainland China. To begin with, though Chan is often labelled a "Hong Kong writer," he has actually been living in Beijing since 1992.[75] Judging by the essays he has written in recent years to express his personal feelings and thoughts, he has already fully integrated into the mainland Chinese literary and intellectuals circles, and as a result, little difference can be discerned between him and those "authentic" mainland writers in terms of focus of intellectual preoccupation and mode of thinking. As far as the novel is concerned, it is reasonable to treat it in the same way as those created by mainland Chinese writers are treated, not only because the novel is completely about China but also because mainland Chinese readers are obviously the target audience. Otherwise, the author would not have "pirated" his own copyright from his publisher to let mainland readers access the novel online for free. Moreover, from the perspective of reception, it is mainland Chinese readers, especially the mainland intellectuals, who are the most interested in the novel and who have had the first and strongest reaction to it.

Because of the unique nature of political fiction with political ideas or political milieu at its core, and also because my own focus of concern is discursive rather than aesthetic, the current study certainly does not fall into the category of pure literary criticism. It requires an interdisciplinary approach and a wide range of knowledge across literature, politics, and intellectual history. In terms of methodology, the present research synthesizes the formalistic technique of "close reading" and a historical perspective. Close reading *as a technique of textual analysis* allows me to scrutinize the most significant descriptive details and moments in the text and dig out the implications hidden deep in the narrative structure. This technique is especially productive in reading an oppositional Chinese political novel because, in the Chinese context, the author often has to employ varied linguistic and narrative devices such as metaphor, symbolism, allegory, fantasy, hyperbole, surrealism, linguistic ambiguity, and the like as artistic camouflage to conceal the highly subversive messages contained in the text. My adoption of "close reading" as a method of textual analysis, nevertheless, does not lead me to accept the formalistic philosophy behind it that the meaning of a text can be "closed" and isolated from the outside world and from human experience. Rather, I believe any reading, be it "close" or "distant," is an interpretation; as such, it is unavoidably associated with the interpreter's life experience and, through the interpreter, with the vast outside human world and human experience. To supplement the technique of "close reading," I adopt a historical perspective to look at my findings obtained through close reading. In the process of analysing the texts of these political novels, I also occasionally compare them with Western political novels in an attempt to broaden the hermeneutic horizon of Chinese political novels. The research extensively cites Western political philosophers from Hannah Arendt, Antonio Gramsci, and Michael Oakeshott to Michel Foucault. It also references well-regarded studies of Chinese literature and contemporary Chinese politics, society, and the intelligentsia.

The book is composed of six chapters in addition to an introduction and an epilogue. This introduction has traced the history of Chinese political fiction, explored the external social and political milieu and intrinsic dynamic for the rise of oppositional political novels in the early twenty-first century, and discussed the new mechanisms and channels that commercialization and the internet provided to Chinese writers to circumvent censorship. Chapter 1 analyses the main themes and the historical and epistemological value of these political novels. Linking these themes with the sociopolitical reality of contemporary China, the chapter also offers an overview of Chinese society, the intelligentsia, and the general public in post-Mao China, with a focus on the serious problems facing today's China. Chapters 2 to 6 are "close readings" of the five novels. These chapters are arranged in chronological order according to the publication dates of the Chinese originals of these novels. The epilogue discusses the limitations of ideological transgression of these oppositional political novels and the narrative strategies adopted by Chinese writers to circumvent censorship through examining the relationship between aesthetics and ideology, and between the immediacy of human experience and the abstractness of idea in the political novel.

Chapter One

Destruction of Communist Myths

Because political fiction is rooted in its sociopolitical milieu and reflects the spirit of the age, discussion of the sociopolitical milieu becomes essential in reading a political novel. The sociopolitical milieu serves merely as the "background" for the creation of a non-political novel; in a political novel, however, it becomes an essential part, constituting the very subject matter. It is on this ground that Irving Howe claims a novel like *Nineteen Eighty-Four* "must first be approached through politics."[1] Howe's statement actually points out that political ideas and political milieu are the core of a political novel, and all other elements of the novel – structure, plot, characterization, narration, and so on – derive from that core. This characterization is the defining feature of the political novel and the meta-principle for interpreting it.

Oppositional Chinese political novels also function as a barometer of the Chinese sociopolitical climate in the early twenty-first century. As mentioned earlier, what distinguishes these oppositional Chinese novels from previous Chinese political fiction is that the latter merely targets the specific flaws of the Chinese one-Party system, whereas the former question its fundamental principles and challenge the moral and political legitimacy of the Chinese model. Focusing on the changed "political triangle" in Chinese society – the relationship of the Party, the intellectuals, and the people – in the post-Mao era, these novels ruthlessly, though often in subtle ways, shatter the myths about the relationship between the Party and the intellectuals, and between the Party and the people, painstakingly constructed by the state propaganda machine, and subvert the Party's glorious and messianic self-image as the benevolent saviour and representative of the Chinese people and the guardian of enlightened knowledge and the intellectuals. These novels also expose the predatory nature of the Chinese model of development and the far-reaching and profoundly disastrous impact of state ideology and mainstream discourses composed of Darwinism and extreme nationalism upon the values, views, and mentality of the Chinese people, especially of the younger generations.

This chapter examines the main themes of these novels in the broad context of the contemporary Chinese social, political, and intellectual landscape. Juxtaposing these themes with the sociopolitical reality of early twenty-first century China in which they are rooted, the chapter also illustrates the historical background against which oppositional Chinese political novels emerged. Based on studies of contemporary Chinese politics and society, and synthesizing empirical description and theoretical analysis, the chapter aims at two goals: simultaneously to explore the historical and epistemological value of these novels and to illuminate the social, political, and intellectual landscape in post-Mao China. Given that the themes of these novels honestly and accurately reflect contemporary Chinese sociopolitical reality, the two goals are actually two sides of the same coin.

Them versus Us: Subversion of the Party-People Myth

Due to its essentially imaginary, overselective, and distorted nature,[2] ideology is manipulated by political parties all around the world to serve their own purposes, but it seldom plays so central a role as it does in the Chinese Communist Party. As a "text-centred" political organization,[3] the Chinese Communist Party holds ideology or "thought" as a life-and-death issue for its survival and future. David Apter's and Hans van de Ven's studies convincingly prove that the success of the Chinese Communist Party under extremely harsh and adverse circumstances depends to a large extent on its ability to create and propagate ideology on the part of both its supreme leader and its propaganda machine.[4] Apter believes that Mao played multiple different yet tightly interrelated roles – "storyteller, mythmaker, logician, and philosopher-king" – in constructing the Chinese version of communist ideology, which proved to be a powerful weapon to glorify the communist cause, to persuade or deceive the people, and to slander and attack enemies.[5] As he argues, "what discretionary power Mao actually deployed was based on his ability to make myth appear as logic and acceptable as reality."[6] Of the many myths made by Mao, by his successors, and by the state propaganda machine, the most powerful, beguiling, and deceptive is the one concerning the relationship between the Party and the people. This myth claims that the Party is the saviour, guardian, and representative of the Chinese nation and that the relationship of the Party and the people is one of fish and water; it became the cornerstone and the source of political legitimacy for Communist Party rule in Mao's China. Clearly, the secret code behind this myth is nationalism. There is no doubt that this Party-people myth played a decisive role in helping Mao and Chinese Communists win support from the Chinese people and eventually the power of the entire country in the Chinese Communist revolution. This myth is why Suisheng Zhao claims that the real source of the legitimacy of the Chinese Communist state is not Marxism but nationalism.[7]

Because the Party-people myth is the cornerstone of Communist rule in China and the real source of political legitimacy for the Chinese Party-state, it is only natural to find that it occupies a sacred position in the Chinese political and intellectual sphere, and is not allowed to be tarnished by anyone for any reason. Chinese intellectuals and writers are well aware of this red line; they have already reached acquiescence on this issue and almost unanimously kept silent about it over decades under Communist domination. When a few brave souls dared to transgress the red line, they were punished severely. During the Yan'an period, the price that Wang Shiwei paid for shattering the myth by pointing to the separation of the Communist leadership from the people was his life.[8] In the early 1980s, Bai Hua was harshly criticized nationwide for his highly influential film *Kulian* 苦恋(Bitter Love), whose main theme is that, whereas the people love the Party, the Party seems not to care about the people at all.[9] Liu Binyan was persecuted in the Mao era and forced into exile in the post-Mao era for exposing the "demonic" nature of the Communist rule, which not only does not represent the people but whose agents are actually "monsters" devouring people.[10] All these cases serve as good examples and serious warnings to the intellectuals and writers of the consequence of transgressing the red line.

With the emergence of oppositional Chinese political novels in the early twenty-first century, contemporary China witnessed for the first time in its history a group of writers – though each of them worked independently and separately – who abandoned the political acquiescence and transgressed the most significant red line drawn by the Party. Even though these writers acted in a highly cautious, tactical, and subtle way, their works all contain plenty of messages intended to subvert the Party-people myth in one way or another. In *Such Is This World*, for instance, borrowing a Party official's words, the relationship between the Party and the people is defined as that between "us and outsiders." The confrontation between the Party and the people is claimed to be not about right and wrong but about winning and losing – or precisely, not about truth, morality, or legitimacy but about power. The depiction of the regime putting conscientious intellectuals and even ordinary people under surveillance and busying itself controlling information and suppressing dissidents, while ignoring the life and death of the people in the entire nation during a deadly epidemic, completely shattered the Party's claim of representing the interests of the Chinese people. Taking the SARS episode as an allegory, the novel implies that the Communist dictatorship is a disease fatal to the welfare of the Chinese people. In *Lenin's Kisses*, the county chief considers himself the emperor and all people under his jurisdiction his subjects. In the novel, the relationship of the ruling elites (the agents of the Party) and ordinary people is portrayed as that of "wholers" and the disabled, which indicates that, in the eyes of the ruling elites, ordinary people are simply "disabled" and inferior to them in every aspect. *The Fat Years* is much more audacious than the other four novels in exposing the mendacity and deception of the Communist myth. The novel indicates explicitly that there is no such a thing as a fish-and-water relationship between the Party and the people; instead, the Party treats the people as merely slaves or the mob in the Hobbesian sense. In order to control the society and maintain its rule, the regime shows no hesitation or mercy in using fascist means to persecute and torture those regarded as threats to its rule. The novel makes it clear that the Party has already degenerated into a self-serving interest group after Tiananmen. *The Seventh Day*, along with *The Fat Years*, shows that the Chinese state controlled by the Party has been reduced to a ruling machine manipulated by the political elites in collusion with greedy businessmen to prey on ordinary Chinese people. The relationship between the Party-state and the people is presented in both novels and in *Lenin's Kisses* as one between a predator and its prey. In *Wolf Totem*, the dictatorial Communist Party-state is portrayed as the destroyer of traditional Mongolian culture and the Mongolian way of life; as such, the antagonistic relationship between the Party-state and Mongols – part of the broadly defined Chinese people – is articulated. In all five novels, the relationship between the Party-state and the people is depicted as adversarial and hostile: them versus us.

The observations made in these novels honestly reflect the Chinese sociopolitical reality and are also supported by scholars' studies. The essence of a dictatorial regime, where a dictator or, at most, a tiny ruling elite monopolizes power in a country, determines its oppressive, exploiting, and predatory nature, even though all dictatorships claim to represent the interests of people. In Mao's China, the exploiting and predatory nature of the Chinese Party-state was to a large extent covered up by its strategically egalitarian policy, which produced the illusory image of an equal and just China. To be fair, in Mao's China, the faith in communism on the part of the Chinese Communist Party and its pursuit of social equality seem to have been more sincere and more serious than in the post-Mao era, which partially explains the Maoist brand of egalitarianism. A much more significant reason for the Maoist egalitarian practice is that, because of the stark poverty that the nation faced during that period caused by the Party's devastating policies and absurd political movements, the regime had to strike hard at the greed and corruption of officials to prevent the repeated occurrence of famines and starvation, and ultimately to maintain its rule. The stark poverty of the whole nation at that time also meant that the country did not have much public wealth for corrupt officials to embezzle or steal. Clearly, the ostensible equality and justice in Mao's China were largely a result and manifestation of the stark poverty of the nation and of the regime's strategic policy for its own survival.

The predatory nature of the Chinese Party-state becomes conspicuous in the post-Mao era, when the so-called Chinese economic "miracle" achieved through the exploitation and abuse of the people at the bottom of society generated tremendous wealth for the regime to squander and for its agents to embezzle and steal. Minxin Pei coins the term "developmental autocracy" to dub the Dengist mode of development – now widely known as the Chinese model – characterized by its combination of political dictatorship and market economy.[11] All developmental autocracies including the Chinese regime, according to Pei, are predatory due to their fundamental guiding principles. As he argues, the ultimate goal of economic growth for a developmental autocracy is "regime survival" rather than the welfare of its people.[12] In order to survive, the regime will inevitably enact predatory policies and practices to strengthen itself and to weaken the people in order to reduce their capacity to rebel. Therefore, as Pei concludes, though economic growth should be a favourable factor for political opening and the development of democracy in the long run, in the short term, it might become an effective means for a developmental autocracy to justify its rule and to temporarily strengthen its control.[13] Starting from his theory of developmental autocracy, Pei further points out that the Chinese model of development is in essence "crony capitalism," at the core of which is "collusive corruption by elites."[14] In other words, the Chinese model of development is by nature a mode of production by which the political and business elites collude to prey on the underprivileged and the poor.

The observations of these writers of oppositional political novels and Minxin Pei's conclusions have been proven by the Chinese sociopolitical reality in the post-Mao era. It is common knowledge that the low-end manufacturing industry ("made in China"), infrastructure construction, and the real estate industry are the backbone and main engine for the Chinese economic boom. These are all labour intensive and low technology sectors because of the low degree of mechanization in the country, which leads to what many economists and sociologists term the "population dividend" (*renkou hongli* 人口红利) of Chinese economic development. As such, it is fair to say that the working class is the major contributor to the Chinese economic "miracle." Despite this fact, ordinary people do not benefit from the economic boom; on the contrary, they become losers and even victims of the "miracle" they themselves created. Because of the lack of protective laws and institutions, and functional social security and insurance systems, because of the discriminatory and predatory policies implemented by the local governments,[15] and because of the collusive corruption of government officials and businessmen,[16] these underprivileged people are severely exploited. Not only do they have to work in extremely harsh, dangerous, and sometimes poisonous conditions,[17] but they are often excessively underpaid or even unpaid.[18] For those "peasant workers," a term referring to the people who come from the countryside to work in the city and have made substantial contributions to China's economic boom, things became even worse. In addition to enduring similar exploitation as other city workers, they also have to suffer additional discrimination as "rural residents" in the city. In most cases, they have to bear the pain of separation from their children. Those "left-behind children" (*liushou ertong* 留守儿童), in the care of their grandparents in the countryside, are often subject to all kinds of misery and abuse: hunger, bullying, rape, human trafficking, child slavery, and even murder.[19] To be sure, the Chinese economic success is achieved at tremendous expense to the welfare, happiness, health, and even lives of those struggling at the bottom of society.

Even though it is ordinary people who created the Chinese economic "miracle," the enormous wealth produced by them flows into the coffers of the governments and the pockets of businessmen and corrupt officials. In this way, the unbridgeable gap between rich and poor, the confrontation between the Party-state and the people, and the unprecedented, massive social inequality have been generated in such a short time in post-Mao China. Moreover, under the current system, the poverty and the abject social status of the wretched will be inherited by their children and grandchildren, just as the later generations of the new rich will inherit the wealth and privileges from their forefathers, due to the inequality of the two groups in accessing education, employment, and other important social resources and opportunities. In other words, in today's China, social status is hereditary, which is why China today is widely called *pindie shidai* (拼爹时代): an age of "daddy determinism," a time in which a wealthy and powerful daddy means everything.[20] The Chinese-style "daddy determinism" severely impedes vertical mobility in society and causes the "perpetuation of social strata" (*shehui jieceng de guhua* 社会阶层的固化) in China. The high degree of polarization of Chinese society and the miserable life of the wretched gave birth to a "society falling apart" (*duanlie de shehui* 断裂的社会). In such a society, according to well-known Chinese sociologist Sun Liping, whereas people of the lower social strata have been ruthlessly "thrown out of the social structure," the other groups remaining in the social structure display neither understanding of nor identification with each other. As a result, the whole society experiences great tension to the point of falling apart.[21]

Behind the massive victimization of the underprivileged, the severe social polarization, and the enormous social inequality are state predation and state oppression. Because the paramount goal for a dictatorial regime is its own survival rather than people's interests, naturally, a dictatorial regime will inevitably take advantage of the fruits of economic growth to enrich itself and to strengthen its oppressive capacity. As Minxin Pei incisively points out, "without effective political institutions or structural constraints that curb the predatory appetite of the state, a state that is sufficiently strong to promote economic development unhindered by parochial interests is also strong enough to prey upon society without much restraint."[22] This characterization is exactly the case with the Chinese Party-state. Even worse, in the Chinese context, the "legal" predation by the state often goes together with an additional "illegal" predation caused by the collusive corruption of government officials and greedy businessmen. Consequently, in today's China, under the condition of the monopoly of power and resources by the Party-state and the widespread, rampant official corruption, ordinary people often have to endure double predation. This situation explains the emergence of the phenomenon of "strengthening of the state and the weakening of the people" (*guoqiang minruo* 国富民弱) since the 1990s, an inevitable consequence of the Chinese model.

Based on the political logic of regime survival, the policies the Party-state has adopted for distributing the fruits of the economic growth favour supportive groups, restrict opposing groups, and overlook insignificant groups. In post-Mao China, whereas the elites in different fields including government officials, intellectuals, and entrepreneurs constitute the dominant supportive force for the regime, the ordinary people, being deprived of the rights of political participation and lacking channels to make their voices heard, are actually overlooked by the regime as insignificant for its survival. This stratification explains, at least in theory, why the ruling elites as a group become the biggest beneficiaries of the Chinese economic "miracle," while the ordinary people are the biggest losers and even victims.[23] It also explains why the regime is powerless to fight official corruption and the "government-business collusive network," because it needs the loyalty and support from these corrupt officials and greedy businessmen for survival.

The severity of socioeconomic polarization, inequality, and injustice in China unavoidably stirs up huge discontent and protest in the society.[24] Due to the unresponsiveness, inadequacy, and dysfunction of "institutional mechanisms" to resolve the problems and grievances, and because of the lack of effective channels for political participation and interest representation, these seriously suffering people often have to rely on violent means or take high-risk options of collective protest to voice their demands. This state of affairs inevitably causes confrontation between the government and society, and between the predated and indignant people and the corrupt and greedy ruling elites. All these dark phenomena are presented in the novels *Lenin's Kisses*, *The Fat Years*, and *The Seventh Day*. *Lenin's Kisses* demonstrates how the government treats ordinary people as merely a "money tree" and exploits them with cruel means. It also exposes the normalization of cruelty and dehumanization in contemporary China under the Chinese model of development. *The Fat Years* paints a panoramic picture of the enormous social inequality and social injustice in contemporary China, as exemplified by the phenomena of child slaves, class discrimination, the unbridgeable gap between city and countryside, and other issues. *The Seventh Day*, through its description of some commonly seen and notorious events in today's China such as "forced demolition" and the emergence of "the mouse tribe," persuasively proves that the so-called Chinese economic "miracle" is stained with the blood of ordinary people struggling at the bottom of society.

The political logic behind the presentations of these novels asks the following questions: If a state is controlled by one single political party whose ultimate goal is its own survival and which thus implements policies to prey on ordinary people to strengthen its own oppressive capacity, how is it possible that it can represent the interests of people? If the ruling elites, the agents of the Party-state, regard the people as "outsiders," "subjects," or even threats to the state, how is it possible that the relationship of the Party and the people could be like that of fish and water? Undoubtedly, the presentations of these novels and the underlying political logic ruthlessly shatter the Party-people myth painstakingly constructed over decades by the state propaganda machine.

From Critics to Servants: Changed Role
of Chinese Intellectuals after Tiananmen

Even though intellectuals play a significant role in all societies, it is rare to see them occupy such a privileged and crucial position as in Chinese society, given the extraordinary reverence and even awe that Chinese people show to words, knowledge, and educated people. The Chinese Communist Party is obviously well aware of this significant code in Chinese society, and always takes its relationship with the intellectuals as a top priority, evidenced conversely by the many political campaigns that exclusively targeted intellectuals in China.

Considering the privileged and critical role that intellectuals play in Chinese society and the symbolic significance of the relationship between the state and intellectuals, it is only natural that the Chinese Communist Party throughout its history attempted to disguise itself as the guardian of knowledge and intellectuals. As early as the 1930s, Yan'an was portrayed by the Communist propaganda machine as "the holy land for intellectuals and progressive youths" (*zhishi fenzi he jinbu qingnian de shengdi* 知识分子和进步青年的圣地). In the twenty-first century, the Chinese Communist Party continues to claim that it "represents the progressive course of China's advanced culture" (*daibiao Zhongguo xianjin wenhua de qianjin fangxiang* 代表中国先进文化的前进方向). In the Party-intellectuals myth created by the state propaganda machine, the notorious political movements whose sole goal was to purge and persecute the intellectuals in the Mao era, especially the Anti-Rightist Campaign and the Cultural Revolution, are reconstructed as a deviation from the Party's fundamental guiding principle regarding intellectuals rather than an embodiment and culmination of it. From the same political logic, to preserve the Party-intellectuals myth intact, the Tiananmen Massacre, in which intellectuals were the major actors and victims, has been completely erased from official history and from the memory of China's younger generations.

In these oppositional political novels, however, the glorious and messianic image of the Party as the protective angel for enlightening knowledge and intellectuals is completely subverted. In *Such Is This World*, exposure of the Party's control of information and suppression of conscientious intellectuals is the dominant theme. Through the portrayal of different types of intellectuals from different generations, the novel indicates that suppression of non-conformist intellectuals and critical voices is a policy consistently implemented throughout Chinese Communist history. It also implies that the many political campaigns exclusively targeting intellectuals during the Mao era are not deviations from the Party's fundamental principle regarding intellectuals but rather extreme embodiments and culminations of the regime's consistent, oppressive policy. The novel exposes how the terror of the Tiananmen Massacre, along with the Party's renewed policy of buying off intellectuals with material rewards and social status, completely destroys intellectuals' willpower and courage to rebel against oppression, turning them from representatives of social conscience to mouthpieces for the oppressive Party-state. The relationship between the intellectuals and the Party-state is also a dominant motif in *The Fat Years*. The novel provides a detailed, vivid, and incisive depiction of the astonishing, massive moral depravity of the Chinese intelligentsia and of how the deceptive propaganda completely distorts the personality and mentality of the younger generation of Chinese intellectuals. Both novels expose the same fact – that the Chinese Party-state has always treated intellectuals merely as instruments of its rule but never as an independent, constructive, and corrective force for society. As such, both novels ruthlessly shatter the Party-intellectuals myth long established by the state propaganda machine.

Indeed, the relationship between the Party-state and intellectuals remains a crucial part of contemporary Chinese politics and social life. The Party-intellectuals relationship not only serves as a barometer of the Chinese political atmosphere but also determines to a large extent the direction of the country's development. Given the dictatorial nature of the regime, naturally the Party has always played the dominant role in its relation with the intellectuals. Moreover, to exert the maximum control possible, the regime has continuously upgraded its strategies of control to adapt to the changing domestic and international political situations. In Mao's China, Chinese intellectuals, regarded as disloyal and disobedient by the Party, had long been the object of surveillance, persecution, and re-education, and their political status was far below that of the "revolutionary masses," including workers, peasants, and soldiers. Moreover, during that period, the regime adopted a heavy-handed means of thought control. Not only was its punishment of the real or potential transgressors extremely harsh and even brutal, but the scope of its persecution was also incredibly massive, as many political campaigns targeted the entire intelligentsia. After Mao's death, the Dengist new policy has fundamentally changed China in many respects, including the relationship between the state and the intellectuals. In the post-Mao era, as China opens up to the outside world, the regime's control over thought and intellectuals has greatly loosened under the pressure of both the international community and domestic democratic forces. The control certainly is still there, but the means or tactics of control have undergone many dramatic changes, mostly positive.

First, the Maoist heavy-handed thought control through punishment or even elimination of the body, including forced labour, imprisonment, corporeal torture, and execution, has been replaced by more "lenient" means such as forced exile, surveillance, house arrest, and similar means, aimed to restrict and block the spread of thought in the post-Mao era. Basically, the new strategy focuses on the intellectual's thought rather than on his or her body. The principle underlying this changed strategy is that your body might be free, but your thought is not. The advantage of this more "humane" strategy is that it can shield the Party-state against criticism from the international community and domestic democratic forces, but it does not cause remarkable damage to the efficiency of thought control.

Second, the nationwide massive political campaign against the entire intelligentsia commonly seen in the Mao era has been gradually replaced by the strategy of "killing the chicken to frighten the monkeys" in the post-Mao period. By isolating the most defiant and influential dissidents from the rest of the intelligentsia and severely punishing them, this strategy gives prominence to the symbolic significance of punishment, stressing its warning, deterring, and intimidating effects. It also works to divide the intelligentsia and destroy their sense of unity, which, ironically enough, was a positive side effect of the Maoist massive political campaigns against the entire intelligentsia. The disintegration of the Chinese intelligentsia since the 1990s can be at least partially ascribed to the effectiveness of this strategy.

The third change operates on the procedural level of punishment. During the Cultural Revolution, the punishment for "thought crime" could be very arbitrary and brutal. Even the death penalty could simply be pronounced at a "mass criticism meeting," without going through even a superficial legal procedure. In the post-Mao era, however, not only does the punishment usually go through a legal procedure, but the charges and means of punishment have also become more diverse, subtle, and cunning. The regime has moved away from such highly controversial charges as "attacking the Party," "attacking socialism," or "conspiring to overthrow the government" to punish dissidents. Instead, it charges the political and intellectual dissidents with ordinary crimes such as tax evasion, whoring, using drugs, and other similar offenses, which not only serves to smear the glorious image of the intellectual but is also less likely to provoke criticism.

The fourth and most significant change is reflected in the shift of the guiding principle for thought control adopted by the Party-state.

Rather than resorting to punishment as the major device, the Party-state relies mainly on rewards to co-opt intellectuals into becoming colluders, especially after Tiananmen. To be sure, in both the Mao and post-Mao eras, the Party-state adopted a mix of stick and carrot for thought control, but the emphasis is reversed in the two periods. In Mao's China, though the regime also used rewards such as recruitment into the Party or into Party-controlled professional organizations to co-opt intellectuals, the punitive approach dominated. In the post-Mao era, however, the Party relies more and more on rewards. In the years immediately after Mao's death, realizing the crucial role that intellectuals play in society, the Party started the process of reconciliation with and co-option of the intellectuals. The rehabilitation of those intellectuals persecuted during the Cultural Revolution and other Maoist political movements and Deng's official announcement of the intelligentsia being part of the working class – nominally the leading class as prescribed by the state's constitution – epitomized the new approach. However, despite all these efforts to pacify the intellectuals and to ease their latent animosity towards the Party accumulated during the long period of Maoist heavy-handed control,[25] the strategy of luring and buying off the intellectuals was not yet the Party's first choice before the Tiananmen crackdown. The series of political campaigns launched by the Party in the 1980s – from criticism of the movie *Bitter Love*, the "anti-spiritual pollution" campaign, to the "anti-bourgeois liberalization" campaign – conveyed very clearly the Party's message that warning, intimidation, and punishment were still the dominant means of thought control. This approach can be explained by several factors: at that time, the intellectuals still held a basically vigilant and critical attitude towards the Leninist Party-state; the Party was still quite confident in and satisfied with the effect of the "time-honoured," heavy-handed means of control; and the Party-state did not yet have sufficient economic resources to lure and buy off the intellectuals.

The bloody crackdown that took place on Tiananmen Square in 1989 and the ensuing economic boom changed everything. The shocking effect of the crackdown compelled both the Party-state and the intellectuals to reflect on their previous stances and strategies, and to reposition themselves in the rapidly changing reality. The reflection and readjustment on the part of both the Party-state and the intellectuals have brought about a new relationship between the two since the 1990s. As far as the Party-state is concerned, though ordinary Chinese people and the intellectuals have no way to know the Party's real attitude – behind its asserted confidence in its rule and its future – towards the Tiananmen democratic movement or its real response to the downfall of the Soviet Union and the Eastern European socialist bloc, the shock and fear that the movement and the Communist collapse brought to it must have been enormous. Moreover, the Party-state must also have been shocked by the magnitude of Chinese intellectuals' strength and their influence upon the general public. Logically, we could assume that the Party-state, witnessing the fierce opposition from the intelligentsia and the overwhelming threat to its rule, must have realized the extreme importance of winning support from the intelligentsia for its survival; consequently, it must have rethought its policy for dealing with intellectuals.

All this turmoil is clearly demonstrated by the Party's treatment of intellectuals in the aftermath of the Tiananmen crackdown. Despite the harsh tone that its propaganda machine adopted to denounce the democratic movement, the regime's treatment of the participants, the overwhelming majority of whom were intellectuals, was rather restrained and rational. The strategy of punishing only a few leaders of the movement while pardoning and pacifying the rest of the participants proved highly effective in relieving the intellectuals' fear and, consequently, in stabilizing the entire intelligentsia. Clearly, the regime began to co-opt intellectuals right after the end of the crackdown. After that, co-option has become a consistent policy for the Party in dealing with intellectuals. Since the mid-1990s, as economic growth bore fruit, the Party-state has accumulated enormous wealth to carry out its policy of luring and buying off intellectuals. Since then, co-option has become the dominant device adopted by the regime for thought control, and it has proved very effective in winning over the intellectuals and silencing their opposition. The greatest advantage of this strategy lies in that it makes the intellectuals willing to submit to the Party-state without the feeling of coercion. *The Fat Years*, through its presentation of a former chief editor of the leading intellectual journal, *Reading*, and a senior fellow from the Chinese Academy of Social Sciences as examples, provides a detailed and vivid depiction of the profound effects of the Party's co-option policy upon the intellectuals.

In the relationship between the state and intellectuals, despite the dominant role of the Party-state, the intellectuals' attitude towards the Party and their reaction to its rule, as well as the impact of the external environment, domestic and international, are also of great importance. Just as the Party's guiding principle and strategies of thought control have gone through a drastic shift in the post-Mao era, Chinese intellectuals' attitude towards the Party-state and their mentality have also undergone a profound transformation in the period – from critical and contentious in the 1980s to submissive and cooperative since the

1990s – with the Tiananmen crackdown as a dividing line. Moreover, the rapidly changing domestic and international environment, especially the rapidly accelerating, all-round commercialization of the Chinese society and China's gradual integration into globalization since the 1990s, has also exerted a significant influence upon the intellectuals' mentality and stances.

China in the 1980s is often compared by mainland Chinese intellectuals to the May Fourth period and consequently dubbed the "new enlightenment era." Indeed, the 1980s do share one thing, among many others, with the May Fourth era: intellectuals acting as critics of power and the status quo. As a result, Chinese intellectuals had a "contentious relationship" with the Party-state during the 1980s.[26] The critical stance, the sense of social responsibility, and the moral courage of Chinese intellectuals in the 1980s are mainly ascribed to two factors: the political openness of the 1980s and the relatively simple socioeconomic environment at that time. Intriguingly, though in the 1980s the intellectuals upheld a critical attitude towards the state and had a contentious relationship with it, the two parties were by no means in complete confrontation. Rather, their relationship can be best described as a dialectical synthesis of conflict and complementation. One major reason the Party and the intellectuals could maintain a rather cooperative and constructive relationship at that time is that the two parties shared the common belief in democratization and political reform, and moved in the same direction, though their respective understandings of the nature of these two concepts and of their realization in society might have been different.

Then the democratic movement and the Tiananmen crackdown occurred. The crackdown came as a huge shock to both the Party and the intellectuals. The bloodshed in the square terrified the intellectuals and ruthlessly shattered their utopian dream of changing China through enlightenment and cultural criticism, making them realize both the strength of the regime's resolve to maintain its monopoly of power and the impotence of knowledge and ideals in the face of a formidable dictatorial state. The fear, disillusionment, and despair caused by the shock effectively silenced the intelligentsia until 1992, when Deng's "tour to the south" triggered a dramatic change in the sociopolitical atmosphere of the country. But the readjustment of the intelligentsia began immediately after the crackdown. In the years following Tiananmen, a large number of Chinese intellectuals withdrew from the intelligentsia and turned to business, a veritable "tide of intellectuals diving into the commercial sea" (*zhishifenzi xiahai chao* 知识分子下海潮). Many others returned to their studies, becoming pure academics under the banner of "setting up academic norms" (*jianli xueshu guifan* 建立学术规范); this realignment gave rise to the phenomenon of "thinkers faded away while scholars came to the foreground" (*sixiangjia danchu, xuewenjia tuxian* 思想家淡出, 学问家凸现). Still others turned into technocrats due to the "professionalization of bureaucracy." Additionally, a number of elite intellectuals, who were highly active and influential in the 1980s, were forced into exile. After readjustment and reshaping, the Chinese intelligentsia of the 1990s differed profoundly from that of the 1980s in many ways.[27]

First of all, the Chinese intelligentsia, loosely united under the enlightenment discourse and common goals in the 1980s, rapidly disintegrated in the 1990s and divided into different cliques or sects, which fought against each other seemingly more for intellectual and moral superiority than for truth.[28] In some sense, the disintegration of the Chinese intelligentsia in the 1990s is understandable, given the rapidly changing and increasingly complicated social reality in China as well as the increasingly diversified perceptions of it on the part of intellectuals. In the 1980s, when China had just launched the process of reform and opening up, the problems caused by the new policy were largely invisible. The simplicity of the sociopolitical reality at that time made it relatively easy for the intellectuals to maintain a rather united view. Moreover, the major mission of the intellectuals in the 1980s was to justify the cause of reform by criticizing the disastrous Maoist social practice and promoting modern values. It was not hard for the intellectuals to reach a consensus on this mission. In the 1990s, however, the sociopolitical and economic reality of China changed profoundly. The unprecedented combination of market economy and political dictatorship, the all-round commercialization of the society, China's integration into globalization, and the increasingly deteriorating social conditions brought about many new phenomena and questions. Unlike in the 1980s, when the major question facing the intellectuals was whether or not China should be reformed, in the 1990s the intellectuals were confronted with the question of how to reform, and they were also expected to provide diagnoses of and potential solutions to the extremely complex and diverse social problems facing China. Obviously, the extreme complexity of the socioeconomic condition in 1990s China made it very hard, if not impossible, for the intellectuals to reach a unified vision, and the disintegration of the intelligentsia thus became inevitable.[29] Of course, that complexity is not the only reason for the disintegration and sectarianization of the Chinese intelligentsia since the 1990s. Scholars point to the oversimplified, dichotomous mode of thinking, which has been cultivated and developed over half a century of war and class struggle during the Communist revolution, as another major cause. Whereas Geremie Barmé refers to this mode of thinking as "ideological extremism," characterized by its "sectarian narrowness and virulence,"[30] Chen Sihe dubs it "the thinking of war" (*zhanzheng siwei* 战争思维).[31]

Compared with the 1980s, the overall atmosphere of the intelligentsia and their attitude towards the Party-state also underwent a profound transformation in the 1990s. The Tiananmen Massacre and the terror it brought about completely dissipated the atmosphere of idealism, utopianism, and optimism that had prevailed over the intelligentsia in the 1980s. Under the dual lure from both the Party and the market, the overwhelming majority of Chinese intellectuals chose to surrender to the Party, and consequently abandoned their role as a social conscience and their independent and critical stance. Indeed, after Tiananmen, Chinese intellectuals – except for a few steadfast dissidents, who were marginalized, isolated, and under surveillance by the Party – self-consciously keep silent before the problems and even atrocities inherent in the system. After abandoning their role as the social conscience and critics of power, Chinese intellectuals quickly turned to material gains and mundane achievements along with the tide of commercialization and consumerism. All these factors gave birth to an intelligentsia with a completely different character, mentality, and values. Whereas the Chinese intelligentsia was dominated by idealism in the 1980s, it was consumed by cynicism – a combination of moral nihilism, stark utilitarianism, and hedonism – in the 1990s.

Chinese intellectuals' changed role and mentality naturally opened the door to co-optation by the Party, an opportunity that the Party certainly did not neglect. This situation helps explain the effectiveness of the Party's new strategy in controlling the intellectuals. After Tiananmen, those intellectual elites themselves formed an "interest group" or became spokesmen for interest groups, which led to their mental vulgarization and moral corruption. Gan Yang, a well-known Chinese intellectual, criticized the Chinese intelligentsia for contracting the "syndrome of collective moral corruption" (*jiti daode fubai zheng* 集体道德腐败症). According to Gan, the Chinese intelligentsia has lost the "basic sense of morality and justice," because they understand "freedom" as "a privilege possessed by a minority of people not as a right enjoyed by all," and they also keep silent and indifferent faced with the predation upon ordinary people by a tiny minority of the privileged.[32] *Such Is This World*, through portraying three different types of intellectuals, paints a vivid and intriguing picture of the division within the Chinese intelligentsia and the moral depravity of Chinese intellectuals after Tiananmen. *The Seventh Day*, by showing how the media and university professors collude with the government to cover up the truth of the horrifying "forced demolition," suggests that Chinese intellectuals have degenerated into mouthpieces of the oppressive Party-state.

To be sure, the seemingly more harmonious relationship between the intellectuals and the Party-state since the 1990s definitely does not result from a weakening of the Party-state's capacity of control but from the former's submission to the latter. In the post-Mao era, Chinese intellectuals, especially the elite groups, actually face a dilemma. On the one hand, they seem to enjoy more privileges and more autonomy than before; on the other hand, they also have more to lose: their hard-gained social status, fame, and the enormous wealth that they have obtained through the market and through rewards from the Party-state for political conformity. Consequently, the cost of political defiance for an elite intellectual in the post-Mao era would be even higher than it was in the Mao era. As such, wealth, social status, and fame become an invisible fetter for intellectuals, who become their own wardens and censors. In *Such Is This World*, we witness an intellectual who, under the tremendous fear caused by the Tiananmen Massacre and the lure of wealth, fame, and power, falls all the way from a conscientious critic of government in the 1980s to a shameless academic who willingly serves as a mouthpiece for the Party and shows cowardice and selfishness in the face of state oppression and injustice after Tiananmen. In *The Fat Years*, we meet another academic who turns from a somewhat non-conformist scholar to a model worker and docile counsellor to the government under the lure of the tremendous privileges and benefits provided by the Party-state. We also see another scholar who, extremely contented with the wealth and privilege he enjoys, regards recognition by the Party as the greatest achievement in his life.

Through the juxtaposition of the motifs and themes of these political novels and the Chinese reality with regard to the relationship between the Party-state and the intellectuals, the historical and epistemological values of these novels become clear: they shatter the illusory and deceptive Party-intellectuals myth constructed by the state propaganda machine and aim to restore the truth about the relationship between the two groups. As we will discover later, one of the most significant contributions of these novels is that they reveal the effectiveness of the Party-state's new strategy for controlling intellectuals – buying them off with extravagant rewards – and the profound moral depravity of Chinese intellectuals after Tiananmen.

Nationalism as State Ideology

Apart from subverting the myths of the "political triangle" constructed by the state propaganda machine, these novels also reveal the profound and disastrous impact upon Chinese society of nationalism, which has been elevated to the status of state ideology in the post-Mao era. In *Such Is This World*, readers witness that Chinese internet users employ the discourse of extreme nationalism to condemn, threaten, and attack those conscientious intellectuals who expose and fight against the control of information and oppression of thought. *The Fat Years* portrays an even more horrifying picture: the younger generations of Chinese take the Party's propaganda as absolute truth, and their view of right and wrong is completely inverted; they do not hesitate to persecute their own family and take fascist action against those regarded as enemies or threats to the state in the name of nationalism. Although *Wolf Totem* seems ostensibly to beat the drum for nationalism, "on the deeper narrative level," however, the novel *unconsciously* and allegorically reveals the disastrous consequences that extreme nationalism and social Darwinism brought to the Mongolian people and culture as well as to the Chinese nation in general.

The discoveries made in these novels are both supported by scholars' research and proven by Chinese social reality. As mentioned earlier, theory or ideology plays a crucial role in the construction of moral superiority and political legitimacy for the Chinese Communist Party, evidenced by the fact that every supreme leader of the Party – from Chairman Mao to the current general secretary Xi Jinping – created a "thought" to work as a guiding principle for the Party. Though the Chinese Communist Party claims to be a Marxist party, in reality it is nationalism rather than Marxism that constitutes the core of its ideology. As Suisheng Zhao convincingly argues, because the Chinese Communist Party came to power "through a popular, anti-imperialist war, the very essence of the legitimacy of the communist state was not Marxism but nationalism."[33] David Apter also insists that Marxism, due to its self-contradictory and "idealistic" nature, serves merely as a theoretical shell for communist ideology; it does not possess any practical ability to guide real revolutionary actions. "Classical Marxism has little to say about socialism," he argues, offering no "specific socialist political mechanisms of rule and institutions of government."[34] As such, "Marxism, which claims to be the ultimate materialism, is in fact the ultimate idealism."[35] In the Chinese context, to overcome the self-contradiction and emptiness of Marxism, the Chinese Communist Party fills the Marxist theoretical shell with nationalism, establishing nationalism as the guiding principle for its policies and action.

Indeed, given the overwhelming power and impact of nationalistic discourses and sentiments upon Chinese society, the Communist Party has consistently manipulated nationalism for its own purposes. Throughout its history, the Party has endeavoured to create a glorious, messianic self-image as the only representative of the nation. During the revolution, nationalism was used by the Party to demonize and attack its major opponent, the Kuomintang, which was smeared by the Communist propaganda machine as a "bulldog of American imperialists" and a "traitor to the Chinese nation," to overcome the localism prevailing in the rural area and mobilize the peasants,[36] and to win sympathy and support from the people. After the Communist victory in 1949, when the slogan of "the Party is the people's party" had been well instilled in people's minds, nationalism became a powerful weapon employed by the state to maintain national unity, to gather people's loyalty, to attack the state's enemy, and to claim the Party's political legitimacy. In Mao's China, whenever a social catastrophe occurred as the result of the Party's devastating political movements or policies, it was always "American imperialists" or "Russian Soviet revisionists" who were to blame. Nationalism served as the most effective tool manipulated by the regime to cover up its own wrongdoing and crimes, and to deceive people at that time.

After Mao's death, nationalism went through an ebbing period during the "culture fever" in the 1980s, when China began to open up to the outside world and Chinese intellectuals launched another "enlightenment movement" in an attempt to replace traditional Chinese culture with modern Western values and views. The decline of nationalistic discourses and sentiments was only short-lived before they regained momentum after the Tiananmen Massacre, when the government felt the necessity and urgency to eliminate the influence of liberalism and cosmopolitanism – the dominant trends in the 1980s – and to replace them with what the Party wanted to fill people's minds. Fully aware of the emptiness and futility of the so-called Communist ideals, the Party rediscovered nationalism.

Suisheng Zhao provides a convincing and insightful explanation of the trajectory, intrinsic logic, and reasons for the rediscovery of nationalism by the Party-state after Tiananmen. According to Zhao, Mao's utopian social practices, implemented from the late 1950s to the 1970s, with the Cultural Revolution as their culmination, resulted in disastrous consequences. They started the process of the Chinese people's gradual alienation from Communist ideals. Deng's "thought liberation movement," whose original goal was to "eradicate all ideological and psychological obstacles to market-oriented economy," unexpectedly and paradoxically "resulted in the widespread demise of communist ideology" and the crisis of faith in socialism, Marxism, and the Party.[37] The historical facts exposed in the discussions and debates during the "thought liberation movement" convinced the Chinese people that Maoist Communist utopianism was the root cause of China's recent disasters. As a result, "the near-total collapse of public faith in communism threatened an already-eroded state legitimacy and created an opportunity for the popular advancement of alternative visions of China's future."[38] This opportune opening explains the rapid emergence and efflorescence of Western liberal ideas in the Chinese intelligentsia and Chinese society in the 1980s, which culminated in the Tiananmen pro-democratic movement. "A lesson that the party leaders, reformers and conservatives alike, learned from the Tiananmen incident was that political indoctrination of the younger generation became an urgent need."[39] To restore its own political legitimacy, the Party-state once again adopted nationalism. The reason for the Party's rediscovery of nationalism as an instrument to overcome the crises facing itself and the nation is not only because nationalism always proves itself a ready and effective tool to elicit a sense of unity and engender loyalty to the state in citizens, but also because the Party believes that nationalism is the sentiment and belief shared by all Chinese people, regardless of their social backgrounds and political stances. Because of the purely pragmatic nature of nationalism in post-Mao China, disciplined by neither a set of values nor established principles, Zhao coins the term "state-led pragmatic nationalism."[40]

Indeed, in post-Tiananmen China, along with economic growth, cultivation of nationalistic sentiments among the people is the major effort made by the Party-state to restore its own political legitimacy and to rebuild a belief system for the society.[41] With full awareness of people's resistance to the terrifying Maoist "thought movements," the Party-state in the post-Mao era relies less on coercion and more on seductive means for propaganda and thought control. It subtly wraps nationalism in two more acceptable and accommodating sentiments: patriotism and nostalgic identification with tradition. Here lies the ultimate secret behind and the driving force for the two conspicuous phenomena since the 1990s: the "patriotic education campaign"[42] and the emergence and flourishing of the "national studies fever" (*guoxue re* 国学热).[43]

The nationwide, all-encompassing "patriotic education campaign" represents the Party's major effort to restore its political legitimacy in the ideological realm after Tiananmen, and the course, nature, and significance of the campaign have been fully studied by many scholars.[44]

Several features make this campaign more effective than the old-style Maoist "thought movements." First, unlike the Maoist political movements, which usually put stress on attacking and destroying "hostile and harmful" ideas or beliefs, the "patriotic education campaign" aims mainly at cultivating the sentiments and beliefs judged by the Party as "positive and healthy." In other words, the ultimate goal of "patriotic education" is to forge a new mentality, new values, and a new belief system for the entire society in the long run, which explains why this campaign focuses on young people. Second, in sharp contrast to Maoist political movements, which were always carried out through the disturbance and interruption of the routine of everyday life, the "patriotic education campaign" adeptly immerses ideological indoctrination into daily activities such as schooling, tourism, the mass media, entertainment, and so on. Rather than relying on violent means commonly seen in Maoist thought movements, the Party-state employs school curricula, historical events and sites, cultural relics, festivals, storytelling, movies, and songs to carry out its "patriotic education."[45] These strategies prove to be not only much more acceptable to people than the violent Maoist means but also much more effective in shaping and transforming people's mentality.

The so-called "patriotic education" is by nature an indoctrination using a distorted history of modern China aimed to glorify the Party and to justify its rule. The intent is to evoke nationalistic sentiments in the people. In order to achieve this purpose, the history of China after the late Qing is reduced to two themes: how the foreign imperialists and invaders inflicted humiliation and suffering upon the Chinese nation over a hundred years; and how the Party saved China from its past misery and created a happy and bright "new" society for the nation. What makes the post-Mao "patriotic education campaign" differ from the previous Communist education about history, according to Zheng Wang's study, is that it replaced the Maoist "victor narrative" – that the Chinese Communist Party led the country to destroy the exploiting classes and invaders, won the revolution, and saved the nation – with a new "victimization narrative" that blames the West for China's suffering.[46] Jamil Anderlini provides a more explicit and detailed explanation and an incisive analysis of this phenomenon. He argues: "This campaign replaced the historical narrative of class struggle eventually won by the Communist party with a strong focus on China's struggle with the foreigners. It transformed China from a glorious victor into a weak and persecuted victim."[47] He adds: "The selective teaching of history – emphasising the brutality of foreign invaders and ignoring atrocities or mistakes by China's leaders – is intended to boost the party's legitimacy by cultivating a nationalistic, anti-Western victim mentality among Chinese people."[48]

After Tiananmen, another important intellectual and social phenomenon manipulated by the Party-state for its own service was the so-called "national studies fever" – the sudden popularity of traditional Chinese culture – which emerged in the mid-1990s and dominates the Chinese intellectual and cultural sphere in the new century. Although it is not clear whether this activity was brought into being under the Party's order, there is no doubt that it has received full support and abundant funding from the government since its birth. Lei Yi, a well-known historian and social critic, points out that "the direct push of state power" is the most important driving force for the "national studies" boom in the twenty-first century.[49] Dong Enlin provides a detailed and thorough account of how the government utilizes all kinds of channels and resources to promote and support the "cultural studies fever" through its own organs and other institutions and social media controlled by it since the mid-1990s.[50]

To be sure, promotion of traditional Chinese culture is by no means something new in post-Mao China. Even in the heat of the "culture fever" during the second half of the 1980s, whose dominant theme was to promote modern Western theories and values and to criticize Chinese tradition, studies of traditional Chinese culture made by Li Zehou, Tang Yijie, Chen Lai, and other pre-eminent scholars constituted an important voice within the intelligentsia.[51] The studies of traditional Chinese culture in the 1980s, though not without political implications, were in essence an independent intellectual and cultural activity, with no state power involved. Moreover, the "national studies" of the 1980s aimed at a well-balanced and critical assessment of Chinese tradition, with Western culture as a reference; they were definitely not a eulogy to China's glorious heritage for political purposes. In sharp contrast, the "national studies fever" of the 1990s possessed an explicit political nature and carried an important political mission: to reconstruct the political legitimacy of the Party-state. Lei Yi points out:

In reconstructing the state's "legitimacy," the rapid revival of "national studies" or traditional culture displays a high degree of control over culture by state power in a country with an almighty system. Through the resurrection of traditional culture, "national studies" becomes the vanguard and has been incorporated into the discursive system of national rejuvenation, patriotism, socialism with Chinese characteristics, reinforcement of national cohesion, and national cultural security. This process of encoding and incorporating "national studies" or traditional culture into state ideology also reveals the complicated relationship between state power and scholarship and culture: on the one hand, it reflects state power's control and use of traditional culture; on the other hand, it also reflects the state power's need for and increasing reliance on traditional culture.[52]

Some Chinese intellectuals from the New Left camp define the revival of traditional Chinese culture as a "movement of cultural nationalism."[53] Echoing the Party-state's logic, these intellectuals also regard the "national studies fever" as an important weapon to fight against the "Western cultural camp" for ideological hegemony.[54] In the new century, with the support of the enormous wealth accumulated from the "economic miracle" and under the Party's tight control, "national studies fever" has gone beyond the borders of China, as illustrated by the establishment of the many Confucius Institutes all over the world. Some regard the establishment of Confucius Institutes as the paramount effort made by the government to promote the "national studies fever" internationally.[55]

Although nationalism has always been at the core of state ideology since the beginning of Communist rule in China, and after Tiananmen the Party-state has also consciously utilized nationalism to rebuild its political legitimacy damaged by the massacre, before the Xi Jinping era, nationalism was always wrapped in either a political covering of Communist ideology or a cultural covering of the preservation of national tradition. As a result, state nationalism in the first three decades of the post-Mao era was rather rational, moderate, and defensive – a sharp contrast to populist nationalism, which is often radical and belligerent.[56] Under Xi Jinping, however, the political nature of nationalism is laid bare: "the grand restoration of the Chinese nation" (*zhonghua minzu de weida fuxing* 中华民族的伟大复兴) constitutes the core of the so-called Xi Jinping Thought, and the state machine works at full capacity to propagate nationalist discourses and fan nationalist sentiments. Consequently, nationalism has not only begun to dominate the general public but has also gradually conquered the intellectuals, a group supposed to be more immune to the Party's propaganda than ordinary people. At the bottom of society, nationalism easily converges with populism, forming an "anti-foreign" mentality: whenever a problem occurs in China, it is always blamed on an invisible "foreign hostile force" – usually a subtle reference to the United States or a "force" led by it.[57] In the Xi era, therefore, the distinction between state nationalism, cultural nationalism, and populist nationalism has been blurred, and nationalism becomes a value and stance universally accepted by all groups of the nation – the ruling class, the intellectuals, and the general public alike. Kevin Carrico incisively points out this development:

> Nationalism in China today is a core ideology not only in the sense of a ruse by the ruling class, but also in the sense of a collective misunderstanding of the world that nevertheless provides its believers, including its assumed managers, with the mistaken illusion of complete understanding. What is becoming increasingly apparent in the Xi era is that the general populace is not alone in its susceptibility to such belief: the same elites who fostered and who were to manage these ideologies can also in turn be managed by them.[58]

Under Xi Jinping, nationalism has not only become more pervasive and influential in Chinese society but has also become more aggressive and radical, evidenced by the government's "hardline policies in Hong Kong, escalating threats against Taiwan, mass detentions in Xinjiang, and political interference operations the world over" in the name of defending China's national interests;[59] and by the general populace's extremely hostile attitude towards those whose speeches or behaviour is considered to be "damaging China's national interests or harming Chinese people's feelings."[60]

After three decades of continuous, intensive indoctrination of nationalism since Tiananmen, at whose core is the propagation of the glory of the Party and the viciousness of "Western hostile forces," the effect has become very evident today. The most serious consequence that nationalistic propaganda through "patriotic education" has brought to China is that it distorts the world view and values of China's younger generations.[61] A salient illustration of this consequence is that today more and more young Chinese earnestly believe that the Chinese one-Party system is superior to Western-style democracy and that the Party-state's thought control and even the suppression of dissidents are necessary measures to maintain China's stability and prosperity.[62] Zhu Xueqin, a well-known liberal-minded mainland Chinese intellectual, identifies nationalism and populism as the two most harmful spiritual diseases in China since the May Fourth era.[63]

Ideologization of Morality, Hedonism, and Political Acquiescence

The distortion of the values, views, and mentality of China's younger generations is merely a symptom of the current massive moral and spiritual crisis, a major theme in the novels under consideration. Exposure of the all-round moral crisis in present-day China, for instance, is a dominant theme of *Lenin's Kisses*. This novel demonstrates how vulgar materialism and the pursuit of hedonism trample human dignity and human values, distort people's views and beliefs, corrupt people's hearts, and eventually lead to the dehumanization of society. It points to unrestrained power, stark utilitarianism, and official corruption as the ultimate sources of the nationwide moral crisis. The novel also suggests that the moral crisis and the mentality shaped by it constitute a favourable condition for the survival of the Chinese regime and the sustainability of the Chinese model. *The Seventh Day* reveals how the Chinese model of development has produced a spiritual wasteland in China, where ordinary people are deprived of their voice in the face of brutal predation; injustice and inequality prevail; positive human feelings and relations are destroyed; wealth becomes the sole criterion to judge the value of human beings; and people show callous indifference towards the suffering and misery of others. *The Fat Years* portrays a bleak picture of how Chinese intellectual elites have been bought off by the Party-state, becoming part of the oppressive state machine, and of how Chinese people slavishly submit to dictatorship in exchange for material prosperity. The novel also indicates that the inculcation of extreme nationalism and social Darwinism by the state creates a hotbed for the birth of extreme trends like fascism. *Such Is This World* exposes the grim fact that ordinary Chinese people work as accomplices with the regime in thought oppression and in their own victimization, while intellectuals sell their souls and conscience to the Party-state for power, social status, and wealth.

Now that the moral and spiritual crisis is an ongoing, daily experience for all Chinese, it is impossible that the Party-state is unaware of it. To be fair, when the Party-state launched the "patriotic education campaign" and fanned the "national studies fever" to promote nationalistic discourses and sentiments all over the country, it aimed not only to restore its damaged political legitimacy but also to establish a rationalized system of belief and values that would be functional for the nation. Why did the effort fail?

Two major factors might account for the failure: the ideologization of morality in contemporary China and the wide spread of hedonism in Chinese society after Tiananmen. To begin with, well-known political philosopher Michael Oakeshott's insight into moral life provides us with an inspiring perspective and analytical device to probe this phenomenon. Oakeshott distinguishes between two forms of moral life in human society. The first form is "customary morality": "a habit of affection and behavior," "the unreflective following of the tradition of conduct in which we are brought up."[64] The acquisition of this form of moral life is accumulative, unreflective, and imitative, in the same way as we acquire our native language. It "gives remarkable stability to the moral life from the point of view either of an individual or of a society."[65] It provides the stability, sustainability, and flexibility necessary for a sound society. The second form of moral life, according to Oakeshott, is "reflective morality" – "the reflective application of a moral criterion."[66] This form "appears in two common varieties: as the self-conscious pursuit of moral ideals and as the reflective observance of moral rules."[67] Oakeshott believes that this form of morality is "dangerous in an individual and disastrous in a society" on certain grounds.[68] Consistent moral reflection may damage moral habit, and pursuit of moral ideals always tends to be perfectionist. As such, this form of morality has little power of self-modification due to "its inelasticity and its imperviousness to change."[69] Most importantly, the pursuit of moral ideals means obsession with one ideal leading to "exclusion of others, perhaps all others."[70] It can be inferred that this form of morality is highly vulnerable to manipulation by individuals or organizations for ideological hegemony, thought control, or even oppression. Because of these reasons, Oakeshott believes that this form of morality would bring disaster to society. However, no society, Oakeshott argues, is dominated by only one form of morality; it is always a combination of both. In the combination, one form always predominates. In light of Oakeshott's argument, the most desirable situation should be that customary morality dominates. Unfortunately, in contemporary Western society, as Oakeshott deplores, the second form prevails, which brings serious moral and social problems to Western societies.

Oakeshott's diagnosis of the moral problems for contemporary Western societies can be properly applied to the moral reality in contemporary China, where the situation is even worse. Radical antitraditionalism,[71] the Communist revolution, and the all-round corruption of intellectual and political elites, who are traditionally looked up to as moral models for ordinary people to emulate, have substantively damaged customary morality in Chinese society. As a result, reflective morality – or precisely, the pursuit of moral ideals – has become the dominant form of moral life. In a country where the Party imposes strict control over intellectual, moral, and spiritual realms, it is only natural to find that moral ideals are shaped by state ideology and that moral development is regarded merely as a part of the propagation of state ideology and the construction of the grand Communist project. In the Mao era, a minority of people were labelled "class enemies," ostracized from society, and treated with cruelty, while the majority (the so-called "revolutionary masses") were called upon to emulate a few "Communist moral models," such as Lei Feng, created by the state propaganda machine. Even judging by common sense, the Maoist moral construction was bound to fail, because a moral system that requires people to completely ignore their own interests and to sacrifice themselves only for others and for the grand Communist cause runs counter to human nature, and as such is irrational and impractical. In the post-Mao era, the Party-state has abandoned many inhumane, absurd, and unrealistic elements in the Chinese moral system associated with the Maoist ideology of class struggle and attempts to reconstruct a rationalized moral system centred on nationalism by a more acceptable means. But this effort has also been in vain. Why?

The Party-state's effort at moral construction, centred on nationalist discourse and sentiments, relies heavily on the education of a selective, distorted, and even false history. In an age of the internet and globalization, no matter how hard the state tries, the effort to control information and to hide facts from people is bound to end in failure.[72] With the wide application of the internet and the massive scale of exchange with the outside world in culture, trade, and many other important fields, it is impossible for any government, even with the assistance of such powerful technology as China's Great Firewall, to completely block information from the outside world and to fully cover up historical truth. Thus, the glorious image and moral ideals built on selective, distorted, and fabricated facts are bound to collapse sooner or later. Therefore, the attempt to establish a rationalized moral system based on moral ideals constructed with the education of a selective, distorted, and false history can only create a moral environment of hypocrisy, duplicity, and mutual suspicion. Moreover, distorted history education will inevitably produce distorted personalities and distorted values and world views, which are obviously detrimental to the construction of a sound and rationalized moral system for the nation. Simply put, it is impossible to construct a rationalized moral system that would be functional in the long run based on fabrication and falsehood.

Moreover, in constructing its nationalistic discourse, the Party-state incorporates too much social Darwinism. Darwinism, according to James Pusey, is not only "the first Western 'ism' widely to be accepted by Chinese"[73] but was also the dominant modern Western theory before the May Fourth era.[74] Pusey's research shows that Mao Zedong was greatly influenced by social Darwinism, and his famous statement that "political power grows out of the barrel of a gun"[75] obviously echoes the Darwinist overtone. The political catchphrase in the Deng era that "one will be bullied if falling behind" (*luohou jiu yao aida* 落后就要挨打)

also suggests the notion of the law of the jungle. After the Tiananmen Massacre, the Chinese Party-state subtly embedded social Darwinism into its educational policies in order to restore its damaged political legitimacy. As Zheng Wang's study convincingly demonstrates, in the "patriotic education campaign," the Chinese Party-state adeptly manipulated social Darwinism to glorify itself and to justify its rule by exaggerating the humiliation and oppression inflicted on a weak China by the much more powerful West.[76] It is common knowledge that social Darwinism, by appropriating the law of the jungle and applying it to human society, completely denies the function of morality in society. As such, it is amoral. It seems self-contradictory and paradoxical to build a moral system on amoral or immoral principles. Additionally, the Chinese brand of social Darwinism spreads hatred towards Western countries and Japan. It is hard to imagine that a rationalized moral system built on baseless hatred towards other cultures and nations will not eventually collapse.

Apart from the distorted nationalistic education, hedonism as a product of Dengist economic determinism, which permeates society in the post-Mao era, constitutes another major cause for the unprecedented moral crisis in contemporary China. It is widely assumed that hedonism is a phenomenon unique to the post-Mao era, because Mao's China, apparently dominated by asceticism, had nothing to do with hedonism. Jiwei Ci, however, in a book exploring the transformation of Communist ideology and the social ethos in contemporary China, propounds an original theory invalidating this assumption. The principle of hedonism, according to Ci, has been at the core of the Chinese Communist practice throughout the history of the Chinese Communist Party, in both the Mao and post-Mao eras alike. The only difference between the two periods is that, whereas in the post-Mao era hedonism is the ultimate goal of life openly and avidly pursued by Chinese people, in the Mao era it was disguised as "economic asceticism." In Maoist ideology, according to Ci, the practice of asceticism for a short period was viewed as the necessary means and path to achieve the long-term goal of hedonism.[77] As Ci explains, the practice of communism in China before Tiananmen was by nature a utopian project. Whereas Mao tried to achieve the project by political means, Deng attempted to reach it through economic development. When the Chinese utopian project ended up a complete failure, as exemplified by the Tiananmen crackdown, the whole nation immediately plunged into nihilism. Nihilism quickly turned into hedonism when the market economy brought material prosperity to China after 1992. Because hedonism is the guiding principle underlying Chinese Communist ideology, the trajectory from utopianism to hedonism via nihilism in Communist China, according to Ci's interpretation, is actually a process of the self-revelation of hedonism.[78]

The dual forces after Tiananmen – the indoctrination of extreme nationalism and stark hedonism nurtured by Dengist economic determinism and vulgar materialism – gave birth to a new generation with a somewhat split and distorted mentality. On the one hand, the younger generation displays a "self-interested, apolitical pragmatism," characterized by obsession with material satisfaction and ostensible indifference to politics. Whereas Dengist economic determinism and the accompanying hedonism and consumerism obviously account for their materialistic orientation, the reasons for their "political nonchalance" are rather complicated. Simon Elegant, in a highly insightful essay on China's younger generation – whom he dubs the "Me generation" – enumerates several possible factors responsible for the seeming nonchalance towards politics of young Chinese: their sense of impotence before politics, their satisfaction with the status quo and with the government, and their fear and weariness of Chinese politics as a psychological consequence of the horrible political movements in China's recent history. Elegant believes that the Me generation's materialistic mindset and seeming political indifference constitute a favourable condition for the survival of Communist domination.[79]

On the other hand, those highly materialistic and seemingly politically indifferent "peace lovers" can be ignited and mobilized instantly by a very simple nationalistic appeal and could turn highly belligerent in no time. Joseph Fewsmith, at the very beginning of his well-known book on Chinese politics and intellectuals after Tiananmen, expresses his surprise and confusion with this phenomenon in his comments on the bombing of the Chinese embassy in Belgrade by the United States in 1999.[80] It becomes quite clear that the seemingly apolitical stance of young Chinese actually is not truly apolitical at all; instead, it is a social positioning in a post-totalitarian Party-state with strong political implications. Indeed, it is hard to believe that, in a post-totalitarian regime, where political power still dominates almost every aspect of social life – though in a way quite different from the Mao era – and where the state machine painstakingly and systematically indoctrinates a political consciousness of anti-Western nationalism in the whole society, its people's mindset can be apolitical. If the ostensible "political nonchalance" of young Chinese people is a direct result of their feeling of impotence before a formidable state machine and their fear of the horrible consequences of political participation as demonstrated by the terrifying Maoist political movements, then the seemingly "apolitical" attitude itself is political.

The seeming "political nonchalance" of Chinese people is in essence what Antonio Gramsci dubs "political acquiescence" – the "spontaneous consent" given by the dominated to the ruling class in a society.[81] In the context of post-Tiananmen China, where the Party-state completely lost its political legitimacy, the political acquiescence is actually a deal made by the Chinese people with the Party-state: to use their tolerance of the Party's dictatorship in exchange for material prosperity.[82] Moreover, because nationalism is almost the only content that the younger generation has received for political education, it is only understandable that they can be ignited only by nationalist appeal while seeming "apolitical" in many other aspects of politics. When nationalism becomes not only a political requirement but also, and more importantly, the highest moral principle, it is only natural to see that abundant moral corruption and even cruelty against humanity can be performed openly and unrestrainedly under the banner of nationalism in today's China.

Summary

Deeply rooted in the social, political, and intellectual soil of early twenty-first century China, oppositional political novels provide a sketch of its rapidly changing sociopolitical reality. Focusing on the darkness behind the Chinese economic "miracle," they critically reflect on the disastrous consequences of the Chinese model of development. Dealing with the three most important dimensions in Communist China – the Party, the intellectuals, and the people – as well as some most influential trends in contemporary China, such as nationalism and social Darwinism, these novels transgress the "prohibited zones" drawn by the Party, question the fundamental principle of the one-Party system, and challenge the moral and political legitimacy of the Chinese model. Through solid and persuasive descriptions of the sociopolitical reality in Communist China, these novels subvert some fundamental myths created by the state propaganda machine to justify Communist domination and restore historical truths about the relationship of the Party-state, the intellectuals, and the people. These novels also paint a bleak picture of how indoctrination of extreme nationalism and social Darwinism through selective, deceptive, and even false historical education distorts the mentality, values, and world views of the younger generations of Chinese and brings a moral crisis to the nation.

Chapter Two

Wolf Totem: Paradoxical Eulogy to a Culture

With a circulation of over five million copies since its publication in 2004, Jiang Rong's novel *Wolf Totem*, a winner of the Man Asian Literary Prize, stands out in the history of contemporary Chinese literature. The extreme popularity of the novel becomes especially remarkable because "serious" literature in China has been largely marginalized by the commercialization of the society since the 1990s and the rapid rise and explosion of internet literature in the twenty-first century.

This semi-autobiographical novel focuses mainly on the life experience and thoughts of Chen Zhen, an "educated youth" sent down from Beijing during the Cultural Revolution to the Inner Mongolian grassland to work as a shepherd in a fictional place named Olonbulag. Through his eyes, the novel depicts a spectacular and thrilling picture of the lives of Mongolian wolves and nomadic Mongols, who struggle with fierce wolves, ruthless climate, and formidable political oppression. It also provides a vivid and intriguing account of the traditional Mongolian way of life and cosmology, centred on the wolf totem and the worship of nature. Chen's reflection on traditional Mongolian culture and on its relationship to Chinese culture and to the entire human civilization also constitutes an important part of the novel. Mongolian values, beliefs, and way of life are presented mainly through the wolf totem and through the speeches, thoughts, and actions of the old man Bilgee, an experienced and well-respected herdsman, who can be regarded as the spokesman for traditional Mongolian culture. The old man's conflict with the highest Communist leader of the region, Bao Shungui, who disdains traditional Mongolian cosmology as backward, superstitious, and barbaric, symbolizes the antagonistic relationship between the Mongolian people and Communist rule. The most interesting and significant part of the novel is the episode of the protagonist raising a wolf cub. This episode, with its nuanced and convincing description of the disposition, emotions, and growth of a wolf, is not only artistically intriguing but also discursively revealing as political allegory.

Howard Goldblatt, the English translator of the novel, emphasizes the "paradoxical role" of wolves in people's lives as presented in the novel.[1] Paradox is indeed the key to understanding not only the role of wolves but also the main themes of the novel, as well as all the sensation it created among readers. This perception is also supported by many other critics. Howard Y.F. Choy, for instance, in a highly profound and insightful review of the novel, articulates some of its most significant discursive paradoxes presented: "It critiques Confucianism in light of militarism, calls for environmental protection and sustainability according to the law of the jungle (or, in Jiang Rong's own term, 'grassland logic'), and advocates 'peaceful' survival of the fittest through territorial expansion and a renewed space race."[2] Jeffrey Wasserstrom argues that "one of the trickiest things to unpack about the whole *Wolf Totem* phenomenon is how it can simultaneously involve a tale so subversive that the author needed to remain anonymous, and yet find the novel being promoted in the official press."[3] Haiyan Lee considers the novel "a most unlikely bestseller" and thinks that "from the start, it has been riddled with paradoxes."[4]

Indeed, paradox is at the core of the novel and displays many aspects on different levels. First of all, paradox is contained in the main theme of the novel. On the one hand, the novel presents a charming picture of the coexistence and interdependence of humans and wolves in the grassland. The two rivalling species fight against yet depend upon each other for survival; they both are guardians sent down by Tengger, the Mongolian heaven, to protect the grassland and will reunite in Tengger after death. On the other hand, the intoxicating picture of the symbiotic and interdependent relationship between human beings and wolves does not lead to the universally accepted human values of mutual understanding, mutual respect, equality, and peace among species, peoples, and cultures but to social Darwinism, cultural and racial chauvinism, and the law of the jungle. Second, the protagonist laments the decline and demise of the traditional Mongolian way of life under Communist dictatorship but does not realize that this decline is precisely the consequence that the political logic he worships will bring about; it is the inevitable fate of a weak minority culture faced with a formidable tyrannical power. Third, the protagonist claims that he loves and worships the wolf deeply, and plenty of evidence supports his claim. But he shows his "love" and "worship" for the wolf cub through fettering it and depriving it of all its freedom and dignity as an animal. As a result, his confinement and abuse of the wolf under the guise of "love" and "worship" finally lead the animal to the loss of its identity and death. Fourth and finally, on "the level of surface manifestation," the novel advocates social Darwinism and nationalism, two sociopolitical streams sanctioned and supported by both the mainstream May Fourth discourse and state ideology; on the "deeper narrative level,"[5] however, the novel reveals the horrible consequences that these state-sanctioned ideologies and policies bring to the Mongolian people and to the entire Chinese nation.

The many paradoxes or discursive self-contractions in the novel diversify and enrich its implications and draw attention from both its supporters and critics, which eventually accounts for its high popularity among the Chinese readership. Moreover, the reception of the novel – its popularity, the extreme breadth of its readership, and the huge controversy over it – also sheds much light on the intellectual landscape and the people's mentality in present-day China.

Wolf Totem and Mongolian Correlative Cosmology

As indicated by the title, wolves play a central role in the novel. With its vivid, nuanced, and convincing presentation of the disposition, behaviour, and emotions of the wolf, the novel constructs a cosmology centred on wolf totem and worship of nature, which upholds the notion of the interdependency of humans, animals, and nature under Tengger. Completely different from the image of the wolf commonly seen in Chinese folk tales or children's books – a devilish animal characterized by its incredible cruelty, cunning, and greed – wolves in this novel are portrayed as dignified and lofty beings, superior to their human competitors in almost every aspect. They are crystallizations of virtue, intelligence, and strength.

To begin with, wolves "have a strong collective spirit; they stick together. It is not in their nature to abandon one of their own."[6] Old man Bilgee adopts the term "pack mentality" to describe wolves' collective spirit. As he explains, the reason wolves can dominate the vast Mongolian grassland, whereas much larger and more powerful animals like tigers are not even able to survive out there, is that the latter lack the kind of "pack mentality" possessed by the former. He says:

> Tigers make a kill for themselves, not for other tigers, not even for their mates or offspring. But wolves kill for themselves and for the rest of the pack, even those that can't be in on the kill – the old, the crippled, the nearly blind, the young, the sick, and the nursing females ... A wolf takes

care of the pack, and the pack takes care of each wolf …Wolves are more family-oriented than people, and much more united.[7]

Because of the "pack mentality," a pack of wolves are always well-organized, highly disciplined, and extraordinarily united. Even if in great danger, they retreat "in orderly fashion, maintaining the ancient organizational unity and group formation characteristic of grassland wolves," without "any of the confusion commonly seen among fleeing birds and other wild animals."[8] It is this collective spirit or "pack mentality" that makes wolves the rulers of the grassland.

Wolves are also brave, noble, and have a strong spirit of self-sacrifice. To avoid being a burden for others and to protect the best interests of the pack, a wolf is ready to accept the fate of being killed by the alpha wolf or killing itself in an extremely dangerous situation. With "their hard bones, hard hearts, and survival skills," Mongolian wolves are "tough as steel";[9] they possess the "death-before-surrender spirit"[10] – that is, they will fight to the last breath and die with dignity rather than surrender to their enemies. "You can tame a bear, a tiger, a lion, or an elephant, but you cannot tame a Mongolian wolf."[11] On one occasion, readers witness a severely wounded female wolf, who chews off its own injured leg for survival, refuse to show a trace of fear and submission in the face of two armed hunters; instead, "defiantly, it stared at its enemies, not for a minute forgetting its dignity." There is a "look of savage righteousness" in its eyes.[12] On another occasion, readers see a wolf being chased to the brink of a cliff, with no way out, who manages to loosen the rocks around it and bury itself alive rather than surrender to humans.[13] The wolves possess "spiritual power that would shame and inspire awe in humans."[14] "Neither food nor killing was the purpose of the wolves' existence; rather, it was their sacred, inviolable freedom, their independence, and their dignity."[15]

Contrary to the common presumption that wolves are extremely greedy, the novel indicates that wolves are definitely not as greedy as humans; instead, they are very reasonable and rational, possessing a sense of fairness. As old man Bilgee testifies, "wolves won't bother people and their animals as long as they have food to eat."[16] Their attacks on domestic animals and occasionally on humans are actually motivated by the intention to survive from starvation or to rebel against the tyranny and extreme greed of humans. For instance, the most fierce and most violent fight presented in the novel – the one between wolves and humans when the former launch a massive murderous attack on over one hundred military horses – is caused by the greed and cruelty of human beings in the first place: people not only pillage all the gazelles that the wolves have killed and stored for food to survive the grim winter on the Mongolian grassland but also launch a large-scale fateful campaign to steal wolf cubs in an attempt to eradicate all wolves in the area, which greatly infuriates these unconquerable creatures.

Wolves show deep love and affection for their families and pack members, best demonstrated by a mother wolf's love for her children and her care for others' cubs:

> There were many stories about the love of a mother wolf for her cubs. In order to teach them to hunt, she'd take great risks to catch a live lamb under daunting circumstances; in order to protect her cubs in the den, she'd fight hunters to the death; for the cubs' safety, she'd carry them to a different place each night; and to feed them, she'd gorge herself to the point of bursting, and then empty the contents for them. And in the interest of the pack, females who had lost their cubs nursed others' cubs.[17]

A mother wolf's love is so profound and selfless that it can extend to human orphans, even though humans are their chief enemies.[18] Wolves are also animals full of feelings and emotions, just like human beings.

As clearly illuminated by the growth of the wolf cub raised by Chen and by many other pieces of evidence, wolves have superb adaptability, wisdom, and ability to endure challenges and hardships in extremely harsh climates and adverse environments. They prove to be masters of the strategies and arts of war, "unmatched at climatological warfare."[19] They are always able to figure out the best way to fight a war or to overcome a crisis. Once, a pack of wolves attacked a large flock of sheep in a stone enclosure, eating a dozen and killing more than two hundred. Because the wall of the enclosure was too high for wolves to climb over, and there were also no breaches for them to get in, people simply could not figure out how the wolves carried out the seemingly impossible slaughter. They could only resort to their old belief to explain the mystery: the wolf can fly. Only after a meticulous investigation led by the local police chief was the secret finally uncovered. The murderous attack proves to be a masterpiece of wolves' ingenuity and cooperative spirit. It turns out that the wolves took turns to function as a springboard for their fellow wolves to leap into the enclosure to eat their fill; then they came out over the "bridge" that they built with the carcasses of sheep they had killed. Wolves are also extremely patient and determined. In order to catch a prey, a wolf can hide in a place for a whole day in an extreme climatic condition, watching its target, and find the best time to launch its attack.

Perhaps because of the superb abilities that wolves possess, Mongols look up to wolves with reverence and awe. They believe that wolves have divine powers. Each time wolves make a large-scale killing, they will make some mysterious circular paths on the spot. Mongols believe these "wolf circles" are "spiritual signs" made by wolves to acknowledge their gratitude to Tengger. Old man Bilgee explains:

> Tengger sent wolves down to the grassland as protectors of the Bayan Uul sacred mountain and the Olonbulag. Tengger and the sacred mountain are angered each time the grassland is endangered, and wolves are sent to kill and consume the offenders. Every time they receive this gift, they joyfully run circles around it until they've tramped out a path as round as the sun and the moon. That circular path is their acknowledgment to Tengger, a sort of thank-you note.[20]

Besides, the wolf is the only animal on the grassland that howls into the sky – an act regarded by Mongols as evidence that wolves can communicate with Tengger directly.

Mongols' worship of wolves as supernatural beings is most explicitly demonstrated by their long-lasting tradition of sky burial. "Over centuries, the herdsmen and hunters of the grassland returned to Tengger with no burial and no markers, and definitely no mausoleums. Men and wolves were born on the grassland, lived there, fought there, and died there. They left the grassland exactly as they found it."[21] When a herdsman died, his body was taken into the wilds and laid out in open view for the wolves to eat. "It was called a sky burial owing to the belief that the wolves could fly to Tengger, taking the human soul back with them, just like the magic eagles of Tibet."[22] Whether the soul of the deceased can enter Tengger or not depends on the virtues, or their lack, of the life lived. Therefore, the wolf totem is closely related to the Mongolian view of life and death. "Since all the herdsmen of the Olonbulag would one day wind up in the bellies of wolves via the sky burial, they had, for millennia, been at peace with the idea of death."[23] Underlying the sky burial, there is also a unique Mongolian view of values and of the relationship between humans and wolves. By feeding wolves with human remains, according to old man Bilgee, the sky burial turns humans from "meat-eaters to eaten meat."[24] As he explains, "we grasslanders eat meat all our lives, for which we kill many creatures. After we die, we donate our meat back to the grassland. To us, it only seems fair, and it's good for our souls when we go up to Tengger."[25] There is clearly a sense of fairness and mutual respect between humans and animals in the ritual of sky burial.

Based on wolf totem and the worship of the grassland, Mongols have constructed a unique cosmology. As indicated by the idea of the "wolf circle" as a thank-you note to Tengger and the notion that wolves can fly and take human souls back to heaven after death, Mongols believe that everything under Tengger – humans, wolves, gazelles, livestock, and the grassland – are linked to each other, composing a symbiotic system. This view is actually a Mongolian version of correlative cosmology.[26] It is hierarchical, as its components occupy different positions and possess different significance. Old man Bilgee uses the terms "big life" and "little life" to illustrate the hierarchy. According to his interpretation, "out here, the grass and the grassland are the big life. All else is little life that depends on the big life for survival. Even wolves and humans are little lives. Creatures that eat grass are worse than creatures that eat meat."[27] According to this theory, whereas gazelles, who can eat and destroy more grass than any mowing machine, are the biggest scourge for the grassland, wolves, who kill gazelles and other herbivores, are the protectors of it. In this correlative cosmos, wolves play a dominant role. This pre-eminence is why Mongols regard the wolf as their deity and totem.

Wolves not only safeguard the grassland, the home of Mongols, but also shape Mongols' character, identity, values, and way of life; they are also intricately intertwined with the history of the Mongolian people. Despite its status as a "physical enemy" for Mongols, the wolf has been revered by Mongols as their totem, mentor, and saviour. In the process of fighting against wolves over centuries, Mongols have emulated and learned from wolves; consequently, they share many moral virtues and qualities with the wolves: they are tough, brave, intelligent, and unselfish, possessing a collective mentality and the spirit of self-sacrifice. To some extent, wolves define the identity of Mongols. The protagonist Chen Zhen believes that "if there'd been no wolves, those great war counselors and leaders, there'd have been no Genghis Khan, no golden tribe, no wise and brave Mongol fighting horsemen."[28] Old man Bilgee also says: "Anyone who doesn't eat wolves' food is not a true grassland Mongol. There would be no Mongols without it. In days past, when Mongols were driven to the brink of destruction, they survived by eating wolves' food."[29] He adds: "Wolves are the Mongols' benefactors, sometimes their saviors. Without them there would have been no Genghis Khan, and no Mongols."[30] Legend has it that one of Genghis Khan's ancestors survived a great catastrophe by following a wolf pack and feeding on the food left by the wolves. In this sense, wolves symbolize Mongols and the history of the Mongol people.

Social Darwinism, Reverse Chauvinism, and Nationalism

Among the many paradoxes and discursive self-contradictions in the novel, a conspicuous one concerns its interpretation of Mongolian correlative cosmology. Ironically, the beautiful notion of the interaction and interdependence between "the big life" and "little lives" and between humans and wolves does not lead the protagonist and his friends to such positive values and beliefs as cultural pluralism, equality, and mutual respect among species, peoples, and cultures. On the contrary, it is utilized to confirm and propagate social Darwinism, cultural and racial chauvinism, and the law of the jungle.

Unlike traditional Chinese correlative cosmology, which is essentially anthropocentric,[31] the Mongolian version of cosmology as presented in the novel is wolf-centred. According to this theory, in the Mongolian hierarchical cosmos, though humans and wolves are both acclaimed as protectors and safeguards of the grassland, they occupy different positions in the system. Mongols believe that wolves possess divine power, and as such they are superior to humans in every aspect: wisdom, strength, and morality. It is precisely based on the view of the superiority of wolves over humans that the protagonist and his friends claim that the Mongolian race and culture are superior to the Chinese race and culture – stark racial and cultural chauvinism. Given that the protagonist and his friends are all Chinese, it is proper to dub this claim reverse racial and cultural chauvinism.

In the novel, the origin of the chauvinism can be traced to the extremely oversimplified, problematic, and preposterous dichotomous view of the world upheld by the protagonist and his friends: that human history in general, and Chinese history in particular, is a process of confrontation and interaction between wolves and humans, and between the values, views, and cultures derived from these two species. According to this world view, the history of China is interpreted as a process of the interaction and contention between two forces: nomadic Mongolian culture and agrarian Chinese culture, which is the mainstream culture created by the Han people, the dominant ethnic group in China. Whereas the former is symbolized by the wolf and characterized by the asserted qualities or virtues of the wolf, the latter is symbolized by domestic animals, with sheep and dogs as the most evident exemplars, and characterized by their qualities. To painstakingly promote the idea of the superiority of wolves over humans and Mongolian culture over Han Chinese culture, the novel is replete with statements like "Mongols are meat-eating wolves and Han Chinese are grass-eating sheep"[32] and "Chinese are as cowardly as sheep."[33] Howard Y.F. Choy provides an inspiring analysis of this oversimplified and misleading dichotomous mode of thinking. He points out:

> The novelist proposes to introject Mongolian otherness onto Han selfhood in antitheses of nomads/farmers, carnivores/herbivores, brutalism/domestication, liberalism/Confucianism, and wolf worship/sheep spirit. In these simple binary pairs the former is deemed good, brave and intelligent, whereas the latter is bad (if not evil), weak and stupid. Such binary oppositions present to us not only a clash of nomadic and agrarian civilizations but also, because the latter is derogated to the rudimentary stage of world history, a crisis of superiority and inferiority complexes.[34]

Surprisingly yet understandably, the Chinese students do not feel offended by these contemptuous and insulting comments about Han Chinese and Han culture made by Mongols at all; instead, they wholeheartedly identify with and accept these sayings. In one place, the protagonist deliberately links the scene of a group of sheep silently watching other sheep being slaughtered by wolves directly to the famous "slide show incident" delineated by Lu Xun, where a group of Chinese numbly and silently watch a fellow Chinese being beheaded by Russians,[35] to highlight the symbolic analogy between animal and culture. The two types of culture sometimes are simply referred to as "wolf culture" and "sheep culture," respectively. Similar to the absolute superiority of the wolf over other animals in Mongolian cosmology, the Mongolian "wolf culture" as presented in the novel is also absolutely superior to the Han Chinese "sheep culture."

As a manifestation and a result of this view of the natural world and of different cultures, the novel is full of praise for wolves and "wolf culture" and has stark contempt for domestic animals and "sheep culture." Whereas the wolf is eulogized as the "noblest, most treasured, and most beautiful" creature on earth,[36] an "almost magical beast" with unfathomable wisdom,[37] representing the "perfection of evolution" and "Tengger's masterpiece,"[38] sheep and dogs are considered stupid and despicable animals, who are only slaves to people. In the novel, every trait of the wolf is lauded ardently without any reservation – even its ingratitude to the human who feeds it is viewed as a sign of dignity and grace. When it comes to domestic animals, in sharp contrast, even their virtues are disparaged as signs of weakness and disgrace in disguise. For example, a dog's loyalty and obedience to its master are despitefully considered traits of subservience and slavishness. Old man Bilgee expresses this antithesis between the two kinds of animals in the most explicit way:

> How can you speak of wolves and dogs in the same breath? Dogs eat people's shit; wolves eat people; by eating shit, dogs are nothing but slaves to humans. But wolves eat human corpses to send the souls into the bosom of Tengger. Wolves and dogs [are] as different as heaven and earth.[39]

Parallel to the heaven-and-earth difference between the two types of animals, the difference between Mongolian and Chinese culture is also enormous. Mongolian culture, according to the protagonist's interpretation, is far superior to its Chinese counterpart in almost every aspect. First of all, the former is asserted to have a "much longer history" and "greater natural continuity and vitality" than the latter.[40] Whereas the main ideas in the Confucian thought system are claimed by the protagonist to be outdated and decayed, the central spirit of the wolf totem remains vibrant and young.[41] The protagonist also believes that Mongolian culture was created and passed down by "the most advanced races in the worlds," and it is "one of the truly valuable spiritual heritages of all humanity."[42] Traditional Chinese culture, by contrast, was created by inferior Han people, who are "narrow-minded individuals with tunnel vision,"[43] and based on a "small-scale peasant economy."[44] What makes traditional Chinese culture especially inferior, according to the protagonist, is that it upholds a "top-down philosophy" valuing seniority and unconditional obedience, eradicating competition through autocratic power, and consequently has greatly weakened the people's nature.[45] In the protagonist's eyes, traditional Chinese culture is the bane of all the suffering and humiliation inflicted upon Han Chinese over thousands of years.[46] Therefore, the protagonist believes that Mongolian culture represents the hope and future for China. He alleges: "There'd be hope for China if our national character could be rebuilt by cutting away the decaying parts of Confucianism and grafting a wolf totem sapling onto it."[47] He adds: "The Chinese, with their weak dispositions, are in desperate need of a transfusion of that vigorous, unrestrained blood."[48]

The superiority of Mongolian culture over its Chinese counterpart, in light of the protagonist's interpretation, is not only because the former was created by the "most advanced races" and has a longer history and greater vitality, but also and more importantly, because it has made much greater contributions to the world. The greatest accomplishment and "contribution" to the world that Mongols made, according to the protagonist, is that they once founded "the largest empire in the history of the world"[49] and conquered most of the Eurasian continent with their "advanced military capabilities and wisdom."[50] Throughout the novel, the "military miracle performed by Genghis Khan"[51] is ardently lauded:

> The arrival of Genghis Khan and his Mongol horsemen on the scene led to a rewriting of the history of China, from the Jin and Southern Song on. So too the histories of Central Asia, Persia, Russia, and India. Gunpowder, invented in China, was introduced to the West by Mongol hordes as they cut their murderous swath through Europe and Asia, bringing down the castle of feudalism in the West and sweeping away all the obstacles to the emerging system of capitalism.[52]

Shockingly and ironically, here even the Mongols' "murderous swath" is considered a glorious and laudable "contribution" to the world, a driving force for social progress – destroying feudalism and bringing capitalism to the West. In another place, the protagonist further states:

> In world history, nomads have been the only Easterners capable of taking the fight to the Europeans, and the three peoples that really shook the West to its foundation were the Huns, the Turks, and the Mongols.[53]

Again, aggression is acclaimed a glorious contribution to world history. According to the protagonist, Mongols, along with "Westerners," are the creators of the modern value system. As he asserts, "the most advanced people today are descendants of nomadic races … They cherish freedom and popular elections, and they have respect for their women, all traditions and habits passed down by their nomadic ancestors."[54] It seems that Mongols and Mongolian "wolf culture" are the dominant, if not the sole, driving force in the development of human history as well as the rise of the modern world.

Readers with even a basic knowledge of human history in general, and China's history in particular, would find that this explanation of human civilization and its modern transformation is not only oversimplified but also distorted. Undoubtedly, the Mongolian people and Mongolian culture have made substantive contributions to world history and human civilization. But the novel obviously exaggerates the accomplishments of Mongols and their influence upon human history. The Yuan dynasty, an ancient Chinese dynasty founded by Mongols lasting for less than a century, is one of the shortest major imperial dynasties in Chinese history. Only during that period had Mongols and their culture exerted significant influence upon China and the Eurasian continent. During the rest of Chinese history, Mongols, like all other minority ethnic groups in China, have been under the domination of the Han majority, and their culture, values, and beliefs have also been transformed by mainstream Chinese culture. As explicitly indicated in the novel, over centuries under the influence of the Han people, those Mongols who reside outside the Mongolian grassland have already abandoned many of their indigenous values and way of life, and gradually adopted those of the Han people. Worldwide, especially in East Asia, mainstream Chinese culture, with Confucianism at its core, has definitely exerted a much more profound and far-reaching influence upon other cultures and other peoples than Mongolian culture. Moreover, Mongolian culture is not in fact older than that of Han or pro-Han agricultural peoples, because Mongol-style nomadism could not exist prior to the invention of agriculture and above all metal-working by settled people nearby.

Compared with the factual inaccuracy and historical distortion, the world view and political logic underlying the historical presentation in the novel are even more problematic and shocking. What makes some of the thought expressed in the novel – the part about Mongolian and Chinese culture – truly terrifying is its blind worship of power: it brazenly and openly propagates the law of the jungle, the cold-blooded logic of power as representing truth and virtue. This outlook explains why many scholars, both within and outside China, criticize the novel for promoting fascism.[55] The protagonist Chen Zhen and his two best friends, Yang Ke and Zhang Jiyuan, who share the same world view and values, use power or violence as the sole criterion to judge things in both the natural world and human society. Zhang makes this principle very clear by saying: "A fighting spirit is more important than a peaceful laboring spirit."[56] Accordingly, Mongols are judged as one of the "most advanced races" in the world, because they have incomparable militancy and aggressiveness,[57] and because their "military miracle" had once conquered nearly half of the world. This view also explains why Confucianism with its advocacy of "pacifism," its emphasis on education and devotion to study, is placed in a pejorative and critical light, and regarded as outdated and decayed.[58] Underlying the judgment is obviously the same logic that the protagonist uses to eulogize wolves: the law of the jungle.

Behind the historical distortion and worship of violence is the protagonist's distorted view of values. Following the law of the jungle, the strong are equated with virtue and justice, whereas the weak are considered sin or disgrace. Showing sympathy for the weak is regarded as shameless and despicable. After witnessing the extremely bloody scene of a pack of wolves cruelly murdering and fatally injuring hundreds of gazelles, especially when he sees the despairing and helpless look in a highly frightened gazelle kneeling at his feet, the protagonist cannot help but curse the cruelty of the wolves while showing sympathy for those "warm, beautiful, and peace-loving herbivories."[59] But he is harshly scolded by old man Bilgee for his softness. Later on, after calming down, he eventually realizes the "cowardliness" of his thought and behaviour, and feels regret and shame about his sympathy for the "enemies of the grassland." Here is clear evidence of the protagonist's acceptance of social Darwinism and the law of the jungle. Following the same logic, the protagonist shows sheer admiration for the wolf cub when he feeds the cub with a bitch's milk and witnesses that it drives away all the puppies of the bitch with violence and monopolizes all the nipples. Similarly, it is only natural to see that the protagonist, a Han Chinese himself, is more than happy to accept the mocking and even insulting remarks made by Mongols about the Han people and mainstream Chinese culture, because he truly believes that the Han people and their culture are far inferior to Mongols – the "most advanced race" on earth. Obviously, when the protagonist loudly and ardently lauds the "military miracle made by Genghis Khan" of cutting a "murderous swath through Europe and Asia,"[60] he completely ignores the enormous deaths, sufferings, and disasters that the Khan's aggression brought to the victims. It seems that, in the protagonist's eyes, only power matters, and all other things, including human lives, amount to nothing. The protagonist's blind worship of another people and another culture – which are greatly reconstructed by his own imagination and bias in the first place – while baselessly discriminating against his own people and culture is a clear sign of racial and cultural chauvinism, though expressed in a reverse form. Guided by the law of the jungle, social Darwinism, and racial and cultural chauvinism, the protagonist and his kindred spirits seem to lose the sense of morality: the basic judgment of right and wrong.

Despite the loudness and seriousness of the author's voice in ostensibly spreading Mongolian racial and cultural chauvinism, it is oversimplified and problematic to take the author's message literally and uncritically. After all, the allegedly "superior" Mongolian culture and the Mongolian way of life have been almost destroyed by the supposedly "inferior" Han Chinese under Communist domination, which conversely and paradoxically invalidates the claim of the supremacy of Mongolian culture. Undoubtedly, Jiang Rong truly admires the Mongolian race and Mongolian culture. But it seems that what he admires more is the power, vitality, and aggressiveness inherent in the version of Mongolian culture he has constructed. The real purpose behind his extravagant eulogy of Mongolian culture is to transplant the vitality and aggressiveness contained in Mongolian culture to the Chinese nation and to rejuvenate an impotent China seen to be plagued by submissiveness and slavishness in recent centuries, as Lu Xun and his May Fourth peers did before. For Jiang Rong and many of his readers with an extreme nationalistic mindset, behind the ostensible Mongolian cultural chauvinism actually stands a dream of (Han) Chinese cultural chauvinism that would combine the culturally superior complexity of ancient Han people with the aggressiveness of the Mongols. That combination would create a Chinese race ready to conquer the world. Here we see a mixture of the common nationalistic and social Darwinist discourse, propagated by the state during the "patriotic education campaign" and the "national studies fever," and the residues of the May Fourth radical antitraditionalism. In some sense, we might say that the excessive praise of Mongolian culture by the author is actually an inverted version of Chinese nationalism. Intriguingly, when Jiang Rong used stories of the Mongolian wolf totem to subtly promote Chinese nationalism, he not only echoed the "victimization narrative" – that a weaker China had been humiliated and bullied by a stronger West in recent centuries – which has been constructed and indoctrinated by the state propaganda machine; he also employed, probably unconsciously, the same strategy adopted by the Party: to build a nationalistic discourse based on selective and distorted historical facts. Hereby readers witness a high degree of similarity and homogeneity in content, structure, and mechanism between the mindset of an individual and state ideology.

A Wolf Destroyed by the "Wolf Logic"

From an intellectual perspective, the true value of the novel is not the "thought" – those nationalistic and social Darwinist discourses – explicitly and loudly articulated through the protagonist's and his friends' speeches and reflections, but the historical facts presented in the novel and the political implications underlying those facts, which are evidently based on the author's personal experience and observation of the social reality of Mao's China. Here we see the most meaningful thematic self-contradiction of the novel caused by the author's somewhat split mentality. On the one hand, nurtured by the mainstream May Fourth radical antitraditionalism and the belligerent Maoist revolutionary ideology, he wholeheartedly embraces and loudly eulogizes cultural chauvinism, social Darwinism, and extreme nationalism. On the other hand, the grim reality that he experiences, witnesses, and honestly presents in the novel of how Mongolian culture is suppressed and finally destroyed by an oppressive Communist regime *objectively* subverts those radical and pernicious nationalistic and social Darwinist discourses that he himself promoted. In the novel, the destruction of the Mongolian way of life by the devastating Maoist social practices is sometimes exposed explicitly, taking advantage of the novel's setting during the Cultural Revolution. The Cultural Revolution, as mentioned earlier, is defined by the Party as a social disaster; as such, limited and well-balanced criticism of it is permitted in contemporary China, as long as the criticism does not go so far as to question the Party line or challenge the Party's political legitimacy. In most cases, however, exposure of the Communist oppression of the Mongolian way of life and criticism of the social Darwinist worship of power proceed in an implicit and often allegorical way. The episode of the protagonist raising a wolf cub not only constitutes the most significant part of the novel's plot line but also serves as a political allegory to illuminate how the "wolf logic" – worship of the strong and disdain of the weak, the law of the jungle – ultimately destroys an innocent wolf. Most importantly, the way the protagonist raises the wolf cub and the discourse he adopts to justify his behaviour serve as an allegory to demonstrate how the Chinese Communist regime treats Mongols and other ethnic minorities in China, as well as to show the nature and logic of Communist ideology.

As repeatedly emphasized in the novel, although the process of gradual assimilation and transformation of Mongolian culture by mainstream Han Chinese culture started centuries ago, the imperial rulers in ancient times never implemented policies of deliberate destruction of Mongolian culture and the Mongolian way of life. On the contrary, they respected Mongolian values, beliefs, and customs. Taizong of the Tang dynasty, "the greatest emperor" in Chinese history, not only loved to hunt but also set up a grassland-style tent in his palace courtyard out of admiration for the nomadic way of life.[61] The Manchu rulers of the Qing dynasty prohibited large-scale migration of people from farming areas in order to protect the Mongolian grassland and the Mongolian way of life.[62] As old man Bilgee states, "the Qing emperors ... did not allow their Han subjects to open the grassland to raising crops. Back then, there was no fighting between the Mongols and the Chinese; we were at peace."[63]

In sharp contrast with those ancient imperial rulers, the Communist regime enforces policies that have proved fatal to the traditional Mongolian nomadic way of life, which is condemned by the local

Communist leader, Bao Shungui, as "backward and primitive."[64] Totally ignoring natural laws and the long-cherished customs of the local herdsmen, the Communist government arbitrarily increased the production quotas of the livestock for the local production brigades, which inevitably caused overuse of and damage to the grassland in the long run. Without any respect for the long-cherished customs on the grassland, they ruthlessly break the biggest taboos in Mongolian culture. In order to wipe out a wolf pack, Bao orders the grassland to be set on fire – a crime that would have led to the execution of an entire family by the Great Khans in ancient times – even if old man Bilgee and many other herdsmen strongly protest against the order. Near the end of novel, after removing the conscientious and experienced Mongolian official, Uljii, from the local leadership, Bao monopolizes power in the area. He launches an all-round campaign and utilizes military forces to wipe out wolves on the Mongolian grassland. He also orders farmers and construction workers to move into this area to transform the grassland to farming land. Those farming people, without any respect for Mongols, ruthlessly destroy the environment, things, and animals that are important parts of Mongolian life. Driven by greed and cruelty, they slaughter swans and steal their eggs, and destroy the beautiful swan lake within a few days. They kill with extremely brutal means all the marmots, whose oil and furs are essential in Mongolian daily life, in the "marmot mountain," which had existed there for thousands of years, in just a couple of days. By exposing the incredible cruelty and greed displayed by those farming people in eradicating all marmots in the "marmot mountain," the novel indicates that Communist domination also destroys the traditional Mongolian way and ethics of hunting.[65] The policies implemented by the Chinese Communist regime prove very "successful": within only a couple of years, wolves completely disappear on the Olonbulag; herding dogs, of little use now, are slaughtered and eaten by farming people. These two races of animals, which had played such a crucial role in the traditional Mongolian way of life and, to some extent, even determine the collective identity of the Mongolian people, now have been eliminated from the lives of Mongols.

But the "success" does not bring any benefit to the Mongolian people and the grassland, only disasters. Losing a crucial link in the cycle of the correlative cosmos, the ecological system of the Mongolian grassland collapses very quickly. The consequence becomes visible almost immediately: As early as 1975, "the Majuzi River area, with its lush grass and abundant water, had already been turned into a desert by farming … The Olonbulag regressed by the year."[66] Two decades later, when Chen and Yang come back to the region for a visit, what they see is an endless wasteland caused by desertification; the once wide river with rapid torrents has disappeared, and before their eyes is only a small, narrow brook. Gone also are traditional Mongolian-style yurts, replaced by Han Chinese–style houses surrounded by tall walls. "The Tengger of the grassland was now the Tengger of desert,"[67] as 80 per cent of the Olonbulag pastureland is now desert.[68] Actually, what they witness is the end of the traditional Mongolian way of life and Mongolian culture. "A nomadic herding society was now extinct; even the last trace left by the wolves on the Inner Mongolian grassland – the ancient cave of the wolf cub – would be buried in yellow sand."[69]

The reality that Chen experienced convinces him that "the [Chinese Communist] system was the true origin of the dust storm here."[70] The bleak picture drawn not only honestly and accurately reflects the grim historical fact that Communist domination destroyed the traditional Mongolian way of life, as well as the fundamental values, beliefs, and world view cherished by Mongols for thousands of years, but also subverts the social Darwinist mode of thinking and chauvinist discourse loudly promoted by the protagonist and the implied author throughout the novel. The miserable fate of Mongolian people under an oppressive regime clearly illustrates the horrible consequences for humanity in a world where power, rather than virtue or truth, dominates.

Critical reflection on the cruelty and horror of absolute power and the disastrous consequences it may bring to humanity constitutes another significant contribution of the novel. The theme is demonstrated mainly through the depiction of the protagonist raising a wolf cub. This episode – showing that a member of the dominant ethnic group enslaves an animal worshipped by a minority ethnic group as their totem – serves as a political allegory to illuminate the mechanism of absolute power in general and of the oppression of ethnic minorities by the Chinese Communist regime in particular.

Extremely fascinated with wolves, Chen and his best friend Yang Ke manage to attack a wolf den and steal a litter of seven wolf cubs. "Owing to his deep-seated respect for the Mongol people's totem and his obsessive interest in the profound mysteries surrounding wolves,"[71] Chen decides to raise a wolf cub to study not only wolves but also "human nature, wolf nature, and domestication."[72] Quite understandably, his decision meets with strong opposition and even enmity from the local herdsmen, who worship the wolf as their totem. Old man Bilgee becomes furious with this news; he harshly scolds Chen for his blasphemy to the Mongolian totem and his affront to Mongolian ancestors.[73] Despite all the opposition, enmity, and condemnation from the herdsmen, his own feelings of guilt, trepidation, and sin, and his awareness of his own deed as "an entirely selfish act,"[74] Chen keeps the wolf cub in custody anyway. There is little doubt about the sincerity of Chen's worship and deep feelings for the wolf, because he indeed looks after the cub very carefully and shows deep affection and care for it.

The asserted goodness of the protagonist's intention and his seeming affection and care for the wolf, however, cannot cover up the cruel fact that he deprives the wolf of its freedom and dignity as an animal, turning it into a slave and prisoner. As Haiyan Lee incisively points out, "chained to a pole and confined to a human routine, Little Wolf is no less pathetic than a common domesticated animal destined for the slaughterhouse. The loving gaze that elevates it to a mythic being is also an epistemological gaze that reduces it to a lab creature."[75] The confinement is torture to the wolf, both physically and spiritually. Fettered and confined within a very small area by a long chain, the cub has to endure the unbearable summer heat on the Mongolian grassland and the ruthless attack from mosquitoes. It also has to endure the fear, suffering, and exhaustion of being moved from place to place within a cage, due to the nomadic lifestyle of the herdsmen. During the last trip of its forced migration, the now grown-up wolf's resistance causes a fatal injury to its throat, and the unstoppable bleeding from its throat finally leads to its death. Another serious and fatal physical abuse the wolf suffers is that Chen and Yang, to prevent the now half-grown wolf from hurting people, permanently damage its sharp fangs, the most important weapon for a wolf to survive in the wilderness; their damage means doom for the wolf even if released.

Compared with the physical torture it suffers, the spiritual bitterness the wolf experiences is even more severe and harmful. Being in the custody of a human not only deprives the cub of the opportunity to live with its family and its own race but also shatters its feeling of belonging, bringing an enormous spiritual and identity crisis. The isolation from its own race causes the wolf to lose some essential qualities that define it as a wolf. First of all, under the interference and suppression of its human master, it misses the chance to learn how to howl from the wolves, and consequently, it is unable to howl like a real, wild wolf. This deficiency causes a real problem for it, because it "did not comprehend the nuanced differences in the varying howls, nor did he know how to respond."[76] As a result, it is ignorant of the hierarchy and protocol within a wolf pack.[77] Likewise, the strange howls it makes are also confusing and unintelligible to other wolves. In other words, the cub loses the ability to understand and speak "real wolf language."[78] This loss of language is the greatest existential problem facing the little wolf, the root cause for its identity and spiritual crisis. Unable to communicate with its fellow wolves, it is finally abandoned by them, becoming an "outsider" and an "alien" to its own race.[79] The isolation and alienation put the cub into a "deathlike despair"[80] and bring it endless loneliness, sadness, and agony.

As the wolf grows up day by day, its desire to break the chain to gain freedom becomes stronger and stronger. However, now with its great strength and power as a grown-up animal, each struggle hurts and worsens the injury to its throat. Finally, as mentioned earlier, its violent struggle during a forced migration brings mortal injury to its throat, and it bleeds out. Here is the scene of the last moment in its life:

> The cub strained to push himself up and drag himself over to sit in front of Chen, his mouth hanging open, the tongue lolling to one side. Bloody saliva oozed from the corner of his month as he sat there looking at Chen, like watching an old wolf, as if he wanted to tell him something. He was breathing so hard he couldn't make a single noise … The cub's strength vanished and his front legs began to tremble violently.[81]

What does the wolf cub try to tell Chen? Needless to say, it tries to protest against and condemn his tyranny and cruelty! To give the wolf a "noble" death, Chen, following the traditional Mongolian way of treating wolves, kills it himself with a spade. This act is the end of the wolf cub's life. It is also the ultimate result that the protagonist's self-proclaimed "love, affection, and worship" for the cub bring to the pitiful animal – lifelong imprisonment, endless physical torture and spiritual bitterness, continuous injury, and miserable death.

As demonstrated clearly in this episode, the oppression of the weak by the strong, the tyranny of absolute power, is often conducted in the name of noble causes and sublime goals. Sometimes it might indeed be motivated by good intention, at least as claimed by the oppressor. But all those beautiful words and the self-proclaimed goodness of intention cannot cover up the cruelty and evil of the oppressor and the destructive consequence it brings to the weak and the oppressed. Actually, beneath those beautiful yet illusory claims is always the extreme selfishness of the oppressor's intention. In this episode, despite the protagonist's self-proclaimed sublimity of his intention to raise the cub, he unconsciously betrays his ultimate motivation to imprison the wolf: for his own entertainment. On one occasion, the protagonist mentions that, by raising the cub, "he could enjoy a good drama nearly every day."[82] On another occasion, he confesses that "to imprison the cub and deprive him of his freedom and happiness" serves to help him go through the seemingly endless winter on the barren, uninhabited, and lonely land.[83] The protagonist repeatedly claims that he is often seized by a sense of guilt and sin, and that he feels saddened and sympathetic for the cub's miserable condition, which is completely caused by him. But his alleged sense of guilt and sympathy obviously never overcomes his selfish intention. Readers might doubt whether his self-proclaimed sense of guilt and sin is sincere or not in the first place.

This episode showing a wolf being murdered by the "wolf logic" – worship of violence and power, and apathy for the suffering of the weak – can also be read as an allegorical reference to the Chinese government's mistreatment of China's ethnic minorities, especially those bigger and more influential ones with long-lasting, unique religious beliefs such as Mongols, Tibetans, and Chinese Muslims. By juxtaposing the protagonist's abuse and destruction of the wolf cub and the Communist oppression and destruction of the traditional Mongolian way of life, readers have no difficulty finding the similarity or homogeneity of the two events in both structure and political logic. Just as the protagonist claims that his abuse of the wolf cub is motivated by good intentions, the Chinese Communist government also justifies its deprivation of the religious freedom of ethnic minorities and oppression of their traditions by asserting that it does so in the best interests of the ethnic groups – to save them from their allegedly "backward, ignorant, and uncivilized" ways of life. Similarly, in both cases, the self-proclaimed benevolence of the oppressor brings nothing but fatally destructive consequences to the oppressed: the death of the cub in the former case and the extinction of the traditional Mongolian way of life and wolf totem in the latter. In other words, the abuse and murder of the wolf cub by the protagonist and the oppression and destruction of Mongolian and other ethnic minorities' cultures and ways of life by the Communist regime follow the same political logic. In both processes, the oppressors adopt the same strategy: they justify their cruelty and tyranny through pure theorization while completely ignoring facts and the real experience of the oppressed.

In the novel, the cruelty, horror, and evil of Communist domination and all other kinds of despotism are most explicitly demonstrated by the scene in which the Communist leader, Bao, orders his soldiers to torture and exhaust a wolf to death. During the all-round campaign to wipe out wolves, Bao and several other military men detect a giant wolf. Driving two vehicles and with guns in their hands, they could easily take the wolf down with a bullet. However, motivated by the greed for a fine pelt with no bullet holes in it and by the cruelty to entertain themselves with the wolf's suffering, the humans decide to capture and skin the wolf alive. Taking advantage of human technology, they force the wolf to keep running at the highest speed for a very long distance in an attempt to inflict the maximum physical torture upon the animal. Finally, using up its last bit of energy, the wolf suddenly stops and sits down on the ground. It is so exhausted that even when Bao stabs its mouth with a bayonet, it has no reaction. The Communist leader laughs and says in a mocking tone: "We've chased it stupid."[84] Hereby the cruelty and evil of the Communist leader and the horror of absolute power are revealed in the most explicit way.

The tragic stories of the wolf cub and of Mongolian culture bear profound political connotations. The death of the wolf and the destruction of Mongolian culture explicitly demonstrate the horrible consequences of the political logic worshipped by the protagonist – a combination of the law of the jungle, social Darwinism, and chauvinism. The miserable fate of the wolf and Mongolian culture makes it very clear that, if the protagonist's political "ideal" – the "wolf logic" – dominates the world, the world definitely would not become a better place as he imagines; on the contrary, it would turn into a hell of oppression, torture, cruelty, and death. The implications underlying the episode of the wolf cub and its allegorical reference to the Communist treatment of Mongolian culture actually subvert the dominant theme of the novel – the social Darwinist and chauvinist view of the world. Ironically and intriguingly enough for the author, his portrayal of the tragic fate of the wolf cub and Mongolian culture, which is based on his real life experience on the Mongolian grassland, objectively and perhaps unconsciously denies the mainstream May Fourth discourse and state ideology that he consciously affirms in the novel, which has been indoctrinated into him through education and propaganda. Here, readers witness a self-contradiction in the author's mentality and the most meaningful paradox in the novel.

Ideological Hegemony behind a Literary Sensation

According to Howard Goldblatt, it took over three decades for Jiang Rong to complete the novel.[85] Given the enormous time and energy that he put into the novel, Jiang must believe that the "thought" conveyed in it is something original and significant. The truth, however, might disappoint him, as well as many readers, greatly. Despite the seriousness of the author's attitude in creating the novel and the enormous effort he put into it, as just discussed, the main themes expressed in it – the inferiority and decay of traditional Chinese culture, social Darwinism, and racial chauvinism as a disguised form of extreme nationalism – are far from original and thought-provoking; they are actually no more than fictionalized illuminations or extensions of the May Fourth radical antitraditionalism and state ideology painstakingly promulgated by the state propaganda machine.

Despite the hackneyed nature of its discourse, the novel generated unprecedented circulation and commercial profits in modern Chinese publishing history with its frenzied popularity and the magnitude of controversy it has provoked among critics.[86] In addition to its many successes, two achievements truly make the novel stand out from all other modern Chinese novels. One is the incredibly broad range of its readership, which includes people in all walks of life from taxi drivers, street vendors, and housewives to business tycoons, elite intellectuals, and government officials. The other is that, as Haiyan Lee points out, *Wolf Totem* is among the very few modern Chinese novels that have attracted unprecedented international attention largely because of their popularity in China (rather than being ignored or banned in China due to censorship) and have "genuinely stirred up some controversy among international critics and managed to split critical opinion."[87]

Given the huge disparity between the thematic banality of the novel and the magnitude of the sensation it has generated among readers, both inside and outside China, a few questions naturally arise: How is it possible for the novelist to take the hackneyed discourse long promulgated by the mainstream media and the state propaganda machine for an original, personal thought? Why is such a threadbare "thought" able to make huge waves among both intellectuals and the general public? What factors account for the extreme popularity of the novel among such a wide range of readers? What are the political and intellectual implications behind all these contradictions as well as the entire *Wolf Totem* episode?

To begin with, let us first take on the most fundamental question: the reasons for the frenzied popularity of the novel. To be fair, putting aside the main themes of the novel for the time being, we find that several elements of the novel constitute its selling points. Above all, the exotic nature of its subject matter – the thrilling and specular picture of wolves, gazelles, the endless grassland, nomadic Mongols, and especially the many breathtaking scenes of the life-and-death battles between wolves and humans, and between wolves and gazelles on the vast Mongolian grassland – bring a completely different and refreshing experience to many readers, who are bored with the monotony and dullness of life in a narrow urban space of concrete and marble. Besides, the traditional Mongolian way of life and cosmology centred on the wolf totem and the worship of nature and the underlying views of environmental protection and ecological sustainability can easily strike a chord with Chinese readers, who suffer severely from the damage and violation of nature: the unimaginably widespread environmental pollution. The exposure of the oppression and destruction of the traditional Mongolian way of life by Communist domination can also evoke strong passions and sympathetic responses from many liberal-minded readers. The many detailed, vivid descriptions of traditional Mongolian customs, views, and beliefs and the nuanced and convincing account of the disposition, habits, emotions, and growth of the wolf can also attract many readers interested in history, cultural anthropology, zoology, and other fields. Moreover, the abundant, highly contradictory political messages contained in the novel can draw attention from both its supporters and critics, which in turn reinforce its popularity. On top of all these factors, the many unexpected and "lowbrow" advertising and marketing skills used to promote this novel, which are rarely seen in the promotion of "serious" literary works, have also contributed substantively to the sales miracle of the novel.[88]

For all the significance of the contribution of these factors to the popularity of the novel, they are far less crucial than the two other elements contained in the novel: the discourses of nationalism and social Darwinism. This assessment has been proved by plenty of scholarly research and surveys.[89] Surprisingly and sadly, it is not the constructive and liberating ideas conveyed in the novel – respect for nature and condemnation of Communist oppression of traditional Mongolian culture – but the highly belligerent and pernicious ideas that constitute the most powerful momentum for the frenzied popularity of the novel among mainland Chinese readers. This reaction is certainly a deplorable situation, but it is quite understandable against the historical background of post-Tiananmen China, where, as elaborated at length in chapter 1, nationalism and social Darwinism have been inculcated into everyday life routine, especially for the younger generations.

Critics from mainland China provide in-depth and insightful analyses from broad social and psychological perspectives of the Chinese people's collective craze for nationalism and social Darwinism in general, as well as for this novel in particular. Zhang Hong, for instance, explores this phenomenon by juxtaposing *Wolf Totem* and a brood of derivative books, collectively dubbed the "wolf series," with a so-called "emperor series," a sequence of movie and TV products that emerged in China since the mid-1990s, which dramatize and secularize the lives of famous Chinese emperors. He believes that the high popularity of both series reflects, though in different ways, the same psychology shared by ordinary Chinese people: their simultaneous longing for and flattery of power. As he argues, by presenting the imperial palace full of cruelty and dehumanization as an ordinary family saturated with affection and warmth in the "emperor series" and falsely portraying the dispirited and numb Chinese society as a savage and rebellious world in the "wolf series," both series work to simultaneously satisfy ordinary people's hidden desires for power and to glorify oppression, violence, and power. Zhang coins the term "theory of wolf nature" (*langxing lun* 狼性论) to summarize the chauvinist and social Darwinist discourse contained in *Wolf Totem*, which is guided by two principles: the law of the jungle and the supremacy of profit. According to Zhang, whereas the "increasingly swollen mentality of 'the supremacy of nation state' and the illusion of a 'roaring China' since the mid-1990s onwards" provided the hotbed for the worship of the law of the jungle, the commercialization of Chinese society and blind belief in social competition justify the principle of "the supremacy of profit" and the "bandit logic" (*qiangdao luoji* 强盗逻辑). The "theory of wolf nature" as promoted in *Wolf Totem* and its derivatives, according to Zhang, is "a bizarre mixture of bandit logic and philistine philosophy."[90] Writer and critic Lin Xi upholds a similar point of view and insists that the craze for *Wolf Totem* among the general public in mainland China is largely due to its promotion of the philosophy of philistinism, a poplar trend prevailing in China since Tiananmen.[91] Critics Li Jianjun and Lei Da dig even deeper into China's recent history; they believe that Chinese people's worship of the wolf culture is also a result of the inculcation of the Maoist "philosophy of struggle" (*douzheng zhexue* 斗争哲学) over half a century,[92] which has cultivated an aggressive and belligerent mentality among the Chinese people, who are ready to accept the principle of violence and power and the law of the jungle. To sum up, according to these mainland Chinese critics, the major reason *Wolf Totem* is able to attract such a vast readership in mainland China is its clever reprise of the state ideologies in both the Mao and post-Mao eras, which caters to the psychology nurtured by these ideologies – a mixture of extreme nationalism, social Darwinism, and philistinism.

The entire *Wolf Totem* phenomenon fits very well with Antonio Gramsci's notion of "ideological hegemony" in the class society and his conceptualization of "organic intellectuals," and thus can be explained by these theories. Gramsci argues that, in a class society, the domination of the ruling class depends not only on coercive state power but also, and more importantly, on the "spontaneous consent" given to it by the great masses of the population; "this consent is 'historically' caused by the prestige (and consequent confidence) which the dominant group enjoys because of its position and function in the world of production."[93] It forms the social and ideological hegemony of the ruling class. Gramsci's notion of class domination based on the "spontaneous consent" given by the ruled to the ruling group actually points to the ideological homogeneity in a society – that is, in a functional class society, the ruling class, the intellectuals, and the ruled share the same fundamental ideology. The "spontaneity" of the consent that the ruled give to the dominant ideology also underlines the fact that, in a class society, the submission of ordinary people and intellectuals to the ruling class and to the dominant ideology already becomes a collective unconscious for them.

In Gramsci's theoretical formulation, intellectuals play a crucial role in social and ideological hegemony. Gramsci distinguishes between two major "categories" of intellectuals in a class society. One category is "traditional intellectuals," intellectuals who already exist in the preceding historical periods and "represent a historical continuity uninterrupted even by the most complicated and radical changes in political and social forms."[94] Due to their uninterrupted historical continuity and their special qualification, these intellectuals regard themselves as autonomous and independent of the dominant social group in the current society. Gramsci believes that the "ecclesiastics" are most typical of the "traditional intellectuals" category. The other category is "organic intellectuals," intellectuals who are created by a social group or class and in turn give the group "homogeneity and an awareness of its own function not only in the economic but also in the social and political fields."[95] In other words, organic intellectuals are intellectuals "organically" attached to a social group or class. According to Gramsci, any social group, if it wants to develop dominance over a state, must "elaborate" its own organic intellectuals and, at the same time, "assimilate and conquer ideologically" the traditional intellectuals, because "the intellectuals are the dominant group's 'deputies' exercising the subaltern functions of social hegemony and political government."[96]

Gramsci's concepts of "organic intellectual" and "ideological hegemony" shed fresh light on the nature of intellectuals and their fundamental relationship with the ruling class in a nation-state. Gramsci's perception of intellectuals substantially subverts the traditional Chinese view of intellectuals as the social conscience and critics of political power. Timothy Cheek, a leading scholar in modern Chinese intellectual history, emphasizes that "most of Chinese intellectuals are not dissidents today."[97] As he reminds us, "by focusing on dissidents and religious activists, we miss most of what China's intellectuals are doing today and have done over the past century."[98] In another work, Carol Lee Hamrin and Cheek make it very clear that most Chinese intellectuals are actually "establishment intellectuals,"[99] or the "deputies" or "functionaries" of China's ruling class, the Communist Party, to put it in Gramsci's words. They are "organically" attached to the Party and nurtured on state ideology; therefore, they reflect the will of the Party and carry on its ideology. As far as the entire society is concerned, given that strict political control over thought and suppression of dissidents are policies consistently implemented throughout the regime's history, the ideological homogeneity of Chinese society in the Communist era is more pronounced than it is in many other modern states. As a result, apart from a few truly thoughtful works created by brave and conscientious dissidents, the thought conveyed in many intellectual works in Communist China, if politically charged, is often no more than an individualized expression of the mainstream discourse and state ideology in a disguised form. This finding helps explain why Jiang Rong, an "organic intellectual" attached to the Chinese Communist Party, an employee and "deputy" of the Party-state, takes the mainstream discourses and state ideology for his own original thought. The frenzied popularity of *Wolf Totem* among the intellectuals and the general public serves to testify to the extremity of social, ideological hegemony under Communist domination in contemporary China. In this sense, Jiang Rong's status as a political activist and state prisoner because of his participation in the June Fourth democratic movement only reinforces the sense of the omnipresence of state ideology in Communist China.

Summary

A highly intriguing novel based on the author's personal experience and replete with vivid descriptive details, *Wolf Totem* provides a beautiful and charming picture of the traditional Mongolian way of life and belief, centred on the wolf totem and correlative cosmology. This attractive picture nevertheless does not lead to any positive human values but instead to the belief in the law of the jungle, social Darwinism, cultural and racial chauvinism, and extreme nationalism. To some extent, most of the "thought" articulated in the protagonist's speeches and reflections on Mongolian and Chinese culture is nothing more than an individualized reprise of the dominant sociopolitical discourse and state ideology. It is both a result and manifestation of the ideological homogeneity in Communist China, where strict control of thought and oppression of dissidents have been an uninterrupted social practice implemented by the Party-state throughout its history.

For all these intellectual limitations, controversies, and paradoxes, the novel makes a true contribution to modern Chinese literature and thought through its exposure of the destruction of traditional

Mongolian culture by the Communist regime and of the cruelty and evil of absolute power, which, ironically, subverts the extreme Darwinist and chauvinist discourses expressed in the novel. This ideological paradox is the most significant one in the novel. The paradox to some extent results from the somewhat split mentality of the author: whereas his consciousness, nurtured and shaped by mainstream media and the propaganda machine, leads him to state ideology, his unconscious, formed from his personal experience on the Mongolian grassland, objectively denies it.

From the perspective of the broad context of contemporary Chinese intellectual and sociopolitical history, the reception of the novel is as revealing as its content. The immense popularity of the novel, despite the superficiality of most of its thought, demonstrates the magnitude in both intensity and scope of the impact of nationalist and social Darwinist discourses and sentiments upon Chinese society. It also confirms the ideological homogeneity in Chinese society and the cultural hegemony of the Party-state.

Chapter Three

Lenin's Kisses: Absurdity, Dehumanization, and Dilemma of the Chinese Utopia

Yan Lianke is arguably the most politically engaged writer currently residing in mainland China.[1] Because of the audacity and incisiveness of his criticism of contemporary Chinese politics, most of his recent novels have been banned in China. Exposure of the absurd and inhumane logic of China's one-Party rule and critical reflection on the disastrous consequences that the Chinese model has brought to the Chinese people, especially to the downtrodden, are dominant themes running through all his fiction. Three novels – *Dream of Ding Village* (*Dingzhuang meng* 丁庄梦), *The Sunlit Years* (*Riguang liunian* 日光流年), and *The Explosion Chronicles* (*Zhalie zhi* 炸裂志) – can be read as allegories of the Dengist model of economic development. Through the depiction of the bankruptcy of "grand projects" and the disastrous consequences they bring to the villagers in these novels, Yan lays bare the absurdity and cruelty of the Chinese model and its inevitable failure. Two other novels, *The Four Books* (*Sishu* 四书) and *Serve the People* (*Wei renmin fuwu* 为人民服务), both target the absurd logic of the Maoist doctrine and the inhumanity of Maoist political movements. His longest novel thus far, *Lenin's Kisses*, acclaimed "a masterpiece of contemporary Chinese novel of political allegory" by a mainland Chinese critic,[2] represents his concentrated reflection on the absurdity and cruelty of both the Maoist revolution and the Dengist model of development, and the disastrous consequences they have brought to the Chinese people.

Lenin's Kisses features the life of a small mountain village named Liven, whose residents are almost exclusively disabled people. Structurally, the novel is composed of a text and a series of notes, labelled "further reading," to provide explanations of the special terms and phrases that the villagers use in their dialect, which are not quite understandable to outsiders. Whereas the text narrates the life of present-day Liven, the notes relate its recent and remote history. By virtue of this innovative textual structure, Yan Lianke is able to juxtapose the three historical periods in China – the pre-Communist times, the Mao era, and the post-Mao era – thereby demonstrating the continuities and changes in political code between pre-Communist and Communist China, and between the two eras under Communist domination.

The dominant plot line of the novel recounts how an ambitious county chief, Liu Yingque, manages to implement a grand project – to purchase Lenin's corpse from Russia and install it in a memorial hall in his own county for display – to develop the county's economy. In order to raise the enormous funds to purchase the corpse, he orders Liven to organize two special-skills performing troupes to exhibit their disabilities around the country. This scheme proves to be a huge success in the beginning. Within only six months, the Liven performing troupes are able to make sufficient money with their extremely dangerous and sometimes bloody performances to purchase the Communist leader's remains. Happy times do not last, however. Just when everyone from the county believes that a rosy future is around the corner, the project is stopped suddenly by the central government, and Liven residents' beautiful dream is completely shattered. Even worse, near the end of the novel, all members of the Liven performing troupes are kidnapped and detained in the Lenin Memorial Hall, and robbed of every penny they made from their performances. Completely disillusioned with the politics of Communist China, the once ambitious county chief, at the last moment before he steps down, uses his authority to grant autonomy to Liven, allowing it to cut itself off from Communist governance and regain its independence. More surprising, at the end of the story, he breaks both his legs to qualify as a permanent resident of Liven.

In the novel, only odd numbers, traditionally considered inauspicious by Chinese people, are used to indicate chapters and notes. Missing the even numbers, together with "temporal disjointedness"[3] – for example, snow falls in June for seven consecutive days; a winter day is as sweltering as summer in the mountains – and many spooky and surreal scenes presented in the novel, creates a world of absurdity, grotesqueness, and distortion. Yan Lianke dubs the sort of realism he creates with great effort and ingenuity "mythorealism" (*shenshi zhuyi* 神实主义), a literary style based on conventional realism yet incorporating surrealism, magical realism, fantasy, and the grotesque.[4] The ultimate purpose of mythorealism, Yan explains, is to explore and present "a kind of realness that is 'non-existent,' invisible, and covered up by reality."[5] He emphasizes the subjective and spiritual dimension of this kind of realism:

> Readers can no longer see or experience the common logic of life from the story; they can only sense and become aware of the existence of this new,

intrinsic logic with their heart and understand it with their soul. No longer can they capture the beginnings of the story themselves and touch it with their own hands and feet, and it is even less possible to experience and experiment with it in action; instead, they can only access it spiritually and with a wide-open mind.[6]

In an interview with Li Tuo, Yan provides a further elucidation of the origins, significance, and purposes of his mythorealism in China today:

> In current writing, realism has already turned into a pile of garbage and lost its former solemnity, seriousness, and depth. Yet the reality of life has in contrast grown increasingly complex and difficult to comprehend ... Today none of our literary practices can rival the richness, depth, and incomprehensibility of life itself. No realistic writing can express the content of life or encompass the plight of the downtrodden ... Therefore, I think we cannot but use unrealistic and surrealist modes of writing. Only by using surrealistic writing modes can we approach the core of reality and have a chance to unveil the core of life.[7]

In another interview, Yan Lianke makes it very clear that, by virtue of the creativity and originality of his unique mythorealism, he attempts to present those "alien experiences and uncommon stories" of people in today's China and "to make all that does not make sense make sense."[8]

Yan Lianke claims that he created mythorealism to present the complexity, richness, depth, and incomprehensibility of life itself; yet at the same time, he identifies "power" as the most important "writing resource" that the life of today's China can provide to writers.[9] In other words, Yan regards power or politics as the paramount dimension of social life in China today and the presentation of power or politics as a significant motif in literature that reflects contemporary Chinese life. In talking about *Lenin's Kisses*, Yan explicitly states that the protagonist, Chief Liu, is a product of China's "political system."[10] He elucidates his perception from the perspective of the interaction between people and the political system in the Chinese context. As he says, "it is the result of the system having formed and alienated people, and those alienated people merging and interacting with the system. The system inevitably cultivates and produces this kind of person."[11] Because of the intrinsic connection and symbiotic relationship between the official and the Chinese system, Yan's characterization of Chief Liu logically crystalizes his reflection on the Chinese political system.

In *Lenin's Kisses*, Yan Lianke emphasizes the utopian nature of both Communist eras, and his reflection on these two eras, both their differences and continuities, is conducted through the characterization of the two main characters, Granny Mao Zhi and Chief Liu, as well as through the tragic experience and fate of the people of Liven. Through his depiction of Granny Mao Zhi's nightmarish experience during the revolution, and through the juxtaposition of the "heavenly days" of prosperity, peace, harmony, and autonomy that Liven enjoyed before joining the Chinese Communist revolution with its hellish existence under Communist domination, Yan portrays the Maoist revolution as a nightmare for the Chinese people rather than salvation in any sense. Similarly, through his vivid and impressive portrayal of the mindset and behaviour of Chief Liu, the bankruptcy of the grand Lenin project led by him, and the tragic experience of Liven's villagers, Yan exposes the cruelty, dehumanization, predatory nature, and inevitable failure of the Dengist model of development. By paralleling the miserable fate that Liven shares in both the Mao and post-Mao eras, Yan Lianke also reveals the fundamental continuity of the two different Communist periods: in both eras, the Party-state treats its people as merely subjects and tools to maintain its rule; and in both eras, the people of Liven are victims of Communist rule.

In addition to exposing the absurdity and cruelty of the Communist utopias, the novel also paints a bleak picture of a nation consumed by vulgar materialism and moral nihilism. With his description of how Chief Liu and the government led by him are willing to do anything and sell anything in exchange for money, including their long-cherished values and beliefs, historical facts, and even human dignity, Yan convincingly demonstrates that Communist rule is the very source of the all-round moral crisis in the nation. The novel also delineates a grave dilemma that the people of Liven face: even if they are permitted to withdraw from Communist domination and nominally regain their autonomy, they have no future, given that they are encircled by the Communist regime and their mentality and behaviour have been completely shaped by Communist ideology. Through the depiction of this dilemma, Yan draws our attention to the dead-end future that the Chinese model would lead the nation to.

Revolution as Nightmare

The small village featured in the novel, Liven, is located deep in the Balou Mountains in Henan province of central China. What makes the village special is that the overwhelming majority of its residents are disabled people. Legend has it that the history of the village can be traced back to the massive, forced relocation that took place over six centuries ago in the early Ming dynasty, and the origin of the village came out of the pure goodness of humanity – compassion, generosity, and gratitude. According to the legend, during the long, gruelling trudge from northwest China to the central plain, the highest official in charge of the migration, in order to repay the kindness he had received from a deaf-mute woman, allowed a blind man and his crippled son to drop out of the procession and join the woman to establish a new village. It turns out that, before the official became prosperous, the extremely kind-hearted disabled woman, despite her own poverty, had treated him to a big meal when he was starving and begged for food in her doorway. Out of gratitude, the official settled the three disabled people in a valley with rich soil and abundant water resources. To guarantee the long-term welfare of these three people and their posterity, the official left them with many tales of silver and ordered a hundred soldiers to build them a house and help them cultivate a large area of farmland near the river. Later on, after hearing that three disabled people had settled down nearby and were enjoying a heavenly existence, disabled people from throughout the region began pouring in. The deaf-mute woman supplied them with land and silver, permitting them to live and raise families there, and finally established a village. Therefore, the deaf-mute woman is venerated by the villagers as their "ancestral mother."

Founded on human goodness, the village also sustains itself by human goodness. In the village, all people treat each other with kindness and care; they help each other, support each other, and do not let anyone lag behind. Moreover, because they are blessed with rich soil and a geographical privilege, every family in the village lives a bountiful, peaceful, and happy life:

> They all had more land than they could manage, and every family had more grain than they could eat. Everyone asked others to help them out, while at the same time helping their neighbors. During that period, a cripple might use a blind man's legs, a deaf man might use a mute's ears, and a mute might use a deaf man's mouth. The entire village behaved like a large family – peaceful and prosperous, and with no struggles or conflicts.[12]

The villagers of Liven cherish love more than anything else in the world, as demonstrated most explicitly by the story of Sister Hua, an extremely beautiful woman with a minor disability, and her husband. The story has it that Sister Hua's husband was originally a scholar who had passed the highest level of the civil service examination and was appointed to the post of county magistrate. On his way to office, he met Sister Hua and fell in love with her immediately. In order to marry his beloved woman, the scholar gave up his official post, cut off one arm to qualify as a resident of Liven, and lived there as a farmer until he was conscripted by the government as a punishment. The village as portrayed here, isolated from temporal and spatial flow and full of tranquillity, peace, and love, readily reminds us of Tao Yuanming's Peach Blossom Spring, a paradise on earth. "This is a special mode of existence that only the residents of Liven have experienced or can understand. Its uniqueness lies in its freedom, relaxation, substance, lack of competition, and leisure."[13]

The villagers of Liven are guided not only by human virtues but also by common sense and reason, which can be clearly seen from the order of their village meetings. Whenever there is a gathering in the village, the villagers, based on the nature of their disabilities, will find places that make themselves feel comfortable while at the same time protecting their fellow villagers' welfare. In this way, norms and customs come into being naturally. It is accentuated in the novel that these norms and rules are not made or imposed by external authorities but form "spontaneously" over time, based on common sense and the villagers' shared values and beliefs. Moreover, Liven also enjoyed autonomy and self-governance prior to the advent of Communist rule. "For several centuries, Liven never paid grain taxes to any dynasty, province, canton, district, county, or township, and no one from the other districts, towns, or villages … ever came to Liven to collect grain taxes."[14] Obviously, Liven's way of life epitomizes traditional Chinese rural society characterized by its isolation, self-governance, and autonomy. As Jianmei Liu argues, Yan Lianke's charming picture of Liven prior to Communist rule represents a utopian imagination of a small, tranquil, and peaceful community informed by the Taoist ideal of "withdrawing from the world."[15]

Liven's "heavenly existence" is destroyed overnight after Granny Mao Zhi, the revolutionary matriarch, leads the village to the Revolution, a synonym for "Communist rule" in the novel. Here it is necessary to point to an intriguing and meaningful detail in the novel: the two matriarchs of the village – the founding "ancestral mother" and the revolutionary Granny – are introduced to the reader at the same time, despite a temporal abyss of several centuries between them. Introducing these characters simultaneously is no coincidence. On the contrary, it is deliberately designed to juxtapose the two most powerful and influential women in the history of the village and thereby to contrast the different contributions they have made to the village. Whereas the former brought long-term blessing to the village, the latter brought only countless disasters, tragedies, and deaths. Intriguingly, not only these two matriarchs but also the two county heads in different times make a sharp contrast. Whereas the Communist official, Chief Liu, cares about nothing but power, always more than willing to sacrifice his people's dignity and even lives in order to accumulate his own political capital, the ancient county magistrate, Sister Hua's husband, gives up his post and one arm without any hesitation in order to live with the woman he loves. Through the juxtaposition and contrast of the two matriarchs and the two government officials in different times, Yan Lianke is able to compare two different modes of rule – self-government in traditional Chinese society and political dictatorship under Communist domination – and the different mentality and morals of people under the different types of rule. Yan's eulogy to the traditional times and his criticism of the Communist era are manifest.

As discussed in chapter 1, over the decades since its founding, the Chinese Party-state has created numerous political myths to glorify itself and the Chinese revolution in order to justify its rule. One myth claims that the Chinese revolution, despite its grim and even bloody nature due to its life-and-death struggle with its enemies, possesses a rather romantic, tender, and warm-hearted side because of the existence of the sublime "class feelings" – the affection, love, and selfless sacrifice among revolutionary comrades. Yan Lianke's depiction of Mao Zhi's experience with the Revolution, however, destroys this myth by stripping away the fabricated tenderness veiling the bloodiness of the Revolution. In fact, as presented in the novel, during the entire Revolution, Mao Zhi never received even a trace of affection and warmth from her comrades; what she experienced in the process was only cruelty and terror. She saw with her own eyes that her mother, a long-term loyal and steadfast revolutionary, along with two other soldiers of the Red Army, was arrested and wrongly executed as a traitor by her fellow soldiers, and her corpse was laid out in the open on the riverbank unattended for a long time. This shocking and bloody event left a profound and long-lasting trauma in her young heart. "During her time with the army contingent, Mao Zhi had grown up in fear, with gunshots of the enemy and of her mother's execution reverberating through her dreams."[16] Not only was her mother brutalized by the Revolution, but Mao Zhi herself was also a victim of it. She was raped by her platoon leader after she was severely injured in a bloody battle, hid in an open grave with him, and lost consciousness. After that, she was left dying alone in the grave. If it were not for the Stonemason, a poor peasant from Liven and her future husband, who saved her, she would have died long ago. For Mao Zhi, the Revolution means nothing but cruelty, terror, pain, nightmarish memories, and long-lasting traumas.

In addition to its inhumanity, what makes the Revolution especially horrible is its seemingly contagious nature – like a virus, it can infect people's minds easily; once entering into a person's mind, it will not only live there perpetually but will also take every chance to infect others. Mao Zhi's thought and behaviour demonstrate this general truth. Although, as just mentioned, the Revolution brings nothing to her but nightmarish experiences and incurable traumas, Mao Zhi seems to be obsessed with it, as if under a spell. It is not explained in the novel why she behaves this way, but we readers know that in reality it is a result of long-term, deceptive Communist inculcation. After learning by accident that the outside world has already been subject to Communist rule, she takes pains to introduce the Revolution to Liven and finally succeeds. Under Communist domination, however, the prosperity, peace, harmony, and autonomy enjoyed by the village disappear overnight, and the entire village undergoes one devastating political movement after another, which, as it did to Mao Zhi, brings nothing to the village but exploitation, humiliation, terror, suffering, and death.

Not only is the process of the Revolution extremely bloody, but the consequences it brings to the people are even more horrible, clearly demonstrated by the results of all the absurd and catastrophic political movements. The political movements presented in the novel include the Iron Tragedy, the Great Plunder, and the Black and Red Crimes, which allude to the Great Leap Forward (of which the Backyard Steel-Making Movement was an integral part), the Great Famine, and the Cultural Revolution, respectively. Yan Lianke's presentation of and reflection on these political movements shatter some fundamental myths about the Chinese revolution and about the relationship between the Party and the people created by the Communist propaganda machine and expose some essential facts about the Chinese revolution long covered up by the Party.

In contradiction to the Party's claim that the Chinese Communist revolution was motivated by the high degree of "class consciousness" of the Chinese peasants – their somewhat "transcendental" hatred of the landlord class and their spontaneous love for the Party – Yan Lianke makes it crystal clear that the people of Liven do not have any class consciousness, let alone the so-called class hatred, because all the families in the village were equally prosperous prior to the Communist era, and they treated each other like brothers and sisters. Nothing like "spontaneous rebellion against the landlord class" existed in the village. The Revolution is actually an intrusion into the peaceful village rather than a voluntary, homegrown activity initiated by the villagers themselves, even less a salvation for the village in any sense. The external and imposed nature of the Revolution is implicitly embodied in the status of the revolutionary leader of the village, Granny Mao Zhi, who is originally an outsider to Liven. Even after marrying a Liven man, Mao Zhi does not identify herself wholeheartedly with Liven – while "physically living in Liven, her heart was floating in the world beyond the Balou region"[17] – until her husband starves to death during the Great Plunder, which completely disillusions her with the cruelty and horror of the Revolution. Moreover, the act of Mao Zhi introducing Communist rule to the village is motivated less by her consideration of the best interests of Liven than by her somewhat capricious endeavour to spread the revolutionary seed in the village.

Yan Lianke's observation that the Chinese revolution is an intrusion and a destructive force in traditional Chinese society imposed by the Communist Party for its own political agenda reflects the Chinese reality honestly. According to Lucien Bianco's study in *The Cambridge History of China*, due to the importance of kinship in traditional Chinese society – a typical Chinese village is usually like an extended family that can be traced back to the same ancestor – the class hatred, class exploitation, and class oppression in traditional China were actually not as severe as in many other societies. Therefore, class consciousness and the idea of revolution were rather weak among the peasants in traditional Chinese society. Bianco points out: "Certainly the Chinese Communists could not have won power without the peasant armies and the support of so many villagers. Yet without the Communists the peasants would, quite simply, never have conceived the idea of a revolution."[18] Clearly, according to Bianco, the idea of revolution did not "spontaneously" form in the minds of Chinese peasants; rather, it was inculcated in them by the Party through propaganda. Bianco proves with abundant historical facts that the Chinese Communists used "a mixture of abnegation and cunning that aroused not only enthusiasm but also resentment" to "forge victory for the revolution."[19] In a study of peasants' responses to the Chinese Communist Party's mobilization during the period from 1937 to 1945, Bianco concludes that Chinese peasants were "initially reluctant and slow" to answer the Party's calls, and once mobilized, they were "not easily controlled,"[20] which is solid proof of their lack of the class consciousness claimed by the Party. In fact, Yan Lianke's observation and Bianco's study of the Chinese revolution are also supported by the insights of other Chinese writers. Su Tong, for example, also portrays the Chinese revolution as an intrusion into and destruction of traditional Chinese society.[21]

The novel also lays bare another grim fact about Communist rule in China. Even after the end of the Revolution, during the so-called "peaceful period of socialist construction" (that is, the Mao era), the implementation of every major political policy or political movement in Liven was accompanied by state violence. From the first day under Communist domination, there were always guns to be seen at every crucial moment in Liven's history, and the village did not enjoy even one single day of peace during this so-called "peaceful period." The day when Mao Zhi returned from the county seat to declare Liven's submission to Communist rule, she was accompanied not only by county and township leaders but also by two soldiers from the township's militia. "The latter were carrying rifles, and when they reached the entrance to the village they fired three shots in succession" to convene "the village's first-ever People's Assembly."[22] "With the sound of those gunshots, a mutual aid team was formed, and the villagers also entered a cooperative society."[23] After completing the agricultural collectivization in the village, the militiamen left a gun in the village when they departed. Needless to say, "they left the gun with Mao Zhi," the Communist leader of the village.[24] The symbolic implication of the act hereby cannot be made clearer: Communist rule is maintained by the gun. Later on, during the Iron Tragedy, when the villagers are reluctant to hand over their cooking utensils to carry out the Backyard Steel-Making Movement, we again witness that soldiers "all carrying guns" were sent by the government to Liven to subjugate the villagers to its will.[25] Eventually, during the Great Famine, the brutality and brazenness of the state power preying on the villagers of Liven were revealed. One group of people after another, some of whom "arrived in a car and bearing guns,"[26] were sent by the governments at different levels to Liven to collect grains. In the end, every single grain owned by Liven's families was taken away under the threat of the gun; as a result, the once affluent villagers begun to eat grass roots, tree bark, and even dirt, and many starved to death, including the husband of Mao Zhi, the highest leader of the village. The government's action at that time almost amounted to open robbery, which is why the Liven people use the term the "Great Plunder" to refer to the Great Famine. Yan Lianke's depiction showing that every step of the Chinese socialist project in Mao's China was accompanied by guns honestly reflects the social reality of China at that time. It relentlessly shatters the deceptive Communist propaganda that the Party represents the interests of the Chinese people; that the people are voluntary and loyal followers of the Party due to their admiration for its greatness, glory, and correctness; and that they are grateful to it for bringing them happiness.

In addition to unveiling the coercive and violent nature of the Maoist socialist project even during the so-called "peaceful period of socialist construction," Yan Lianke also exposes the astonishing severity and extreme inhumanity of the Great Famine.[27] In two places in the novel, it is mentioned that three out of five people in one family and four out of seven in another starved to death during the famine. In another place, it is stated that there was even cannibalism at that time. Here is what happened to Liven, the once rather affluent village prior to Communist domination, after their grain was stolen by people sent by the various governments:

> People began starving to death.
>   One person died after another.
>   New graves began to appear in the village cemetery. After another half a month, those graves began sprouting like bamboo shoots after a spring shower, and eventually an array of graves as vast as a wheat field appeared in the front of the village.[28]

Though the Great Famine is a common motif for many contemporary Chinese literary works, few writers have ever portrayed it as devastatingly as Yan Lianke does in this novel. The horrifying picture painted here may come as a shock even for those who already have some knowledge of the great catastrophe in Chinese history. Yan's presentation of and reflection on the Chinese revolution and on the devastating Maoist political movements certainly renews our memories of some of the darkest moments in Chinese history.

Contemporary Freak Show: Absurdity and Cruelty of the Biopolitics of a Utopia

As indicated by its English title, *Lenin's Kisses*, which alludes to the fictional Lenin project, a grand program contrived by ambitious Chief Liu to create an economic miracle for the county in the post-Mao era, the novel focuses on the Dengist model of development rather than on the Maoist revolution, though reflection on the latter, as demonstrated by the previous analysis, is an important part of the novel. The Lenin project is the core event in the novel. As such, how to interpret the project constitutes the key to the hidden connotations of the text. Given the surreal and grotesque nature of this project, it certainly cannot be read literally. In fact, when paralleling this fictional project in the novel with the Chinese government's grand plan of developing the economy at any cost in the post-Mao era, readers might quickly discover the analogy between the two events and realize that the former is actually created as an allegory of the latter, since it reveals the defining character, guiding principle, mechanism, and inevitable consequences of the latter in many profound ways. Thomas Chen argues that Chief Liu is "the crossbreed of socialist doctrine and the capitalist will," who embodies the Dengist ideology that combines political dictatorship and economic determinism.[29] As he comments, "Deng Xiaoping is noticeably absent from the novel, yet it is he who seems to be Liu's patron saint."[30] David Der-wei Wang also argues that the novel, in addition to playing with the theme of revolution and desire, presents a vivid picture of the Dengist gospel that "development is an unyielding principle" (*fazhan shi yingdaoli* 发展是硬道理).[31] Additionally, through the juxtaposition of the Dengist project and the Maoist way of rule, the novel also demonstrates the fundamental continuity of the two Communist eras in guiding principle and political logic, thereby unveiling the true face of Communist domination in China.

As mentioned earlier, Jiwei Ci, in a book on the dialectic of the Chinese revolution, made a highly incisive and convincing argument that the Communist project in China, including both the Maoist revolution and the Dengist economic development, is one of utopian nature "inspired by a vision that was essentially hedonistic and materialistic."[32] In the Mao era, according to Ci, because of the extreme poverty the nation faced at that time, the Party had to adopt an ascetic means to pursue the hedonistic ends; as a result, the utopian character of the project was disproportionally heightened by its ascetic surface and by the sublime and grandiose aura of Communist ideals that it claimed to pursue. In the post-Mao era, by contrast, due to the collapse of Communist ideals caused by the Tiananmen Massacre, the relatively "more pragmatic means" adopted by the Party-state for economic development,[33] and the material prosperity that the people enjoyed as the fruition of reform and opening up, the utopian aura of the Communist project faded away while its hedonistic core was revealed. In the Chinese context, according to Ci, utopianism is nothing more than "hedonism sublimated and postponed,"[34] whereas hedonism is a desublimated and vulgar form of utopianism; the two are actually different forms of the same thing. To elevate hedonism to utopianism, it demands "abstraction," a process of anointing hedonism with a layer of sublime and abstract Communist ideals to cover up its vulgar and sensuous core. This process is where propaganda, the inculcation of Communist ideology, comes in. Moreover, utopianism always requires zeal and strong belief. In the Chinese context, given the extreme poverty that the nation faced when the Party launched its utopian project in the Mao era and the seeming unreachability of the promised Communist society, propaganda became a crucial instrument to arouse people's zeal for the Communist cause and to build up their faith in the rosy hedonistic future. Therefore, the Chinese Communist utopian project is inseparable from propaganda.

Ci's perception of the reality of China under Communist rule is obviously shared by Yan Lianke, who portrays the utopian and illusory character of the Lenin project in a vivid and impressive way, with the help of literary devices such as farce, hyperbole, and black humour. As Thomas Chen convincingly argues, the novel is actually an allegory that "challenges both socialist and free-market utopianisms at their very core."[35] As presented in the novel, Chief Liu's home county is the poorest in the district, and people there suffer stark poverty, which, according to Ci, provides fertile soil for the birth of utopianism.[36] To stimulate people's zeal for the Lenin project and to build up their faith in it, Chief Liu draws a beautiful and alluring blueprint for them in an exciting speech. He promises his audience that, after Lenin's corpse is brought back and installed in the mausoleum in less than one year, thousands of tourists will come pouring in every day; they will bring at least a million yuan to the county every day, and money "will be as abundant as autumn leaves on the ground."[37] By that time, the chief tells the villagers, even if they extend their government buildings halfway to the sky and paint the walls and pave the streets in gold, and even if all peasants of the county stop farming and just sit there eating and spending money, they will still end up with more money than they can spend. He expresses his worries about the excessive money they would have in the future:

> By that time, the question will not be how much money we can earn, but rather how we could possibly spend all the money that we do earn. Our primary challenge will be finding ways to spend all that money ... By that point, every family and every household will have so much money that their food will no longer taste fragrant, and they won't even be able to sleep at night. Each household will undergo extreme hardship in their attempts to spend that money.[38]

It can be imagined what a sensation a speech like this would make among the audience, who are so excited that their faces are "glowing with amazement" and their eyes turn "as bright as the sun and the moon."[39] At this moment, no one in the audience would question whether this rosy dream could indeed turn into reality or what meaning they would still find in life when they lost even the taste for food and sleep but only had money. Chief Liu's concern with the difficulty of spending money for people who barely have enough food to feed themselves readily reminds us of Chairman Mao's worry about how the peasants in a poor county in Hebei province could consume so much grain, which they allegedly grew in fields during the Great Leap Forward, right before the Great Famine, during which tens of millions of people starved to death.[40] The parallel between the worries of the fictional county chief and China's late supreme leader helps highlight the absurd, illusory, and utopian nature of the Lenin project and, through the allusion, of the Chinese model of economic development.

Despite the alluring, rosy picture drawn by the county chief, it is no more than a dream at the very beginning. The first and foremost challenge that the chief faces is how to raise the tremendous amount of money to pay for Lenin's remains. It does not take long for the resourceful and clever county chief to figure out a way, however. Highly impressed and inspired by the performance of Liven's people at their annual village festival, he decides to organize the villagers of Liven into two special-skills performing troupes to achieve the goal. The so-called performance, as we shall see later, is in essence to exhibit the disabilities of the villagers at the expense of their health and dignity as human beings. As Carlos Rojas makes especially clear in his reading of the novel, "in *Lenin's Kisses* what is being commoditized is quite literally the very fragmentedness and incompleteness of the villagers' bodies themselves."[41] Here we can already see a sign of cruelty latent in the scheme, and its cruelty and dehumanization display to the fullest in actual performances when the villagers travel around the country.

One of their acts is called One-Legged Flying Leap. To complete the performance, a young man with only one leg, nicknamed One-Legged Monkey, has to leap nine feet over a pool of peas, then over a ten-foot-long bed of nails, and finally over an even broader "sea of fire." It is so dangerous that any minor accident in the process would cost him his good leg or even his life. Nevertheless, it is deliberately designed this way to arouse wild excitement in the audience. Actually, during his first-ever performance on the stage, the man's pants catch fire; the pain is so great that he cries in agony. The fire burns away his empty pants leg, with only a charred circular opening remaining. "The charred pants leg was clearly visible under the spotlights, permitting the audience to see the stump of Monkey's missing leg poking out. That stumplike appendage clearly had two large blisters which were shimmering under the lights."[42] This detail of exposing the stump of a man's missing leg in public not only fully reveals the cruel nature of the performance but also plainly shows that the so-called performance by these wrecked people is nothing but an exhibition of their physical disabilities at the expense of their dignity as human beings.

Another performance is Deafman Ma's Firecracker-on-the-Ear, which is composed of two parts: exploding a string of hundreds of firecrackers over a deaf man's ear, separated from his face only by a thin cardboard; and exploding an explosive as big as a turnip placed on a side of his head. While the first act blackens his face completely, the second causes his face to be "covered in blood and ash."[43] He has to repeat the same act over and over, sometimes two or three times every day. As a result, "the side of Deafman Ma's face was completely disfigured as a result of the six months he spent performing his firecracker routine," and "half of his face became covered with pus."[44] It can be inferred, even based on common sense, that the nightmarish experience must have imposed not only tremendous physical suffering but also profound and far-reaching psychological traumas. This suffering and trauma was the case with all Liven performers.

Among all the performances, the cruellest is the one performed by little Polio Boy. He has to curl up his crippled foot, stick it into a bottle, and then walk around using the bottle as a shoe. To entertain the wildly excited audience, near the end of the performance he will break the bottle and then walk over the glass shards barefooted. At the end of the performance, when he lifts his tiny foot into the air, "blood [is] dripping like rain onto the canvas."[45] During the last performance, in order to wait for Chief Liu to watch the show, he is asked to walk barefooted several times around the stage covered with glass shards:

> He left the stage covered in a thick pool of blood, and every few feet the canvas was marked with one of his bloody footprints. These sticky footprints were initially bright red, but they quickly faded to deep purple, and then to black ... After he finished making six loops, he went to the front of the stage to take a bow, and even lifted his leaflike deformed foot to show the audience. They saw that the glass bottle in which he had originally inserted his foot was gone, and that instead the shards of glass were now embedded in the sole of his foot.[46]

The bloodiness and cruelty as portrayed here certainly would shock many. In their readings of this novel, Shelley W. Chan and Thomas Chen both compare the performance to the nineteenth-century American freak shows.[47] As Chan incisively points out, "the performers of the special-skill troupes are actually no more than trained monkeys in human clothes,"[48] and they represent a manifest case of the objectification and degradation of humanity to "a state of non-human."[49] The horrifying dehumanization embedded in the Chinese model of development reveals the brutality of the biopolitics in contemporary China –

that the so-called Chinese economic miracle is achieved through the exploitation, abuse, and control of the bodies, lives, and deaths of the underprivileged by unrestrained political power. In the process, they are stripped of their social nature as human beings and reduced to "bare life."[50]

Indeed, biopolitics, the management and control of people's lives and deaths by political power, is one of the most significant aspects of reality in contemporary China, most explicitly demonstrated by the government's birth control policies and practices. As such, exposure of and reflection on the cruelty and absurdity of contemporary Chinese biopolitics constitute a pronounced motif in many outstanding literary works. Mo Yan's novel *Frog*, for instance, through a vivid and detailed depiction of the implementation of birth control by state violence over half a century in contemporary China, reveals the arbitrariness, bloodiness, and absurdity of the ever-changing and unpredictable policies and mechanisms adopted by the dictatorial regime to control people's physical existence, lives, and deaths, and the enormous devastating consequences and far-reaching traumas it has brought to the nation. Yu Hua's novel *Chronicle of a Blood Merchant* recounts the story of an ordinary Chinese man who relies on selling his own blood to overcome every major family calamity caused by the Maoist political movements. His novel *Brothers* features the life of a male protagonist who has to receive several plastic surgeries to change his physical appearance in order to make a living in the post-Mao era. Two of Yan Lianke's other novels, *Dream of the Ding Village* and *The Sunlit Years*, both play with the motif of biopolitics in contemporary China. The former narrates the story of how the dream of an ordinary Chinese village's people to turn rich overnight through selling their blood ends up with almost all adults in the village becoming infected with AIDS. The latter portrays how the people in a village try to build a ditch to connect the village to a hidden divine river with the power to prolong their lives past forty years. Meanwhile, they have to sell their bodies to pay for treatment of their current illnesses – men selling parts of their skins to the hospital and women selling sex in the city. In all these novels, we witness a "connection between economic growth and the expenditure of the villagers' bodies" and see that "the villagers give up their rights over their biological bodies for their leaders" in order to develop the economy.[51] The unrestrained and brutal exploitation of the people's bodies for sociopolitical purposes proves the predatory nature of the Chinese model of development.

What make Yan Lianke's depiction in *Lenin's Kisses* more shocking and horrifying is his exposure of the extreme popularity of those cruel performances among city people. As presented in the novel, in order to enjoy the performances, the city people do not hesitate to spend all their money or to miss school or work. During their six months touring all around the country, the Liven performing troupes have turned every city they visit into a carnival. Throughout the novel, no one, except Granny Mao Zhi, ever feels anything is wrong about the shows, let alone questions their immorality and the cruelty and dehumanization embedded in them. On the contrary, during the performances, the audience often demands that the performers escalate the danger of their performances as well as the cruelty. These scenes readily remind us of those cruel moments in twentieth-century Chinese literature portrayed in Lu Xun's "Kong Yiji" and "New Year's Sacrifice,"[52] Xiao Hong's *Tales of Hulan River*, Ba Jin's *Garden of Repose*, Han Shaogong's "Pa Pa Pa," and Yu Hua's "1986" and *The Seventh Day*,[53] where a crowd of heartless spectators entertain themselves with others' suffering. Moreover, these scenes also reveal a grim social reality of contemporary China under Communist domination: the normalization of cruelty and dehumanization. Yan Lianke's depiction of how human suffering is aestheticized for political reasons also reminds us of Walter Benjamin's notion of "aestheticization of politics," by which Benjamin refers to the phenomenon that fascism only grants the masses the freedom to express themselves while depriving them of their actual rights. As a result, the self-alienation of humanity "has reached such a degree that it can experience its own destruction as an aesthetic pleasure of the first order. This is the situation of politics which Fascism is rendering aesthetic."[54]

Whereas the process of the Lenin project in the novel exposes the cruelty of the Chinese model of development, the outcome of the project reveals the predatory nature of that model, though in an implicit and subtle way. In the novel, there is a sharp and highly meaningful contrast between Liven's people and the government in terms of their respective benefits from the Lenin project. For the people of Liven, despite the rosy picture the county chief paints for them and the many promises he makes, and despite the enormity of money they earn during their performance trips, at the end of the day they bring nothing home but suffering, humiliation, fear, nightmarish memories, and traumas. The government, however, accumulates enormous wealth from the project, as the money made by the Liven troupes "[flowed] along the banks' channels and into the county coffers."[55] The county chief and other officials are so pleased with the tremendous wealth the Liven troupes bring to the government in such a short time that they simply call them a "money tree."[56] Even more revealing, near the end of the novel, when the villagers are kidnapped and detained in the Lenin

Memorial Hall for over three days, these same officials, who seem omnipresent and almighty in monitoring the troupes at every step in their moneymaking trip, suddenly disappear without a trace. From all these descriptions, readers might easily draw the conclusion that the Lenin project actually turns into a predatory tool for the government to exploit the underprivileged, even if it might not have been designed that way in the first place. The ultimate outcome of the failed Lenin project – the government is the only winner and beneficiary of it, whereas the ordinary people of Liven, who create the enormous wealth with their sweat and blood, become victims and losers – serves to highlight the predatory nature of the Chinese model of development.

At this moment, we arrive at one of the most important points that Yan Lianke makes in the novel: Whereas the Chinese people were prey to the endless, devastating political movements in the Mao era, they are sacrificed for the grand economic "miracle" in post-Mao China. In both eras, ordinary Chinese people are victims to Communist rule. With his vivid account of the life experience of Liven's people in both eras, Yan lays bare the reality that, despite the seeming difference in policy of the two eras on the surface, the inhuman nature of Communist rule and the miserable fate it brings to the Chinese people remain unchanged. In the novel, the consistency of the Communist rule in China and the commonality of the Chinese people's fate in the two different eras are highlighted by two particular facts with symbolic implications – in both eras the women in Mao Zhi's family are sexually assaulted by Communists, and in both eras the people of Liven fall victim to fateful plunders.

In the novel, Yan Lianke presents a scenario pregnant with allegorical implications: Liven, a village composed almost exclusively of disabled people, is surrounded by a powerful outside world dominated by "wholers" – a term used by the people of Liven to label non-disabled people. During the Great Famine in the Mao era, it is wholers who brandish guns or government documents, take away every grain from Liven's people, and cause many of the villagers to starve to death. In the post-Mao era, the villagers are robbed twice, and both robberies are also perpetrated by wholers. Whereas the robbers of the first group turn out to be the "higher-ups" of the performing troupes, the second group is composed of the driver and a few other wholers who work for the troupes. The double robberies suffered by the people of Liven, and especially their being robbed by their own leaders and co-workers, readily remind us of the dual predation suffered by Chinese people as discussed in chapter 1: the "legal" predation by the government through predatory policies and practices, and an additional "illegal" predation inflicted by the collusive corruption of government officials

and businessmen. In both Communist periods, the robberies are conducted openly, and the perpetrators do not feel any regret about their
crimes. During the Great Famine, for instance, when a wholer comes to
rob Liven's villagers of grain, he even questions his victims in a right-
eous tone while walking out the door with a sack of grain: "How is
it that you blind people are living better than us? Who ever heard of
disabled people leading better lives than able-bodied people?"[57] He
loudly announces to the victims: "We haven't come to steal your grain,
we were sent by the government."[58] In the post-Mao era, when Liven's
villagers are kidnapped and detained in the Lenin Memorial Hall, a
robber asks them the same rhetorical question: "Do you really think
that you disabled people could overpower us wholers?" He warns and
admonishes his victims: "We wholers *are* your law."[59] Here the logic of
the law of the jungle adopted by the wholers is made very clear.

Given the rich political implications of the images of the disabled
people and the wholers as presented in the novels, it would be naive
to treat the distinction between them merely from a biological perspective. In fact, the people of Liven's disabilities and their distinction
from the wholers as presented in the novel bear profound discursive
significance, which is illuminated by several scholars from multiple
perspectives. Jianmei Liu, for instance, argues that the people of Liv-
en's disabilities and the type of isolated, carefree, and self-reliant mode
of existence prior to the Communist era represent an ideal way of life
as promoted by the Taoist master Zhuangzi.[60] Weijie Song insists that
the distinction serves to highlight the heterogeneity and complexity
of Liven as an existential space. As he argues, "the mythorealist juxta-
positions of healthy people and disabled villagers underline the truth
that Liven is not a homogeneous, abstract, rigid community but rather
a complex, heterogeneous, partly closed, and partly open space full
of contingent contradictions and temporary reconciliations."[61] Both
Thomas Chen and Carlos Rojas hold the notion that the people of Liv-
en's disabilities symbolize their "marginal, subaltern, and vulnerable"
social status.[62] Chen points out: "Happy villagers can also be taken to
represent the poor, the powerless, and the oppressed in a society where
cadres and business elites – the "whole" people – are the ones reaping
all the riches."[63]

In line with Thomas Chen's and Carlos Rojas's perceptions, I believe
that the disabled in the novel represent the marginalized and underprivileged, while the wholers represent the ruling elites, who hold
power and enjoy privileges and thus consider themselves superior to or
"abler" than the underprivileged. In the eyes of the ruling elites, those
marginal and underprivileged people are simply "disabled," inferior in

every aspect. In the novel, the implication of the wholers as a symbol of power is made very clear: whenever wholers appear, they always hold something representing power, such as guns or government documents if they are not officials themselves, and it is always the wholers who inflict suffering and disaster upon the disabled, not the other way around. The linkage of wholers and power is also allegorically affirmed by a surreal incident: one of Granny Mao Zhi's four little nin granddaughters,[64] Huaihua, suddenly and marvellously reassumes growth, turning into a wholer and the prettiest woman in the area, after she starts sexual relationships with government officials and the troupe's higher-ups, who are wholers; the other three, who have no relationship with wholers, remain little nins. From what the wholers say to the disabled people while robbing them, it can be inferred that the guiding principle for those ruling elites is also grounded in their sense of superiority: how could we, the "abler" elites, allow those "disabled" ordinary people to lead better lives than us? This statement is clearly a social Darwinist view and follows the law of the jungle, which lays bare the essence of Communist rule in today's China.

"With Money, Anything Is Possible"

As discussed earlier, forty years of implementing the Dengist model of development has not only created an economic "miracle" but has also brought about many grave problems, of which moral crisis is one of the most serious. This crisis was caused by the collapse of Communist ideals as a result of the complete failure of the Maoist ascetic pursuit of utopianism and voluntarism, by Dengist vulgar materialism and the stark utilitarian and nihilistic means used to achieve it, and by the politicization of morality concocted by the regime for its own agenda, as discussed in chapter 1. In everyday life, the moral crisis displays itself most manifestly in loss of belief, money fetishism, and moral nihilism. It is an ongoing phenomenon in present-day China and a real experience of every Chinese in everyday life.[65] Yan Lianke's novel provides a vivid and accurate picture of this ongoing moral crisis in today's China and explores the reasons for it.

In the novel, when a self-proclaimed Singapore business tycoon expresses his doubt to Chief Liu about the feasibility of purchasing Lenin's remains, the county head dismisses it with a confident laugh. He tells the guest: "With money, anything is possible."[66] These words uttered by the Communist official are the gospel in the Deng era, and Chief Liu's confidence proves to be well grounded in the reality of today's China. To give his deceased mother a magnificent funeral, the

Singapore tycoon, a native of Chief Liu's home county, asks the local leader to help him find more people to attend the funeral as her "filial sons," and promises to offer 10,000 yuan for each "filial son" in return. With the lure of money, Chief Liu easily organizes a filial procession consisting of more than two thousand people, whose wailing "scared off all of the crows and sparrows on the mountain."[67] This comic picture makes it clear that, in today's China, filial piety, the highest virtue in traditional Chinese ethics, becomes a commodity. Actually, as presented in the novel, not only filial piety but anything can be purchased easily with money: human dignity, obedience, chastity, and so on. Money fetishism and vulgar materialism, the defining features of the Chinese model, are displayed to the fullest.

The worship of money is only one end of vulgar materialism; the other end is stark utilitarianism along with moral nihilism: to get money, one can use any means and do anything. To make money, people can trample on their most cherished values and beliefs. Just as filial piety, the paramount traditional Chinese virtue, is treated as an object of trade, the allegedly "sublime and glorious" Communist ideals and values are also treated as commodities, evidenced by the plan to purchase Lenin's corpse and exhibit it for money. For money, people falsify history, fabricating or abusing historical facts and figures, legends, folk tales, and other historical and cultural events. They also tell stark lies about nature and people to attract potential visitors. To establish that the mountain used as an attraction has had a long history, they put plaques on trees in the forest, claiming that the hundred-year-old trees are three hundred or even five hundred years old, and that the five-hundred-year-old ones are eleven hundred, nineteen hundred, or even two thousand years old. To increase the mysteriousness of their identity and the appeal of the performing troupes, they can modify or fake any person's identification. Not only can ordinary people's lives be modified, but the great Communist leader Lenin's identity and life experience can also be fabricated to attract visitors' attention. For instance, they claim every single brick in the Lenin Memorial Hall has its own story, and every stone is directly linked in some way to Lenin's life. In sum, in order to attract customers, there are no social and moral boundaries that cannot be transgressed, no values and beliefs that cannot be trampled, and no truth, be it historical or natural, that cannot be falsified or fabricated.

More valuable than the novel's description of the phenomenon of the moral crisis is its penetrating enquiry into the reasons for the crisis, which is conducted mainly through the characterization of Chief Liu. The decisive impact of the county chief upon the morals of the entire county is presented mainly in two ways: how he promotes money fetishism and moral nihilism around the county with utilitarian and immoral policies to develop the economy; and how he, the highest moral authority in the county, sets a bad example for the people with his immoral character and corrupt behaviour, helping create a social environment characterized by the normalization of immorality.

As just mentioned, throughout the process of the Lenin project, there is transgression of social and moral boundaries, trampling of long-cherished values and beliefs, and falsification of historical and personal truth. It all happens under Chief Liu's direct leadership, as the narrator makes very clear: "The county chief has overseen all the plans, and any changes would have to be approved by him."[68] The novel provides a detailed and vivid account of how Chief Liu develops the economy in his township when he is in charge of the township's business. For example, one policy he makes decrees that every village can only have ten men stay behind to lead a group of women and the elderly to work in the fields, while the rest of the village's young men and women must go out to find work. They are not allowed to return home in less than three to six months; otherwise, their families will be fined and punished. Liu tells the villagers that they can steal and loot if they have to, but no matter what, they cannot remain at home working the land. It turns out that the chief is not joking or playing with words here; as we will clearly see later, he literally means that in order to get rich, the villagers can steal, loot, or do almost anything. In the novel, three cases demonstrate most explicitly the stark nihilism and immorality of Chief Liu's philosophy of economic development.

The first incident happens in a family in which all of the children are girls. Chief Liu sends the two oldest daughters to the provincial city to find work. Within half a month, the girls use up all their money and are famished. For fear of being punished by the chief for going home early, they have to stay in the city working as prostitutes. As a result, they make a lot of money in a very short time; their family becomes rich quickly as a consequence, and they are able to build a new house within half a year, which pleases Chief Liu greatly. "Yingque led all the cadres in the township to their home to host an impromptu meeting, bringing the parents flowers and hanging a plaque on the wall of the house. The officials even issued congratulatory letters, stamped with the township's seal, to those two girls who were out selling their flesh."[69] The caricature drawn here reflects exactly the phenomenon commonly seen in post-Mao China – being poor is more shameful and despicable than being a prostitute (*xiaopin bu xiaochang* 笑贫不笑娼). The congratulatory letters to the prostitutes stamped with the government's seal help highlight the decisive role that the state plays in the nationwide, grave moral crisis in China today.

The second case also concerns prostitution. One day, more than a dozen young women from Chief Liu's township are caught by the district police for engaging in prostitution. The police call Chief Liu and ask him to go to the city to fetch them. As soon as he leads the women out of the police station, however, he releases them and addresses them:

> You have the ability to make a Public Security Bureau Officer divorce his wife, disrupting his family so much that his wife and son leave him. You have the ability to become a madam and teach other women to follow in your footsteps. You have the ability to send money home, enabling your family to build a tile-roofed house and permitting the entire village to have electricity and running water, such that the village will erect a good-merit stela celebrating your good deeds.[70]

Obviously, the chief does not think that the women have done anything wrong. He not only does not condemn them but also encourages them to continue and develop their careers as prostitutes, which is illegal and immoral in the country. He even instigates them to break up the families of public security officers who stand in their way of wealth and instructs them on how to drag more women into this illegal business. The message the chief conveys here cannot be clearer: If anyone blocks your way to make money, then his family deserves to be torn apart. Even if you are a prostitute, as long as you can make money to get yourself, your family, and even your village rich, then what you do is "a good deed" and deserves a "good-merit stela" to be erected in your honour. The philosophy of vulgar materialism, stark utilitarianism, and moral nihilism as presented here indeed grasps the essence of the guiding principle for economic development adopted in post-Mao China. This message is a vivid reflection of Deng Xiaoping's famous white cat–black cat theory: "No matter whether a cat is white or black, it is a good cat as long as it can catch mice."

The third case is related to stealing. A man from the township who goes to the city to find work is captured for stealing a motor from a factory. He is sent back to Chief Liu for penalty. Unexpectedly, the punishment the chief lays out for him is that within three years he must set up a factory in his village. After leaving Chief Liu's office, the man immediately returns to the city without even going home to see his parents. It is said that he goes to the provincial capital or cities in the south "to develop his skills."[71] What kind of "skills" does he develop in the city? No one knows, but we can only imagine. Not surprisingly, however, he indeed manages to establish a small factory in his village years later, which must have made Chief Liu very pleased. This story once again proves that, for Chief Liu, any means can be justified in order to get rich, and money is bigger than anything else in the world. With his vivid and detailed descriptions of how Chief Liu develops the economy in his home county, Yan Lianke convinces us that vulgar materialism and the nihilistic and utilitarian policies adopted by the Chinese Party-state for economic development are major causes of the massive, grave moral crisis in China today.

In addition to nihilistic policies, government officials' corrupt and immoral behaviour is another major contributor to the moral crisis. The Chinese regime tends to eulogize its system as a meritocracy: rule by the able and the talented. It is worth noting that, in the Chinese intellectual and political tradition, virtue is considered an integral and crucial part of talent for a politician. In traditional Chinese culture, government officials not only represent the political authority to maintain social order but also serve as the moral authority and moral exemplars for ordinary people. This tradition is a result and manifestation of the "integration of sociopolitical order and cultural-moral order" during the two thousand years of Chinese imperial history.[72] Given the long-lasting Chinese tradition of the integration of political and moral authority, the impact of government officials' character and behaviour upon the morals of the entire society cannot be overemphasized. The Communist regime obviously inherits this imperial tradition and adopts it for its own agenda. As Jiwei Ci incisively points out, in contemporary China, "the Party-Government is the only institutional initiator and authorizer of moral norms."[73] As such, "those who make up the authority behind the norms, that is, the Party-Government as embodied in its officials at various levels, are the same people who must play the role of exemplars in acting on the norms."[74]

Clearly, Yan Lianke understands this Chinese political tradition and the social reality of today's China very well, and reflects them in his characterization of Chief Liu. As mentioned earlier, there are two revolutionary cadres featured in the novel, Granny Mao Zhi and Chief Liu, but they are portrayed in completely different ways. Granny is depicted more or less as a tragic hero of moral integrity; although she leads Liven to Communist rule and brings oppression and suffering to the village, she risks her life for the villagers during the Maoist political movements and keeps fighting for the village's autonomy after Mao's death. Chief Liu, by contrast, is delineated as a despicable cartoon character who cares about nothing but power. Although he is not completely evil – he at least shows gratitude to his foster father – he is undoubtedly an immoral person and a corrupt official. Right after his social status changes from worker to cadre, he seduces Mao Zhi's beautiful daughter, Jumei, on his first business trip to Liven for "socialist education" and fathers four girls. Nevertheless, he never acknowledges his relationship with his biological daughters and their mother, and instead treats them coldly – an explicit sign of his lack of morality.

Instead of focusing on his immorality as an individual person, the novel puts more stress on Chief Liu's moral depravity as a government official. Unlike many Chinese officials seen in real life or in artistic works, whose corruption often takes the form of receiving bribes or using public power for personal wealth or sex, Chief Liu's corruption is displayed as excessive obsession with power and abuse of power. After he takes the post of county chief, with the Party secretary temporarily absent from his post to study in Beijing, Chief Liu begins to possess absolute authority and power over the entire county, and he soon comes to feel and behave like an emperor. Indeed, under the current Chinese one-Party system, the number one leader at any level of the government, be it the village, township, county, province, or the entire nation, holds absolute power within his jurisdiction, just like an emperor in ancient times.

In the novel, there are plenty of depictions showing how Chief Liu behaves and is treated like an emperor. For instance, when ordinary people go to his office for business or even when they see him in the street, they must first kneel down and kowtow to him. When people visit him in his office, if he is taking a nap, they have to kneel on the ground outside waiting until he wakes up. When he attends a meeting, he demands that the audience applaud before he speaks. When he goes to see a performance in a theatre, he must be seated in the central position so that when the performers bow to the audience, they seem to bow directly and only to him. When he delivers disaster relief funding to the victims on behalf of the government, he can decide at will which household receives more or less money based completely on his moods and preferences. In his office, he hangs his own portrait, the same size as Chairman Mao's standard portrait, side by side with the late chairman's. He also hangs his portrait in the so-called "contribution room" in his residence among those of China's ten founding Marshals, just behind the five greatest Communist leaders, Marx, Engels, Lenin, Stalin, and Mao. More surprisingly, he orders people to build a secret room underneath the one where Lenin's crystal coffin is going to be located and to put in an identical coffin for himself. With the help of such literary devices as farce, hyperbole, surrealism, and so on, Yan Lianke exposes the extreme greediness of a low-ranking Chinese official for power.

Chief Liu never hides his feeling of being like an emperor and his view of his relationship with ordinary people. On one occasion, he expresses this attitude clearly when he talks to his wife. Because he often goes away from home for weeks in the name of work, and because he does not care about his wife and their daughter at all, his wife hates him deeply. As a result, the couple often have intensive verbal fights. Once, when he goes home, his wife refuses to sleep with him; he then gives her a tirade:

> I am telling you, your husband is not the same Boshuzi commune soc-school [socialist education school] teacher you originally married. He's not the same turnip-head cadre he once was. He is now the county chief, the emperor of Shuanghuai county, with eight hundred and ten thousand subjects under his commanding, including tens – or even hundreds – of thousands of women who are younger and prettier than you. He could sleep with any of them, if he wants.[75]

Clearly, in the eyes of the Communist county head, ordinary people under his jurisdiction are no more than his subjects and women his playthings. For him, the meaning of being a government official is to enjoy the privilege, pleasure, and sense of superiority that power brings to him. His philosophy of life is very simple: power is his life, and all his efforts in life aim at power. In order to climb up the ladder of power, he can do anything or abandon anything, including family, which makes a sharp contrast with one of his counterparts in ancient China, Sister Hua's husband, who abandoned his post as a county chief and cut off his arm in order to live with the woman he loved. The contrast between the two county chiefs at different times amounts to a subtle criticism of the moral depravity of Chinese officials under Communist domination. Chief Liu's frenzy for power and his reduction of the people in a modern society to the subjects of an emperor in ancient times constitute stark irony and poignant sarcasm aimed at the Chinese Party-state, which claims that its guiding principle is "serve the people."

In the novel, the account of Chief Liu's personal history, especially his childhood experience, is highly significant from a discursive perspective. He is an orphan, adopted by teacher Liu of the local soc-school (short for socialist education school). He literally grows up on socialist nutrition, both materially and spiritually, as he eats at the public canteen and attends the classes at the soc-school for free. As a result, "all of the cadres and Party officials regarded him as a son of the school to the point that many of them stopped calling him by his name and instead referred to him as 'soc-school child' or 'soc-school babe.'"[76] It is simply hard to find another "Communist heir" more pure than him. With the image of Chief Liu as the purest Communist child, Yan Lianke points to the invalidity, futility, and hypocrisy of the so-called Communist ideals and socialist moral education, as his presentation suggests that it is merely a beautiful yet illusory dream to cultivate high moral standards in people with the inculcation of Communist ideology and the propagation of Communist ideals.

For a government official, excessive pursuit of power and abuse of power while disregarding public welfare and public good and trampling on social and moral norms are undoubtedly corruption. From an ethical perspective, this kind of corruption falls into the category of selfishness – obsession with the satisfaction of one's own desires with no regard for others' interests. Ultimately, Chief Liu's mania for power is an expression of his extreme selfishness and moral depravity, which inevitably would exercise a profound and far-reaching influence upon the morals of the entire county, given that, in the Chinese political culture, government officials are regarded as the embodiment and crystallization of moral authority and moral exemplarity.

Arbitrariness of Power, Sustainability of Dictatorship, and Dead-End Future

It is now common knowledge that the so-called Chinese model is a combination of two ingredients: economic determinism and political authoritarianism, characterized by "an economic superpower ruled by a sophisticated and ruthless one-Party dictatorship,"[77] if put in Minxin Pei's words. In *Lenin's Kisses*, Yan Lianke, as discussed previously, not only exposes the absurdity, cruelty, and dehumanization of the Dengist style of economic development but also critically reflects on the nature, workings, and consequences of dictatorship in the economic "miracle." In the novel, Yan's reflection on the dictatorship in contemporary China proceeds along two tracks: on the one hand, he lays bare the arbitrary and formidable nature of power in a dictatorial state, which governs with "slow violence"[78] and terror; on the other hand, he also points to the grim reality that dictatorial state power, despite its arbitrary and horrifying nature, displays a powerful ability to sustain itself through developing submissive mentalities and favourable conditions supportive of its existence among the people. Yan's finding in either direction would disappoint those who hope for a quick end to dictatorship. In addition to his dialectical reflection on the nature and workings of political power under the Chinese model, Yan also provides an assessment of the Chinese model's fate. Despite his affirmation of the Party-state's ability to sustain itself, Yan Lianke, with his allegorical depiction of the fate of the Lenin project and the dilemma that Liven residents face, suggests that the Chinese model will lead the nation nowhere but to a dead-end future, and as such it is destined to fail.

The presentation of the arbitrariness and absoluteness of power in the novel is one of the most pronounced motifs, which is most evidently demonstrated by the characterization of Chief Liu. As discussed earlier, Chief Liu has absolute authority over all organizations and people under his jurisdiction. Not only can he freely arrange the economic activities of any village in his county, he can also, as mentioned earlier, decide on the affairs of an individual household as to who in the family can stay in the village and who must go to work in the city. He regards his relationship with the people in his county as that of an emperor with his subjects. In fact, the absoluteness and arbitrariness of political power in contemporary China under Communist domination are embodied in the relationship not only between officials and people but also among officials at different levels in the hierarchical bureaucracy. Just as the ordinary people in his jurisdiction are merely subjects to him, Chief Liu himself is no more than a subject to his own superiors. Near the end of the novel, when the Lenin project is on the brink of bankruptcy, the provincial governor, Chief Liu's direct superior, summons him. After travelling with his driver for one day and one night without any sleep or food and arriving at the provincial government building, Chief Liu still has to wait outside the governor's office for half a day before the high-ranking official finally condescends to see him. The meeting turns out to be insanely short. "To his surprise, the governor spoke to him only for the length of time that it takes a drop of water to fall from the roof of a building."[79] After that, "the governor gestured for him to leave, the way one might brush away a fly."[80] Despite being regarded as an emperor or even a deity by the people under his own jurisdiction, Chief Liu is no more valuable than a fly in the eyes of his superior. Moreover, not until the end of the meeting does he realize that the only purpose the governor has for summoning him is to humiliate and curse him. After the provincial governor vents his own fury, he does not even give the lesser official a chance to respond. This scene illustrates how the relationship between a subordinate and his superior functions in the Chinese bureaucracy today.

In the novel, more revealing and thought-provoking than his exposure of the absoluteness and arbitrariness of political power in contemporary China is Yan's representation of the sustainability of the dictatorial power. Yan paints a highly impressive yet despairing picture: in the face of the formidable state power's oppression, cruelty, and dehumanization, the people of Liven do not show any intention of rebellion; instead, they slavishly submit to its terror. Throughout the novel, there are countless scenes portraying how people kneel down and kowtow to Chief Liu but not even one moment when readers see people say no to him. It seems that enduring subjugation to dictatorship deprives people of their sense of dignity, desire for freedom, and rebellious spirit and instils an obedient and submissive mentality in them. In the novel, with plenty of vividly depicted scenes, Yan Lianke emphasizes that the reason Chief Liu feels and behaves like an emperor is because his people treat him as an emperor in the first place. "In Shuanghuai, Chief Liu was regarded as an extraordinary figure, comparable to the legendary Qing dynasty emperors Qianlong and Kangxi, or the founders of the Ming and Song dynasties, emperors Zhu Yuanzhang and Song Taizu."[81] Later on, after he declares the launching of the Lenin project and paints a rosy picture of the path forward for the county, "everyone began to regard Chief Liu as a deity, and even peasants in the countryside somehow manage to buy copies of his photograph and hang it up on their walls. They hung his photograph alongside the pictures of the bodhisattvas, the stove god, and Chairman Mao."[82]

In between the many scenes delineating people's worship of Chief Liu, there is a highly revealing one recounting how a pack of old, filthy, and disabled dogs kneel down in front of Granny Mao Zhi begging her for adoption. By paralleling people kneeling down before a dictatorial leader regarded as a deity and dogs kneeling down in front of a human seen as their potential saviour, Yan Lianke emphasizes the Chinese people's slavish submission to dictatorship that deprives them of their dignity and pride as human beings and reduces them to the level of animals. The disability shared by both Liven residents and the dogs helps further highlight the underprivileged and abject status of both groups. Yan Lianke's presentation here adds an insightful footnote to Aldous Huxley's statement that the art of "a really efficient totalitarian state" is that it rules not by coercion but through cultivating its people's "love for servitude."[83]

Here, we actually touch upon the second factor that accounts for the sustainability of dictatorship, a factor logically and discursively interrelated with the previous one: the Chinese people's voluntary acceptance and internalization of the Party-state's ideological indoctrination that is intended to deceive and victimize them. As elaborated in detail in chapter 1 and elsewhere in the book, after the Tiananmen crackdown, economic development has become the new source of political legitimacy for the Chinese Party-state, since the massacre declared the death of the old source of the Maoist people's sovereignty.

To talk people into buying its agenda and to cover up the predatory nature of its policies and practices adopted to develop the economy, the Party-state makes full use of its propaganda machine, creating various deceptive theories and slogans. Among all those theories and slogans, there are two pre-eminent ones: "Development is an unyielding principle" and "Development is the biggest human right" (*fazhan shi zuida de renquan* 发展是最大的人权), which both indicate that economic growth can overwhelm any other human values, including basic human rights, human dignity, and long-cherished beliefs and values. To the Party's great delight, ordinary Chinese people indeed buy its deceptive propaganda and, consequently, become unwitting accomplices in their own victimization, which is vividly presented by Yan Lianke.

In the novel, no other moment better illustrates Chinese people's acceptance and internalization of the Party's propaganda than Liven residents' craze for the "special-skills performances," which are in essence exhibiting their disabilities at the cost of their dignity as human beings, and their strong opposition to withdrawal from Communist domination. When Chief Liu proposes to organize a Liven performing troupe to raise funds for the Lenin project, Granny Mao Zhi is the only person who strongly opposes the proposal, while all the other villagers unanimously support it. When she tells them that the so-called performances are exhibiting their disabilities and as such are a humiliation and exploitation of their dignity, Polio Boy loudly declares: "I am willing to have my dignity exploited."[84] In fact, Polio Boy is not alone on this matter; his thought represents the overwhelming majority of the villagers. This thinking also helps explain why they almost unanimously oppose withdrawal from Communist domination. As mentioned earlier, Granny Mao Zhi, the once steadfast and loyal believer in communism, after experiencing and witnessing the tremendous cruelty and inhumanity of Communist rule in both the Mao and post-Mao eras, is completely disillusioned with Communist rule. Consequently, she is determined to lead the village to withdraw from Communist domination and to restore its autonomy and independence. She assumes that, after suffering so much under Communist rule, the villagers would naturally support this proposal, and there would be no question about it. To her great surprise and despondency, however, when she makes this proposal to the villagers, she meets with almost unanimous opposition, as the overwhelming majority of the villagers vote against it. Polio Boy even announces: "If withdrawal from society means that the performance troupes have to disband, then my family will fight the withdrawal tooth and nail."[85] Other villagers echo him, because they also believe that giving up the opportunity to make money by disbanding their performing troupes is "the ultimate in stupidity."[86]

In the novel, what makes readers feel more saddened and despairing is to see that the villagers, just as they said, do not mind their dignity being exploited as long as they can make money. During their performing trips, when Deafman Ma lies on the ground and explodes an explosive as big as a turnip on his face, covering his face in blood and ash, he actually "smiles" instead of crying or screaming after being told that he will earn a big bonus for that performance.[87] One-Legged Monkey and Polio Boy, in order to excite the audience and make more money, often take the initiative to increase the danger of their performances and the harm to their own bodies. In order to make money, the villagers are willing to jeopardize even their health and lives, let alone their dignity and pride as human beings, which is powerful evidence of their internalization of the Party's inculcation that anything can be sacrificed for economic development, an idea meant to deceive ordinary people into accepting their own victimization for the sake of the economy. Liven residents' thought and actions once again confirm Antonio Gramsci's notion of cultural and ideological hegemony – that the success of the ruling class in a given society relies not only on coercion but also, and more importantly, on the "spontaneous consent" given to it by the great masses of the population.[88]

In addition to people's love for their servitude and their internalization of the Party-state's deceptive propaganda, as Yan Lianke suggests in the novel, the terror of dictatorship and the lure of sensuous and material pleasure work hand in hand to degenerate and isolate people and destroy the trust and unity among them, creating a favourable condition for the survival of the regime. As mentioned earlier, the small mountain village, Liven, was founded and sustained on human goodness before the Communist era. During that time, the entire village was united like a big family; they trusted each other, helped each other, and relied on each other, and all the villagers held high moral standards. All this unity and harmony has changed completely under Communist domination, when the village was divided into different classes, lost its unity and mutual trust among its members, and went through a profound moral crisis. This crisis is most clearly demonstrated by the villagers' experience of being kidnapped and detained in the Lenin Memorial Hall. During their detention, in the face of the threat, extortion, and crime of their kidnappers, every villager, except Granny Mao Zhi, exhibits the darkest side of human nature; they all consider only themselves, and they do not even share food and water with their families. In this way, they are completely isolated and separated from each other and lose their power of resistance as a group, which greatly benefits their enemies. The allegorical scene as rendered by Yan Lianke here affirms Hannah Arendt's perception of totalitarianism.

Hannah Arendt, in her highly influential book on the origins of totalitarianism, provides an incisive and convincing illumination of how totalitarian domination isolates people and makes them powerless. She adeptly points out:

> Totalitarian government, like all tyrannies, certainly could not exist without destroying the public realm of life, that is, without destroying, by isolating men, their political capacities. But totalitarian domination as a form of government is new in that it is not content with this isolation and destroys private life as well. It bases itself on loneliness, on the experience of not belonging to the world at all, which is among the most radical and desperate experiences of man.[89]

According to Arendt, totalitarian government, whose essence is terror, is much worse than any other kind of tyranny, because totalitarian domination not only destroys the public realm of life and isolates people, as all tyrannies have done before, but also destroys the private realm of life left intact by tyrannies. In this way, totalitarian government deprives people of their capacities to think and create, and turns the isolated craftsmen (who still have ability to create) into lonely labourers (who are completely deprived of the capacity to create). By separating people both physically (isolation) and psychologically (loneliness), by destroying people's feeling of belonging, totalitarian government makes people "powerless" and "impotent," because "power always comes from men acting together."[90] Under the Chinese model, the appeal to people's greed for material gain and the evocation of selfish desires to develop the economy only serve to push people's feeling of isolation, loneliness, and powerlessness even further, creating the conditions conducive to the survival of dictatorship.

Despite his affirmation of the formidability and strong ability for survival of the Chinese model, Yan Lianke holds an unambiguously critical attitude towards it, suggesting its inevitable failure through his depiction of the bankruptcy of the grand Lenin project and the tragic experience of Liven's residents. Yan's denial of the Chinese model becomes even more manifest if we compare this novel with his other novels featuring post-Mao era, including *Dream of Ding Village*, *The Sunlit Years*, and *The Explosion Chronicles*. As with *Lenin's Kisses*, there is also a grand project in all these novels: in *Dream of Ding Village*, for instance, it is the blood-selling business aimed to get the village rich overnight;

in *The Sunlit Years*, it is the construction of a ditch connected to a hidden river with divine power, whose water is expected to prolong the villagers' lives beyond the age of forty; and in *The Explosion Chronicles*, it is the construction of the grand high-speed subway and the largest airport in Asia. Again, similar to the fate of the Lenin project, all these grand projects end up in complete failure. Whereas the dream of Ding villagers to get rich through selling blood brings them nothing but AIDS and countless deaths, the divine river in *The Sunlit Years* does not bring life-saving water but pollution and garbage from the city. The economic explosion of the town named Explosion not only does not elate the people there; on the contrary, it frightens them so much that they choose to escape the town and live in the graveyard of their ancestors instead. The complete failure of the Lenin project as well as of the other grand projects in Yan's novels makes his stance especially clear: The hope to build a prosperous and equal China only through economic development with no concern for people's dignity and basic rights is no more than a beautiful illusion. The grand Chinese model leads the nation nowhere but to a dead-end future.

Summary

Lenin's Kisses undoubtedly is a representative work of contemporary Chinese political fiction. Taking advantage of the unique literary device of "mythorealism," the novel exposes the nightmarish nature of the Chinese Communist revolution and the absurdity, cruelty, and dehumanization of the Chinese model of development. It also provides a vivid and convincing account of the grave moral crisis facing today's China and explores the reasons for it. As presented in the novel, Dengist economic determinism, vulgar materialism, stark utilitarianism, and official corruption are the major factors accounting for the moral crisis. The novel also engages in a dialectical reflection on the fate of the Chinese model of development: despite its cruel and predatory nature, it is not expected to perish soon, because it creates a mentality and sociopolitical environment conducive to its survival. Yan Lianke ascribes the strength and sustainability of the predatory model to Chinese people's extreme servitude in the face of oppressive power, their spontaneous acceptance and internalization of the Party-state's propaganda, and the destruction of the people's feeling of belonging and unity and of their rebellious capacity by the terror of dictatorship. Although Yan Lianke appreciates the survival ability of the Chinese-style dictatorship, he unambiguously denies the idea that the Chinese model represents the right path for the nation. Through his vivid depiction of the bankruptcy of the Lenin project and of other "grand projects" in his other novels, Yan suggests that the Chinese model will lead the nation nowhere but to a dead end.

From an intellectual perspective, a real contribution Yan Lianke has made to Chinese literature and thought with this novel, as well as with his other novels focusing on the post-Mao era, is that he draws our attention to the darkness and evil of the Dengist model of development, which has been relatively overlooked or neglected by Chinese writers, whereas the absurdity and cruelty of Maoist rule has already received massive exposure in Chinese literature. Another unique and original contribution of the novel is that it represents and critically reflects on the darkness of the Dengist model of development from the perspective of biopolitics – the management and control of people's bodily existence, lives, and deaths by political power, which is a pronounced feature of the Chinese model.

Chapter Four

Such Is This World@sars.come: Dictatorship as a Fatal Disease

As is the case with many politically sensitive novels in China, the publication of Hu Fayun's novel *Such Is This World@sars.come* also underwent many setbacks due to strict political censorship imposed by the Chinese Party-state.[1] The censor of the book certainly deserves credit for his judgment and expertise, because the novel indeed contains abundant explicit and implicit information that might be considered subversive and pernicious by the Party-state under the cover of a love story.[2] The novel exposes many historical facts and raises many questions that fundamentally challenge the nature and guiding principles of the Chinese Party-state as well as its political legitimacy.

The novel centres on the experience, feelings, and thoughts of a protagonist named Ru Yan, a conscientious, middle-aged, educated woman, during the SARS outbreak in China. It also features the life experience of several other people related to Ru Yan, including her new friends, three intellectuals, Damo, Maozi, and Teacher Wei; her short-lived lover, Vice Mayor Liang Jinsheng; and a few others. Additionally, the novel provides a naturalistic description, with rich allegorical implications, of what is going on in today's China as well as in its recent past. The novel focuses on Ru Yan's three everyday activities: her experience on the internet, her interaction with those intellectuals, and her love story with the vice mayor. By delineating her experience on the internet, the novel reveals the existence of a terrifying yet invisible "old crone" behind the computer screen, who watches every corner of the internet and controls all the information on it. By depicting her interaction with those intellectuals, the novel displays the shocking and far-reaching impact of the Tiananmen Massacre upon the Chinese intelligentsia, the changed mentality of the intellectuals after Tiananmen, and the ultimately antagonistic relationship between the dictatorial Party-state and conscientious intellectuals. By portraying her love story with the seemingly decent vice mayor, the novel exposes the two different faces of the Party, the split and distorted mindset of its members, and the real attitude of the Party-state towards its people. Intriguingly and paradoxically, through the three different channels, the novel uncovers the same truth about the relationship between the people and the Party-state: the people are on one side and the Party-state on the other; the two sides form the paradigm of "them versus us." As such, the novel subverts the Communist claim that the Party represents the people's interests. Additionally, the novel provides a vivid and impressive description of Ru Yan's inner transformation: how she turns from an ordinary academic professional who shows explicit political nonchalance to a "reluctant" intellectual who sees through to the truth of the Party-state and begins to possess a strong defiant political consciousness. In this sense, we could say that Ru Yan actually goes through a process of political enlightenment. Therefore, the novel can also be read as an allegory of the Chinese Party-state and of the intellectuals.

Before engaging in a detailed discussion of the political implications of the novel, it is necessary to point out that Ru Yan's love story with Liang Jinsheng constitutes the major plot line of the novel; it is of high aesthetic value and artistic appeal, even if read from a non-political perspective. The novel provides a nuanced, accurate, and convincing account of the psychological journey that each person in the couple goes through during the relationship. The novel also explores some significant themes, such as the relation of sex, freedom, and the self, the true meaning of life, and other such issues, and the author's reflections on these themes are highly incisive and insightful. All these motifs and themes, however, are beyond the scope of the current research and thus have to be left behind unattended.

"Lockdown" as Social Reality and Political Allegory

When we complete the entire novel and examine it as a whole, we find that "lockdown" – in which people are locked in the dark wards of hospitals, in police stations, in their own houses; websites are shut down by the government; and other such measures – is the most pronounced image in the novel and the key to understanding the connotations of the novel on both manifest and metaphoric levels. "Lockdown" is not only an everyday scene in the society where Ru Yan lives but also a psychological state of being wary of others, distrusting others, and isolating and alienating oneself from others and the outside world. "Lockdown" is also an allegory of the political, social, and existential conditions in the country, where the Party-state has omniscient and almighty power to "lock" any person or anything at will, and where historical truth is "locked" by the Party-state, hidden behind a dark, iron curtain.

In the novel, "lockdown" is an everyday scene and a real experience of people in Ru Yan's world, where the Party-state controls everything. In the beginning of the novel, before the SARS outbreak, readers witness that the website of Damo, a conscientious and disobedient intellectual, has been repeatedly shut down or "locked down" by the government because of its devotion to the discussion of politics and philosophy, and its criticism of China's social ills. Later on, after SARS breaks out, Ru Yan's brother-in-law, Teacher Wei, and many real or suspected SARS patients are locked in dark hospital wards, where the so-called medical treatment completely depends on luck, because the doctors don't even know what causes the deadly disease, let alone how to cure it. During the SARS outbreak, all Chinese people lock themselves in their houses with all doors and windows shut tightly. During the same period, a notorious event occurs: a college student is illegally detained or "locked" in a police station and eventually tortured to death there. On the last page of the novel, we witness another shockingly tragic story: after her mother has been sent for compulsive detox, a little girl is locked in her own apartment, completely forgotten by the police, and finally starves to death in her own house. All these events, often associated with government irresponsibility and abuse of power,[3] run throughout the novel from the very beginning to the last page, making very clear that "lockdown" is a fundamental and omnipresent social phenomenon in Ru Yan's world.

"Lockdown," on a deeper narrative level, also refers to people being locked outside truth. In the novel, many descriptions testify to this phenomenon, but Teacher Wei's life story, especially his death, and Ru Yan's love affair with the vice mayor demonstrate it in the most explicit and profound way. During the SARS outbreak, Teacher Wei is sent to the hospital due to a minor illness caused by overexcitement and exhaustion during an unexpected and highly emotional family reunion. Plenty of evidence shows that it is just a common cold, because all the people who have had close contact with him for quite a few days do not have any problems. But after he goes to the hospital, he is diagnosed as a suspected SARS patient, put in quarantine, and finally dies in the hospital. No one even knows whether he really contracted SARS in the first place or if he actually got infected with it in the hospital or neither. More shockingly, due to his national and international reputation as a well-known theoretician and dissident, the real cause of his death is completely covered up. The official newspaper controlled by the Party announces that he died of a "long disease,"[4] and in this way, all the possible mistreatment and horror related to his SARS experience have been completely erased. Teacher Wei himself, based on his long-term observation of the Party-state and his profound understanding of its oppressive and deceptive nature, makes an accurate and incisive prediction of his fate with SARS before his death. He states: "When it is not, they say it is; when it is, they will say it is not."[5] These words seem to predict his fate with SARS, but actually crystallize his judgment of the Party-state's manipulation of truth: confusing truth with falsehood and inverting right and wrong.

In the novel, the Party-state's manipulation of reality and history – its effort to "lock" people outside truth – culminates in a vivid and highly meaningful description of what happened in the aftermath of SARS, which bears profound allegorical implications:

> There commenced a series of meetings devoted to summarizing the achievements of the campaign against SARS and issuing recommendations at every level, and reporting teams were organized at every level and made the rounds giving speeches. The calamity, panic, rage, desolation, and suffering of a few months before – not to mention the discord, the enforced isolation, the confrontational defensiveness, the back-stabbing and buck-passing – were now transformed in retrospection into an inspiring narrative, a thing of beauty. The TV was filled with scenes of people talking about it and moving both themselves and their listeners to tears. It was very affecting.[6]

In some sense, this description can be read as a footnote to the stories of Teacher Wei and many other Chinese who underwent the same experience and shared the same fate. By turning a fatal epidemic – which was terribly mishandled by the Party-state and, consequently, brought countless unnecessary deaths and enormous suffering and panic to the entire nation – into an "inspiring narrative" of victory, and especially by turning a scandal combining oppression, violence, cruelty, deception, conspiracy, and crime into "a thing of beauty," historical facts have been completely distorted, and people are locked outside the door to truth forever. As a result, common people quickly forgot all the horrible experiences and feelings of the just bygone calamity and immediately returned to the everyday routine of "pleasant dullness."[7] For them, "the preceding panic had been, rather, a kind of psychological entertainment that added a bit of drama to the banality of their lives"[8] and nothing more.

Undoubtedly, exposure of the amnesia imposed upon the Chinese people by the Party-state is a pronounced theme in the novel. As a mainland Chinese critic points out, for Hu Fayun (and for many other Chinese writers as well), fiction writing actually serves as a way to "resist forgetting."[9] Teacher Wei provides an incisive analysis of the reasons for the forced forgetting:

> There's so much in China's past that no one can bear to remember ... The perpetrators don't speak of these things, for they have skeletons in their closet. The victims don't talk about them either, perhaps because it hurts too much, or because the perpetrators don't let them. The years pass, and history gets covered up until the next tragedy.[10]

As exposed in the novel, the cover-up of historical truth occurs not only on the grand public level but also in the private realm. Under the Party-state's tight control of historical truth and collective memory, individual people are often denied access even to their own personal histories – they are locked outside the truth about their own lives. This "lockdown" amounts to the denial of the wholeness and integrity of their identity as human beings. This phenomenon is once again illustrated by Teacher Wei's story.

Despite his status as a long-term, steadfast, and loyal Party member and a well-known Marxist theoretician, Teacher Wei is labelled a member of the "Hu Feng counter-revolutionary clique" and put in jail for several years before the Cultural Revolution. Years later, when he is released from jail and goes home, he sees only an empty house with a few pieces of old and dilapidated furniture in it, and his wife and two children are nowhere to be found. Afterwards, he painstakingly tries to discover their whereabouts and other information about them, but fails. As a consequence, during a period of over two decades, the life of his family becomes a void in his personal memory. Though it is indicated that Teacher Wei, with a strong heart and a profound understanding of the political situation under Communist domination, is not deeply traumatized by this event – which can be inferred from his rather rational and optimistic attitude towards life and from the friendly and comfortable way he treats people – being deprived of the right to access the truth of his personal history does cause confusion and misunderstanding in him about his former wife. If it were not for his later, accidental reunion with his daughter and granddaughter, which provide a chance for him to learn the truth about his former wife's departure, the confusion and misunderstanding would have remained in his heart all his life.

Ru Yan goes through a similar experience, though in a completely different scenario. After a short-lived yet ardent love affair with the vice mayor, Ru Yan suddenly finds one day that the man with whom she fell deeply in love, and who also seemed to love her very much, disappears mysteriously like a drop of water evaporating in the air. His disappearance is so complete and sudden that Ru Yan feels as if her interaction with him were just a beautiful yet illusory dream – to the point that she even doubts whether the man ever existed. Never receiving any news or explanation from him afterwards, Ru Yan is deeply frightened and agonized by the absurdity of her own love story, which has "no ending":

> Ru Yan had read all kinds of romantic novels. Some dripped with sentiment; some were taut with suspense; they might have happy endings or tragic endings, *but they always had an ending*. The story in which she now found herself dragged on ambiguously with no end in sight … This is a horrible ending, worse than any heart-rending and dramatic scenario. It was the death by a thousand cuts, one little slice after another, slowly; one drop of blood after another, with no idea when it would stop.[11]

Obviously, Ru Yan, like Teacher Wei, is also locked outside the truth of her own personal history, tortured by feelings of confusion, disillusionment, and agony. What makes Ru Yan's love story truly "surreal" and "frightening" is not only the outcome itself but also the reason for the outcome. It turns out that what caused this purely private affair to end without an ending is not anything personal but political calculation, a topic that will be elaborated later.

"Lockdown," at the psychological level, also designates a mentality, a state of mind characterized by a combination of estrangement, mutual suspicion, and fear. In the novel, there is a highly meaningful description of Ru Yan's personality and psychology, which illustrates this kind of mentality in an explicit way:

> For many years, in her real life, she had been guarded with strangers, even to the point that she would stay out of conversations that sprang up among passengers in a crowded train compartment. Even with people she knew, she was not accustomed to personal exchanges.[12]

This description should not be read merely as a sketch of Ru Yan's personal traits. If linked with other phenomena of similar nature in the novel, it can be viewed as a summary of the kind of mentality typical of Chinese people. In another place in the novel, the narrator, while commenting on Chinese people loving to wear masks, provides an insightful analysis of the mentality. According to the narrator, by covering up their faces with masks, Chinese people attempt to hide their thinking from others.[13] In this sense, wearing masks betrays the same psychology as when they lock themselves in their houses with all doors and windows shut tightly, showing distrust and fear of other people and the outside world. This attitude is actually an unavoidable psychology of people who are physically or mentally isolated from the outside world, because the unknown often causes fear and suspicion. It helps explain why, during a serious natural or social crisis when people are deprived of the right to access information about the crisis – what is going on now and what is waiting for them ahead – the crisis often brings about panic in society. This scenario was exactly the case in China during the SARS outbreak. Based on this perception, Damo concludes that the Party-state's control of information was actually the real source of the panic in Chinese society during that time, and this knowledge is "something more terrifying than the plague" itself.[14] In the novel, the SARS outbreak is treated as a particular yet typical moment in Chinese Communist history, an example of Communist dictatorship. It highlights the essence of Communist dictatorship in a condensed way. But the novel, for reasons Chinese readers would understand, stops short of saying that Communist dictatorship itself is a fatal virus or disease.

The Terrifying "Old Crone" behind the Screen

What is the reaction of Chinese people to being locked outside the truth of their own lives and of the whole nation, experiencing the enormous pain inflicted upon themselves, or watching their innocent fellow people enduring mistreatment and suffering in locked, dark wards? Hu Fayun also addresses this significant question in the novel. His finding concerning this question, however, is rather despairing: the overwhelming majority of Chinese people display a kind of nonchalance and numbness when faced with the distortion and blockage of truth by the Party-state and its manipulation of history. Being locked in a terrifying dark ward without even knowing they are in it is one of the most distressing phenomena exposed in the novel. This perception readily reminds us of Lu Xun's allegorical scene of an ignorant and numb crowd sleeping soundly in an indestructible, windowless "iron house." But Hu seems more optimistic about China's future than Lu Xun because he suggests that more and more Chinese people will awaken from this political numbness, which would bring hope to the society. Ru Yan is portrayed as such a person. The novel provides a detailed account of how Ru Yan, through her experience with the internet, wakes up from political numbness and eventually sees the true face of the Party-state. Ru Yan's experience with the internet thus can be read as a process of political enlightenment undergone by an ordinary Chinese as well as the making of a non-conformist intellectual.

In the beginning of the novel, Ru Yan is just an ordinary, middle-aged woman leading a leisurely, quiet, and contented life. Having fully recovered from the tragedy of her husband's accidental death, with a stable and easy job as a research fellow at an academic institute, she seems to have nothing to worry about in the world, especially after her only son goes to study abroad at a university in France. What concerns her most now is how to kill time and entertain herself. She finds the internet. When she first enters the internet world, she finds it extremely fascinating and exciting. She joins an online forum for parents who live in "empty nests," as she does, and receives abundant warmth there. She chats with her new friends online, sharing her everyday life experience, feelings, and thoughts with them. She also posts essays about her everyday life and her thoughts on the forum, and their linguistic exquisiteness, artistic sensitivity, and outstanding expressive skills immediately win wide acclaim and admiration for her on the internet. She is recommended as a co-moderator of the forum by her fellow netizens shortly after she joins it. She rejoices that she has found a new home on the internet, warm, encouraging, and most importantly, free.

Her honeymoon with the internet does not last long, however, as her beautiful feeling of a happy, friendly, and free internet world is shattered quickly. One day when she talks online with a couple of netizens about a mysterious disease that has emerged and silently spread in the south, later known as SARS, their messages show up only for a few minutes before disappearing mysteriously. The same thing occurs several times. At first Ru Yan can't believe what is happening right before her eyes, so she posts a message again. This time the consequences become even more obvious: a window pops up on her screen saying that there is a server error and her message is temporarily unable to be posted:

> Ru Yan now realized that in what she had thought was a little salon hosted by herself there was actually an old crone concealed and peering at everything from behind a curtain. Her mood changed in an instant: she was offended and discouraged.[15]

This incident is the first time Ru Yan encounters the invisible "old crone" online. Since then, she has become aware that there is no freedom in the seemingly free internet world at all – everything in cyberspace is also under complete control by an invisible hand, just as occurs in the outside world. Her heart begins to sink.

Later on, as she travels further and further into the internet world, she encounters the invisible "old crone" more and more frequently; in the process, she sees the oppressive and sinister nature of the "old crone" and her omnipresent and formidable power more and more clearly. After SARS breaks out and spreads rampantly in the south, as she posts essays and messages online talking about it and exposing the government's cover-up, she constantly receives warnings, threats, and even personal attacks. Among them, an extremely harsh post directly attacks her for taking the side of "anti-China forces" and for spreading an "unhealthy and corrupting spirit," which does not preserve a "high degree of unanimity with the Party Central" and damages the interests of the nation.[16] Afterwards, when to express her indignation and criticism she writes about the notorious case of a college student who is illegally detained and tortured to death by police, she is attacked as a "hypocrite" and "a traitor to China."[17] This harassment gives Ru Yan the feeling of travelling alone in the night "surrounded by pairs of green eyes in the darkness,"[18] which makes her shudder tremendously. In the meantime, she finds that the atmosphere in the cyber-world turns from amicable to hostile. The originally friendly, peaceful forum is now full of vicious rumours and back-stabbing. One day she receives a mysterious message with vicious intention, disclosing a very private issue about the other moderator of the forum, which frightens Ru Yan deeply, because such information is accessible only to relevant authorities or to one's family, relatives, or close friends. Shocked by the depth of the "old crone's" watch – it can reach the deepest recesses of one's privacy – Ru Yan's feeling about the internet gradually turns from fondness to frustration and finally to fear.

Her fear reaches a peak when she posts an essay online, with photos she has taken as evidence, to expose the incredible atrocity committed by the city authorities towards animals during the SARS period and, consequently, receives fierce attacks from someone. The person not only condemns Ru Yan for "catering to the international China-bashers who are slanderously attacking the [Chinese] government" but also denounces her as a "despicable hypocrite" and calls her a shameless "whore."[19] This "murderous post" provokes a huge wave of follow-up comments, which almost unanimously attack Ru Yan's personality and moral character. Among those commentators, there are even people with whom she is usually on friendly terms. This betrayal puts her in fury, fear, and despair:

> Having read this far, Ru Yan saw stars, as if she'd been whacked with a club, and she had a splitting headache. Her despair was like that of a

dog who is drowning while a crowd of masked thugs, brandishing sticks and pitchforks, eye her balefully from the riverbank. For a moment, she couldn't think at all, but stared dully at the screen, her mind a blank. After a long time she started to weep.[20]

Then she uses her authority as the forum's moderator to delete the "horrifying post" and block the person's IP address. Even after that, "she found herself trembling still."[21] But this post is not the end to her nightmarish experience. Only a short while later, an even more malicious message appears on the forum, posted by the same person using a different username. It makes Ru Yan feel more frightened and furious, and she deletes it and blocks the IP again. But it is no use; in just a second, another post appears. All these posts convey the same message, threatening to expose all of Ru Yan's privacy and her "reactionary" activities to the public, and to make the lives of both her and her son a nightmare. This threat puts Ru Yan in complete despair and panic. It makes her recall "those demonic wraiths which could never be killed no matter how many times you struck them, or those robots which repair themselves after being smashed to pieces."[22] She is so frightened that she even imagines that the monster could clamber out of the screen, sniggering at her. At this moment, she can do nothing but switch off the computer. She does not dare to go to the internet for a very long time.

Nevertheless, that threatening post is not the most horrible moment for Ru Yan. One day, after the end of the SARS epidemic, she randomly goes to the online forum out of pure curiosity. What she finds there almost frightens her to death: not only are her own "highly pernicious and subversive" posts about SARS nowhere to be seen, but the much more "patriotic and positive" messages attacking her have also completely disappeared. The erasure is so thorough that it as if the fierce fight and perhaps the entire SARS episode itself had never happened. In this way, a life-and-death historical period for many people like her brother-in-law, Teacher Wei, and for the whole nation, has been completely deleted from people's memory. Ru Yan is utterly stunned by the unfathomable abyss of "memory void" created by the Party-state and by the omnipresence and almightiness of the invisible "old crone." After that, she never writes anything online again.

Ru Yan's internet experience, as Haiyan Lee incisively points out, constitutes a "daring criticism of the state's habitual suppression of information and censorship practices."[23] It bears multiple political implications. First, it discloses the purpose, mechanism, and weapon of the Party-state in its control of the internet in particular and of information in general. When Ru Yan simply enters the internet world and stays in the private realm, writing only about her family life and personal feelings and thoughts, she seems to enjoy full freedom and autonomy, and is never disturbed by anyone. Later on, when she steps out of the private realm and enters the public sphere to expose the government's wrongdoing and its cover-up of SARS, however, the "old crone" immediately shows up to intimidate her. This depiction illuminates the purpose of the Party-state's control of information and society explicitly: the Party-state attempts to confine or "lock" its people within the private realm and to block their way to public participation. Additionally, Ru Yan's internet experience also exposes the mechanism of the Party-state's control of information and society: the use of terror. It is the fear caused by the horrible encounters with the invisible "old crone" and the many threats and attacks she receives that drives Ru Yan away from public participation in the internet world. This perception proves Hannah Arendt's observation of totalitarianism very well: terror is the very essence of totalitarianism.[24] Moreover, Ru Yan's internet experience also betrays the most important weapon that the Party-state uses for thought control: extreme nationalistic doctrine. Whenever she criticizes the government's wrongdoings, she is attacked for "being a traitor to China" or for "representing the international anti-China forces damaging the interest of the Chinese nation." As mentioned earlier, nationalism is at the core of state ideology in Communist China, and after Tiananmen, propagating nationalist discourses and cultivating nationalist sentiments among its people has become one of the most powerful weapons used by the Party-state to justify and maintain its rule.

Second, Ru Yan's internet experience also proves that the Party-state's dictatorship is a major source of Chinese people's unhappiness and mutual distrust. When Ru Yan initially enters the internet world, before the "old crone" shows up, she feels very happy and excited, and she is also full of trust in others and of hope and optimism for the future. But after she encounters the horrifying "old crone," and subsequently receives continuous attacks and threats for telling the truth about SARS, her feelings of happiness, warmth, and trust completely vanish. Instead, she is seized by suspicion, anxiety, and fear. Though the novel does not explicitly indicate who makes these attacks and threats, plenty of evidence – the vice mayor's statement that SARS is a serious problem and that information about it is "monitored closely";[25] the action of another official, Jiang Xiaoli, who prints out all Ru Yan's posts from the internet; and Jiang's claim that Ru Yan's writings make "some people [in the government] very angry"[26] – suggests that these oppressive activities are at least supported, if not concocted, by the government. This finding not only discloses the true identity of the invisible "old crone" but also makes it very clear that the regime's oppression constitutes the major source of people's unhappiness and mutual distrust. This insight is further reinforced by another experience undergone by Ru Yan – that the interference of the "old crone" is what divides the originally peaceful and united cyber forum into two opposing groups and turns its atmosphere from amicability to hostility. In the process, Ru Yan loses her trust in others and her optimism about the future.

Third, Ru Yan's internet experience also convincingly illustrates that Communist domination, contrary to its claim of representing "people's democracy," is actually in conflict with human nature, and its oppressive character can be easily grasped by human instinct and the human heart. The narrator repeatedly emphasizes that Ru Yan is a person who relies on "her feelings and intuition" to make a judgment. The principle guiding her life is phrased this way: *You can explain the world in terms of correct and incorrect, but I will judge it in terms of good and evil; you use your brain, I'll use my heart.*[27] As an ordinary research fellow at a botany institute, she does not receive any training in political science and also hates all kinds of theories. What motivates her to write down all those seemingly politically charged posts, viewed by the Party-state as subversive and pernicious, is not any kind of highbrow political theory or political agenda but her intuition, conscience, and common sense. Her disclosure of the information about SARS when the government painstakingly covers it up is utterly driven by her conscience – she believes that the cover-up of such a life-and-death issue from the people is wrong – and by her simple intention to warn her net friends to protect themselves against the fatal disease. Ru Yan's experience proves that, despite the enormous propaganda efforts made by the Party-state to glorify its rule and to deceive the people, its oppressive and deceptive nature can be easily recognized by ordinary people merely exercising intuition, conscience, and common sense.

Fourth and finally, Ru Yan's experience suggests that the attempt to strangle thought through oppression, despite its effectiveness as indicated in Maozi's case (discussed later in the chapter) and also seen in reality in contemporary China, does not always work; instead, sometimes it only plants the seeds of freedom and rebellion in people's hearts. As mentioned earlier, originally Ru Yan is just an ordinary woman who, like the majority of Chinese people, is quite contented with the status quo and displays political numbness. Had she not encountered the "old crone" or received the threats and attacks masterminded by the regime, the idea of rebellion would never have occurred to her. It is her encounters with the horrible "old crone" and all the threats and attacks that make her see the true face of the Party-state, the true sociopolitical reality of today's China, and recognize her true feelings and true self, long-suppressed by the regime. In this sense, Ru Yan's experience of oppression is simultaneously a process of political enlightenment and intellectual liberation. It proves that the Party-state's attempt to strangle thought through oppression will also create more and more rebels and enemies for itself in the long run, which will ultimately lead to its own destruction.

The Chinese Intelligentsia after Tiananmen: Cynicism and Division

Hu Fayun also addresses some crucial issues facing the Chinese intelligentsia after Tiananmen that have rarely or never before been touched upon by mainland Chinese writers. These issues include the true relationship between Chinese intellectuals – especially conscientious and critical ones – and the Party, the impact of the Tiananmen Massacre upon the Chinese intelligentsia, and Chinese intellectuals' changed attitude towards the Party-state after Tiananmen.

As discussed in chapter 1, the relationship between the Party-state and the intellectuals is a pivotal dimension in society and serves as an important barometer for the political atmosphere in contemporary China. Despite its consistent oppression of intellectuals and thought, the Party-state creates a self-image as the true patron and protector of knowledge and intellectuals through its propaganda machine. It also asserts that the persecution of intellectuals and suppression of thought in the Mao era were actually an erroneous deviation from the Party line rather than a representation of it. In the novel, through his vivid and thought-provoking description of the life experience of Teacher Wei and his family, Hu Fayun completely shatters the glorious and messianic self-image created by the Party and discloses the never-ending antagonistic relationship between the Party-state and the intellectuals, especially those who are conscientious and critical.

Despite his status as a steadfast and loyal Party member and a well-known Marxist theoretician, Teacher Wei was persecuted, tortured, and imprisoned during the Mao era. The reason for his being branded a counter-revolutionary was more than absurd: he wrote a letter to Hu Feng – an outspoken and brave intellectual, later classified by Chairman Mao himself as the number one rightist in China – to submit an article to a journal edited by Hu; the letter became the sole proof of Teacher Wei's asserted "collusion" with the biggest rightist. He was put in jail for several years for this "crime." Compared with his own misery, the injustice and suffering inflicted upon his family was even more shocking. Shortly after he was imprisoned, his wife left home with their two little children. Only after more than two decades did he learn that her seemingly heartless act was actually motivated by her intention to protect not only their children and herself but also, and more importantly, him. It turns out that she hid from the Party two crucial facts about her personal history and family background: she had been a member of a Kuomintang (KMT)-led youth organization before joining the Communist revolution, and she had a brother who was a KMT military officer and had fled to Taiwan. In light of the Maoist revolutionary principle, which emphasizes the importance of the clear-cut class line and the absolute purity of family background, either secret was fateful for her future; therefore, hiding such information from the Party was considered a serious crime. Unfortunately, after the outbreak of the Cultural Revolution, those secrets were eventually exposed. Their revelation meant doom for the woman. Despite her status as a long-term veteran and a revolutionary cadre who had made substantive sacrifices and contributions to the revolution, she was categorized as a "class enemy" – even worse, a hidden one – immediately after the exposure and subjected to humiliation and torture. Unable to bear the humiliation and brutality, she killed herself under the wheel of a train. Later on, her teenage son, now a child of a "hidden class enemy," also committed suicide due to the unbearable heaviness of humiliation and persecution.

The incredible suffering, cruelty, and death inflicted on him and his family, however, did not beat down Teacher Wei. Instead, they drove him to look deeply into the darkness and brutality of the oppressive one-Party system, turning him from a blind follower of the Party into a truly independent and critical intellectual who dares to speak truth to power. Unlike the majority of Chinese intellectuals, who accept the Party's assertion that the Cultural Revolution was a result of the crimes committed by some bad people within the Party, Teacher Wei, even before the end of the Cultural Revolution, reached the conclusion that it was a systemic problem – something inherent in the system and the Party-state. After the end of the disastrous Mao era, Teacher Wei was rehabilitated and resumed his position as a theoretician. He made full use of the opportunity and wrote extensively to reflect on the devastating Maoist social practice and to criticize the flaws in society, and his "hard-hitting insights ... sent shockwaves through the Academy and the intellectual world."[28] Consequently, "when the campaign against Spiritual Pollution came along, and later the Anti-Liberalization movement, Teacher Wei became a heretic again."[29] As occurred during the Mao period, in Deng's "new era," he was once again regarded by the Party as a dangerous dissident and troublemaker, representing a subversive and pernicious force. Teacher Wei's status as a repulsive dissident and public nuisance in the view of the government during the post-Mao era is most clearly demonstrated by the incredible indifference that government officials displayed towards the misdiagnosis of his disease and then towards his death. As mentioned earlier, after he died from SARS, the government not only covered up the real reason for his death but also prohibited people from commemorating him in any way.

Teacher Wei's life experience in the Chinese Party-state – being persecuted as a counter-revolutionary during the Mao era and treated as a repulsive and dangerous troublemaker in the post-Mao era – very clearly illuminates the Party-state's suspicious, oppressive, and hostile attitude towards intellectuals, especially towards those who are independent and critical. His tragic fate in both historical periods of the Communist regime also proves that oppression of intellectuals and control of thought are the guiding principles of the Party line, consistently adopted by the Party-state throughout its history, during the Mao and post-Mao eras alike. The massive and insane persecution of intellectuals during the Cultural Revolution is a culmination of the Party line – an implementation of it in a radical way – rather than an accidental deviation from it.

Another significant contribution this novel makes to Chinese literature and thought is its critical reflection on the impact of the Tiananmen Massacre on Chinese intellectuals. This novel marks the first time in the history of the Communist regime that a Chinese writer currently residing in mainland China has dealt directly and critically with this bloody event. Despite the abundance of coverage in literature and the media in Hong Kong, Taiwan, and overseas, the Tiananmen Massacre remains the biggest "prohibited zone" in mainland China. The regime has completely erased the event from history books, and as a result, many Chinese of the younger generations do not even know it happened. Under such circumstances, dealing with it constitutes a huge risk for any mainland Chinese writer. Therefore, Hu Fayun certainly deserves praise and admiration for his courage in being the first mainland Chinese writer to address the "forbidden zone."

Hu's critical reflection on the impact of the Tiananmen Massacre on Chinese intellectuals is achieved mainly through the characterization of Maozi, a clever and manipulative intellectual, especially through the presentation of his mental transformation. Maozi grew up with the Party-state and saw with his own eyes the entire course of Maoist social practice, with all its cruelty and absurdity, and the tremendous disaster it had brought to the Chinese people. During his formative years, he was also greatly influenced by Teacher Wei. In the early 1970s, Maozi, Damo, and a few other friends formed a group to study the thought of young Marx – that is, Marx's theory about human nature and alienation rather than that of class exploitation and class struggle. They named this study group *Qing Ma*, short for *Qingnian Makesi* (young Marx). During that period, they often visited Teacher Wei, who, after being released from the prison, started his lifelong journey of critical reflection on the problems of the one-Party system. Maozi and other members of *Qing Ma* regarded Teacher Wei as a mentor and spiritual leader, and received a basic enlightenment about freedom and democracy from him, which constituted an important background for the intellectual development of these young men.

After the end of the Mao era, the higher education system was restored in China. Maozi passed the college entrance examination and went to college. After graduation, he was assigned to a job at the provincial Social Sciences Academy and became an academic. It was the 1980s, the most politically tolerant and intellectually creative period in the history of the socialist state. Given Maozi's life experience and intellectual background, it is only natural to see that he was highly passionate about and active in the "culture fever," at the core of which is the introduction of modern Western values and criticism of Chinese tradition. Like all other Chinese intellectuals at that time, he was an ardent and radical believer in idealism and utopianism, with the view that democracy and freedom would be realized in China very soon. His extreme optimism about China's future was considered unrealistic and naive even by his good friend Damo. Naturally, it is no surprise to see him becoming an extremely ardent activist in the 1989 Tiananmen democratic movement.

As occurred to many Chinese intellectuals, the bloodshed in Tiananmen Square completely shattered Maozi's utopian dream and changed his life forever. The atrocity committed by the government in killing its own unarmed people with tanks and guns, along with the realization that the regime dared to "do the most terrible thing in the world" to maintain its rule,[30] frightened him so much that he nearly became mad. In the days following the massacre, he locked himself in his house, sitting on the bed "like a statue" and unresponsive to anybody or anything. Now and then, he "burst out in a loud sob like the howl of a wolf."[31] Coming to Maozi's place to comfort him upon the request of his wife, Damo only heard him whimpering: "It's too frightening, it is just too fucking frightening. China is finished, finished … it's all over."[32] Ironically and intriguingly, Maozi's madness – no one knows if it was real or faked to protect himself – eventually saved his career and future. It turns out that, in the face of Maozi's "insanity," the director of the Academy, for fear that putting too much pressure on an unstable person might jeopardize his own future, decided to delay his punishment. Fortunately, after a period of time, the overall political atmosphere in the entire country loosened. "Eventually the Director realized that a very large number of people in Beijing were basically just like Maozi. So he decided, sullenly, to let it go."[33]

Back from the brink of the deadly abyss, Maozi changes to a completely different person. He throws away everything he once possessed – his beliefs, values, ideals, and true self – and moves forward in an opposite direction. He makes a free fall from a champion of cultural idealism to a believer in vulgar materialism and stark nihilism, and turns cynical. Like most Chinese intellectuals after the June Fourth Massacre, he completely gives up the belief of intellectuals as a social conscience, and instead takes pursuit of personal wealth, social status, and fame as the ultimate goals in his life. He starts his plan by currying favour with the director of the Academy through giving him a bribe. The bribe is quite unique: it is not money, valuable items, or anything like that; it is an article. Maozi spends abundant time and energy writing an article of high quality, and manages to get it published under the name of the director in a first-tier theoretical journal in the nation. The article turns out to be a huge success. It makes a wave in Chinese academia and is later reprinted by several other prestigious journals. The article wins huge fame for the director, who collects full credit for it, and establishes him as an important theoretician in the nation.

With this success and the subsequent favour from the director, Maozi's own road to wealth and power turns broader and brighter. Afterwards, he gets "one promotion after another," and his reputation begins to spread.[34] Within only a few years, he becomes a well-known scholar in his field, wins several awards, and then receives stipends from the government. He is promoted to director of the Philosophy Department of the Academy. While his friend Damo is struggling at the bottom of the society to make a living, he has everything – "a fine position, a good income, a nice car and a beautiful home, a lovely wife and a promising son."[35] He does not curse the Party and the government any longer; instead, he joins the Party and publishes books to justify the system and praise the Party-state and its supreme leader, Deng Xiaoping. "In candid moments he often said that Deng was The Man, and Maozi gave him unqualified support. Without old Mr. Deng, Maozi would never have had this good life."[36] It seems he completely forgets that this same old Mr. Deng had ordered the army to kill unarmed innocent people, which almost frightened him to death and pushed him to the brink of insanity. Here we see a fallen intellectual who completely loses his soul and conscience in pursuit of personal gains under the lure of the Party-state's incentive system. We also witness the astonishing rapidity of the moral degeneration of Chinese intellectuals after the Tiananmen Massacre.

In the novel, the fall of Maozi is ascribed to cynicism, a mentality prevailing throughout the Chinese intelligentsia since the 1990s, at the core of which is a combination of moral nihilism, hedonism, and extreme egoism. The essence of the mentality is the belief that there is nothing wrong in using any kind of means, moral or immoral, to make oneself well off, which clearly echoes Deng Xiaoping's famous "white cat–black cat theory." In this sense, Maozi's behaviour is indeed an explicit embodiment of cynicism. On one occasion, in response to Damo's criticism of his devising deceptive theories to justify a system that he once hated so much, Maozi declares that he does not care: "Since that summer day, I haven't believed in anything."[37] He not only does not find anything wrong with his behaviour but also questions Damo: "Didn't I tell you that what I write is not what I think, and that this itself is a deconstruction, a kind of black humour for our time? Its significance lies precisely in the discrepancy."[38] When Damo condemns him for being a cynic and nihilist, he responds: "I don't care. I'm better off than I used to be. I am grateful for this era we are in."[39] He feels no shame in writing only "in exchange for money and housing" and selling his conscience and soul.[40] This attitude makes Damo believe that Maozi's behaviour is much more despicable than that of poor labourers or the men of the countryside. As he says directly to Maozi's face, "the way they earn their money is far more honorable than the way you earn yours. What you do is worse than peddling fake medicine."[41]

Even worse, Maozi's success is achieved not only through abandoning his role as a social conscience but also at the cost of his moral integrity as a human being. Damo discovers that Maozi, like many other professors in mainland China, abuses his authority as an academic advisor and exploits his students. It turns out that a large portion of the books published in Maozi's name were actually written by his graduate students, who receive little, if any, credit or pay for their work. More surprisingly, Maozi asserts that what he has done is merely common practice at mainland Chinese universities today, and he feels there is nothing wrong with it. Protecting his hard-gained wealth and social status by appeasing the oppressive regime, he refuses to work together with Damo to organize a commemorative meeting for Teacher Wei. And when Damo organizes one, he is reluctant to attend. This stance is solid evidence of his willingness to submit to the regime and to consciously censor and discipline himself. In addition to his moral depravity, Mao-zi's intellectual creativity as a scholar also declines greatly under the spell of cynicism:

> Damo felt Maozi's most trenchant, energetic, and innovative writings all dated from the Eighties ... But it went downhill after that. Maozi's work became increasingly mediocre and perfunctory, though oddly enough this was precisely the time when his reputation started to spread and he received one promotion after another.[42]

The image of Maozi provides us with a thought-provoking portrait of the moral and intellectual depravity of Chinese intellectuals after Tiananmen. The characterization of Maozi and the depiction of the Chinese intelligentsia are powerful testimonials to what Gan Yang dubs the "syndrome of collective moral corruption of the Chinese intelligentsia."[43] Teacher Wei explains the logical and historical inevitability of the intellectual shift from idealism to cynicism since the 1990s in China. He points out:

> The thing about young people (especially young intellectuals) is that when their idealism burns out, what comes next is philistinism and cynicism. For young people, the temptations of material gain are even harder to resist. When spiritual and moral satisfactions are no longer to be had, the satisfactions of property and power are the best substitute.[44]

Damo traces the origin of Maozi's fall to the tremendous fear he experienced and witnessed during the Tiananmen Massacre, and identifies the terror created by the regime as the ultimate cause for the cynicism of Chinese intellectuals:

> Damo knew that Maozi's case was all about fear. And the fear in which it had begun was nothing to despise. But after the fear, he changed in a way that was painful to contemplate, and that was actually more terrifying than the fear ... To terrify people, he wrote, is more effective than to kill them. Killing disposes of the dissident's body. Terror can transform his soul, turning the most troublesome rebel into a docile slave who will serve as an example to others. What's most frightening is that the fear is rooted so deep in your heart. No one can remove it for you.[45]

Damo's perception proves highly incisive, and it testifies once again to Hannah Arendt's conclusion of terror as the essence of totalitarianism.[46] Teacher Wei also points to the omniscience of fear that people experience in the Chinese Party-state. If we put Teacher Wei's and Damo's explanations together, we can have a more complete idea about the origin of cynicism in the Chinese intelligentsia after Tiananmen: the dual forces of material temptation and terror manipulated by the Party.

Critic Shu Chong, in his review of the novel, provides an incisive analysis of the reasons for the cynicism of Chinese intellectuals after Tiananmen, which strongly supports our previous finding:

> Since the 1990s, most Chinese intellectuals have become conservative and abandoned their pursuit of freedom and democracy, and their criticism of dictatorial power. This turnaround is commonly interpreted as intellectuals being co-opted by the Communist Party and thus becoming the beneficiaries of the system. Many intellectuals are willing to admit their co-optation, as being co-opted indicates one's value ... The political turn of the intellectuals clearly occurred after the June Fourth; therefore, it was mainly a product of fear. The June Fourth created intense fear among the Chinese people, and fear forced many to stay away from politics. Once distanced from politics, they no longer feel the weight of oppression, and so their fear subsides; they perceive their lives to be carefree and become complacent. At this point, if the ruling class hands out material lures, many will even feel highly satisfied.[47]

The novel also provides a sketch of the shifting intellectual landscape in contemporary China, especially the division of the Chinese intelligentsia after Tiananmen. This shift is mainly demonstrated through the changing relationship among the three intellectuals: Teacher Wei, Maozi, and Damo. Because much space has been dedicated to Teacher Wei and Maozi already, I shall focus mainly on Damo here. Damo is an intriguing and unique character, who combines some seemingly contradictory qualities. Once the most brilliant, knowledgeable, and promising figure in the *Qing Ma* study group, he is unfortunately the only one in the group who later on sinks to the bottom of society and makes a living by repairing household appliances for people. Despite his status as an outsider to the intelligentsia and his humble position in society, he often performs the work of an intellectual and does much better than a real one. He creates a website dedicated to serious discussion of philosophy, politics, and criticism of the Chinese system and society, and his profound thought wins him huge internet fame. He is adept at using simple and even coarse language to discuss profound philosophical and political issues – a bizarre combination that seems both refreshing and amusing. Despite his reputation and influence as a famous thinker in the internet world, he dresses, talks, and acts like all other working people. More importantly, he possesses the virtues typical of the working class: he is humble, honest, and warm-hearted. He seems to combine the virtues of both a worker and an intellectual but is devoid of the shortcomings of both. Though struggling at the bottom of society, he harbours no grudge towards people or society but rather holds an optimistic and positive attitude towards life, and his criticism of the system and society is also well-balanced, rational, and constructive. Like Teacher Wei, he never loses his conscience and sense of morality, and has a strong heart and firm beliefs. In this respect, Damo and Teacher Wei contrast sharply with Maozi, who, despite his high social status and wealth, completely loses his true self under the dual pressure from the dictatorial Party-state and material lure, and whose heart and mind turn weak, fragile, and confused.

The depiction of Damo in the novel serves multiple purposes from a discursive perspective. First, his interaction with Teacher Wei indicates the transmittal and continuation of the long-lasting Chinese tradition of intellectuals as the social conscience and critics of power. His sincere respect and admiration for Teacher Wei and his consistently critical attitude towards the regime also suggest that the critical spirit of Chinese intellectuals cannot be eradicated, despite the extreme political oppression by the Communist Party-state. Second, the growing fundamental differences in world view, values, belief, and life path between Damo and Maozi after the Tiananmen Massacre, as well as the disintegration of the *Qing Ma* study group, also serve as an honest reflection of the split in the once united Chinese intelligentsia since the 1990s, a significant social phenomenon elaborated in chapter 1. The stark contrast in political stance between Damo and Maozi, and the tremendous disparity in social status between them as a result, also very clearly illuminates the reason for the split in the Chinese intelligentsia: it is all caused by the irreconcilable contradictions among the intellectuals in their attitudes towards the Party-state. Whereas intellectuals like Maozi, who abandon their conscience and completely submit to the regime, are awarded by the Party with wealth and high social status, those conscientious intellectuals like Damo, who refuse to sell their soul and consistently hold a vigilant and critical attitude towards the Party-state, are ruthlessly thrown to the bottom of the society. Hereby the mechanism of reward and punishment manipulated by the Party-state is made especially explicit. Third, the duality of Damo's status – a subaltern in society but with high moral standards and wisdom – also betrays the complexity of the sources comprising the intellectual heritage of Hu Fayun as well as of the entire generation of Chinese intellectuals. Damo, like Teacher Wei, obviously embodies the May Fourth enlightenment values of democracy, freedom, and individualism. Damo's depiction also displays a residue of the populist world view and ethics left behind by the Maoist class theory: that ordinary people possess both wisdom and virtues, whereas intellectuals and those of high social status are actually selfish, foolish, and hypocritical people. Moreover, Damo's depiction also reveals the inheritance of Taoist anti-elitism and anti-intellectualism, which is clearly demonstrated by Zhuangzi's comparison of a feudal lord to a big thief who steals a state but claims to be a virtuous gentleman possessing benevolence and righteousness[48] and his comparison of people pursuing office and social status to rats chasing rotten meat.[49]

Two Faces of the Party: Ugliness behind a Lovely Mask

The most original, intriguing, and thought-provoking part of the novel is the love story of Ru Yan and Vice Mayor Liang Jinsheng. The love story is remarkable not only because it provides a detailed and vivid account of an uncommon love affair involving a high-ranking government official and a nuanced description of the inner journeys that the couple goes through in the process, but also because it exposes a unique political logic in contemporary China never previously touched upon by any other mainland Chinese writer. For our purposes, I shall discuss only the second theme in the following pages.

As elaborated in the introduction, among the many myths created by the Party and its propaganda machine to justify its rule, the most fundamental one is the Party-people myth – that the Party is the saviour, guardian, and protector of the Chinese nation and represents the interests of the people – which constitutes the cornerstone of the Party's ideology and the very source of political legitimacy for the Party-state. Because of the paramount significance of the myth, it is never allowed to be tarnished by anyone for any reason. Starting from the logic of this myth, there is a red line drawn by the Party for literature: in any literary work, the Party and the socialist system cannot be depicted as negative and destructive forces in opposition to the people's interests; instead, they must be portrayed as positive forces representing justice and hope for the people. In the case of the literature of exposure, as exemplified by anticorruption fiction of the 1990s, darkness in society should be ascribed to the wrongdoings or crimes of particular individuals or specific flaws in the system rather than to the Party line or the system itself. This stipulation forms a unique political logic in contemporary Chinese literature.

What makes Hu Fayun's novel truly original and provocative is that it presents a political logic running counter to the one prescribed by the Party, which honestly reflects the sociopolitical reality in contemporary China: that the Party has already degenerated into a self-serving interest group, and the system – the Party-state itself rather than any individual official – is the major cause of the problems and tragedies of the nation. This recognition completely subverts the Party-people myth, so painstakingly propagated by the Party-state, and exposes the hypocritical and deceptive nature of the Party and its propaganda. Moreover, as presented in the novel, the hypocritical and deceptive nature of the Party is also reflected in the personality and mentality of its members. As a result, hypocrisy and mendacity become the signature character of both the Party as a whole and its individual members. Hu's presentation of this theme is conveyed mainly through Vice Mayor Liang Jinsheng and his relationship with the two female characters, Ru Yan and Jiang Xiaoli.

A.E. Clark, the English translator of the novel, identifies the success in characterization as a major accomplishment of the novel. He argues that the novel avoids a serious shortcoming commonly seen in politically charged fiction in contemporary China: the portrayal of stereotyped and conceptualized characters.[50] Clark's perception proves to be highly insightful, evidenced by the depiction of Liang Jinsheng. Indeed, unlike the flat characters commonly seen in Chinese political fiction, who are either completely good or bad, Liang is a complex character with a multifaceted personality. The complexity of Liang's personality bears profound political implications.

Liang first strikes us as complex by the huge disparity between his image as an individual person and as a government official. Well-educated, well-mannered, very polite, and always speaking and behaving in a proper and pleasant way, he can be said to be a very good man. He does not have the weakness commonly seen in many people of high social status: arrogance. On the contrary, he is unaffected and humble on private occasions. When he goes to visit Ru Yan's mother, his would-be mother-in-law, for the first time, he even shows shyness – a "shortcoming" that makes him look sweet and lovable. In his relationship with Ru Yan, he proves himself to be an ideal boyfriend: considerate, understanding, and tolerant. He is also very romantic, passionate, and energetic. When he knows that Ru Yan loves to eat hotdogs, he brings back a full box of hotdogs from the United States after a business trip; he takes Ru Yan to a moonlight picnic at the Mid-Autumn Festival; he has wild sex with Ru Yan on a sofa in her living room, which fundamentally subverts the image of government officials as boring and pretentious bureaucrats. To our great surprise, this sensible and virtuous man seems to suddenly change to another person when he takes up his role as a government official. He shows unexpected indifference towards Teacher Wei's life-and-death situation, and does not feel there is anything wrong with the government concealing the truth about SARS from its people. Liang's behaviour, however, does not violate the Party-state's regulations and disciplines; on the contrary, his speech, thought, and action comply completely with those regulations and disciplines. It is clear that the huge disparity between Liang as a virtuous and charming human being and as an indifferent bureaucrat indicates the split in his personality and mentality, caused by the conflict between his "human" nature (*renxing* 人性) and his Party nature (*dangxing* 党性), if put in Chinese political terminology.

Another conspicuous feature of Liang is his "invisibility" as a government official. In the novel, there is an intriguing contrast between Liang and Ru Yan in their knowledge of each other. Liang knows almost everything about her, both private and public, taking advantage of his authority and power as a high-ranking government official, whereas Ru Yan knows little about what Liang does as an official, let alone his inner thoughts and beliefs. "Ru Yan had trouble imagining Liang Jinsheng's life as an official. She had never had a clear idea of what her own father did after he walked out the door each morning."[51] Like Liang, Ru Yan's father is also a high-ranking government official. Liang often suddenly disappears, completely cut off from Ru Yan for days or weeks. When he occasionally talks about his job as a vice mayor, he seldom mentions what he does; instead, he only emphasizes how hard, stressful, and dangerous his work is, especially during difficult times like the SARS outbreak, a moment that the nation is going through right now. In this way, consciously or unconsciously, he creates an image for himself as a highly dedicated and dutiful official.

It is true that Liang seems to be a better government official than many others in some ways, but plenty of evidence puts the credibility of his glorious self-image into question. For example, during the Spring Festival, when the SARS virus spreads rampantly through the entire nation, Ru Yan's sister-in-law and many others are hospitalized in critical condition. At this crucial juncture of life and death, however, the government still makes every effort to cover up the truth about SARS. Ru Yan is worried and furious, and she calls Liang. To her great surprise, from the other end of the phone comes not the deadly silence or the worried and tired voice that one would expect under such despairing circumstances but Liang's joking tone and "voices buzz[ing] in the background along with, more than once, merry challenges to drink another round."[52] Obviously, the high-ranking government official is having fun with others at a party or banquet, which readers believe is not something proper for him to do at such a critical moment. This scene, though occurring on a national holiday, still gives readers a strong and highly negative impression of the vice mayor, given the gravity of the situation facing the city. Naturally, suspicions would occur to us: Is this seemingly decent and dutiful vice mayor really as responsible as he self-proclaims? Is it possible that he, like many other Chinese bureaucrats, just poses but actually does not really care very much about the life and death of people? This descriptive detail serves, at least partially, to subvert Liang's self-image as a dedicated and responsible official.

The depiction of Liang's "invisibility" and suspicious irresponsibility as an official discloses two crucial facts of contemporary Chinese politics. One is the tremendous disparity between the people and the government in terms of rights and power. Whereas the government has unlimited and unrestrained authority and power over its people – it knows everything about the people and can do anything it wants – the people not only know little about the government but also have no power to check it. The other concerns the mechanism of the creation of the Party's image in China. Given that the Party always conceals its true face from the people and that Chinese people are also prohibited from talking about the Party – except for singing eulogies to it – the image of the Party is thus self-created or, more precisely, created by the propaganda machine that it controls. As illuminated clearly by Liang's case, the self-image of the Party is often illusory and deceptive, in contradiction with the reality.

In addition to the depiction of Liang, the triangular relationship between Liang, Ru Yan, and another female character, Jiang Xiaoli, also constitutes a highly intriguing and revealing motif in the novel. In many ways, the triangular relationship can be read as a political allegory illuminating the mentality of Chinese officials and the real relationship between the Party and the people. The two women represent not only two different types of female personality but also two different world views, values, and political mentalities. The changing relationship of Liang with them also reflects his changing mentality and political stance.

For Liang, Ru Yan, with her unpretentious, spontaneous, and somewhat naive personality, represents the true self or the original "human" nature unstained by the mendacity and hypocrisy of the bureaucracy. Even after learning about the many critical posts written by Ru Yan, which would potentially affect his own political future, Liang's affection for Ru Yan does not change; his steadfastness indicates his resolve to maintain his true self as a human being, even while performing his official role. In this sense, his love for Ru Yan signals his attempt to pursue the "human" nature instead of the Party nature in his private life. The female official Jiang Xiaoli, by contrast, represents a totally different type of female personality and female mentality. Born into an official family, and later pursuing a career in the bureaucracy, she is a pure "political animal." She is so familiar with the nature, workings, and deepest secrets of the Chinese bureaucracy and the set of schemes she designs for Liang to save his career from the SARS crisis are so successful that even Liang, the vice mayor, laments that, "compared with her, he was just a useless figurehead."[53] Obviously, Jiang Xiaoli symbolizes politics and the Party nature. Liang's rejection of her at the beginning – although he knows very well that she has a crush on him – suggests his intention to keep an independent private realm untainted by political cunning. Because his relationship with the two women reflects two different aspects of Liang's mentality, his story with them can be read as an allegory of his spiritual transformation.

When Ru Yan and Liang first fall in love, they seem to make an ideal couple. They are attracted to each other, appreciate each other, and always feel happy being with each other. Their relationship develops so rapidly that, after only a couple of months since their first date, they already decide on a wedding date. Their harmonious relationship does not last long. It soon faces a huge challenge and a serious crisis when the couple ventures out of the private realm and enters the public sphere. The two lovers, who seldom quarrel about private issues, engage in fierce confrontations on almost every public issue during the SARS period. Whereas Ru Yan, an ordinary citizen and a "reluctant" critic of the government, thinks it wrong for the government to hide the truth about such a deadly disease from its people, Liang, the implementer of the government policy, tries to justify and defend it. Obviously, the ultimate reason for their conflict is the irreconcilable antagonism between their political stances and their roles in society. During their relationship, there are two occasions on which they are in fierce conflict, both related to public issues. One has been mentioned earlier: when the SARS virus has already spread to the entire country and her sister-in-law and many others are hospitalized and struggling at the edge of life and death, Ru Yan learns that the vice mayor is drinking and laughing happily with other officials as if nothing had happened outside the government building. The other occasion is when Teacher Wei is misdiagnosed as a SARS victim. At that point, Liang rejects Ru Yan's request to help transfer him to another hospital because of his status as a politically "sensitive figure." Both occasions concern the government's policy and its treatment of people.

The ardent yet short-lived love affair is put to an end by a long conversation between Liang and Jiang Xiaoli, initiated by the latter. Despite being a minor actor in the triangular relationship, Jiang Xiaoli plays a decisive role. In the novel, Jiang Xiaoli is portrayed as a complicated character with enormous political significance. Rather than a selfish person who plays dirty tricks to destroy others' happiness for her own benefit, she is a woman of high moral standards. Though she loves Liang deeply, after learning that she is not his type, she introduces Ru Yan to him because she knows that Ru Yan is the type of women he admires. She is always willing to lend a helping hand whenever he is in trouble. It seems that she finds happiness in helping her beloved man find his own happiness rather than in possessing him.

In the beginning, she seems very satisfied with the outcome of her matchmaking when she finds that the relationship between Liang and Ru Yan is developing smoothly and rapidly. Her optimistic view of Liang and Ru Yan's future together as well as her view of Ru Yan, however, change drastically and fundamentally after she reads all the essays posted online by Ru Yan to expose the government's cover-up of SARS. She harshly criticizes Ru Yan for her postings and admonishes her not to do it anymore. She warns Ru Yan that such activity not only would put her own career in jeopardy but would also ruin Liang's political future. But Ru Yan refuses to surrender. She posts more essays online to expose the brutality of the government in its treatment of animals during the SARS outbreak,[54] which makes a wave both domestically and internationally. This action irritates Jiang Xiaoli even more strongly and completely changes her view of Ru Yan. Now she is fully convinced that Ru Yan not only is unqualified and unsuitable to be the vice mayor's wife but also should be put on the government's watch list. Feeling obligated to end the potential marriage she initiated, which she believes would destroy Liang's political career, Jiang Xiaoli forces him into a conversation.

The reason Jiang Xiaoli's words work so effectively on Liang is that she proves her political wisdom and acumen – or, more precisely, her cunning – in the test of SARS and saves his career. At the peak of the epidemic, it seems that the situation is completely out of control, and almost everyone loses their hope. As the number one leader of the city in charge of the SARS affair, Liang is destined to be punished later as a scapegoat if he cannot figure out a way to impress his superior and save his career. He is in deep anxiety. At this crucial juncture, Jiang Xiaoli stands up and makes a plan for him. The plan, at the core of which is conspiracy and cunning, proves to be a huge success, as every step develops exactly as she predicted. As the plan is carried out successfully, the people of the entire nation know that the latest research into drugs and a vaccine to treat and prevent SARS, conducted by the scientists in Liang's city under his direct leadership, is nearing success. While the scientists in his city bring the "light of spring to people all over the country,"[55] Liang himself draws attention from national leaders, and his career once again becomes promising. This intervention is how Jiang Xiaoli saves his career and why he is willing to listen to her.

The conversation between Liang and Jiang Xiaoli, though very short, is undoubtedly the most significant part of the novel from a political perspective, the crystallization of its core political messages and the climax of the political allegory. Jiang Xiaoli starts the conversation by straightforwardly putting forth her opinion that Ru Yan is not suitable for Liang. She first enumerates the many flaws in Ru Yan's personality, but quickly stresses that those questions of character and temperament are not significant at all compared with Ru Yan's political stance. The most serious problem with Ru Yan, she tells Liang, lies in that, "on the really big issues, she is not with us."[56] She makes her point very clear: the ultimate reason Liang and Ru Yan are not suitable as a couple is that they belong to different groups. This seemingly simple remark actually discloses the biggest secret of today's Chinese politics: the country has already been divided into two opposing groups. While the Party as represented by the government officials and high-ranking Party members like Liang and Jiang Xiaoli makes up one group, the overwhelming majority of ordinary people like Ru Yan and Damo belong to the other; the two groups are in direct and irreconcilable confrontation, forming the paradigm of "them versus us." Jiang Xiaoli spends the rest of the conversation explaining the political situation of "them versus us" for Liang:

> I know we've got lots of problems right now and have made ourselves look bad. The contradictions between us and the people keep getting worse, and the misconduct of officials keeps getting more common and more odious, almost beyond retrieval. But all these things are for *us* to work out; we can't let outsiders take care of them. If we ever do that, they will screw up not only what we've done but also everything our father's generation built. Read those articles by Ru Yan's friends and you will know what I mean. This is not about right and wrong; it's about winning and losing.[57]

Here the phrase "the contradictions between us and the people" and the repetition of "us" and "outsiders" make the paradigm of "them versus us" especially clear. Following this logic, Jiang Xiaoli judges Ru Yan to be "not the same kind of person we are."[58] She reminds Liang: "Take a close look at her choice of words: she never said 'we,' but only 'they'!"[59] She thus concludes that the contradiction between Liang and Ru Yan is not something trivial but exists "on the fundamental level."[60] Jiang Xiaoli also emphasizes that the struggle between "us" and "outsiders" – or precisely, between the agents of the Party-state and the vast ordinary Chinese people – is not about truth or morality (right and wrong) but about political power (winning and losing). She also suggests that Ru Yan and other "outsiders" – the overwhelming majority of Chinese people – are a potential threat to the Party-state. She tells Liang: "The vital thing is not to let anyone dig up our ancestral grave or cut off our resources. If somebody wants to do that, no matter how many good reasons they give, we must never agree."[61] She repeatedly stresses that the power should be kept in "our" hands, and "we" cannot let "outsiders to take care of" it.

At the end of the conversation, she points to the ultimate source of political legitimacy for Communist rule in China: "You know, some people in my family died for this country. Two of my uncles, and one of my father's cousins. Some in your family too. Let's hope they didn't die in vain."[62] Her logic is very clear: "our" fathers' generation sacrificed their lives to seize power over the country; therefore, as descendants of these revolutionary martyrs, "we" naturally possess the right to claim the power, even if "our" corruption is "almost beyond retrieval." Obviously, she regards public power not as a right owned by all the people of the country but as a privilege inherited by the offspring of a tiny group of ruling elites. This logic, at whose core is the justification of violence and the law of the jungle, sounds horrible, ridiculous, and obviously in contradiction with the universally accepted values of humanity. But it was the dominant theme of propaganda in the Mao era, and is still deeply ingrained in the minds of many Chinese people today and adopted by the ruling elites to justify their rule.

Understandably, this conversation completely shatters Liang's intention to continue his relationship with Ru Yan. After that, he simply disappears from Ru Yan's world like a drop of water evaporating in the air. At the end of the novel, it is hinted that he marries Jiang Xiaoli, and the two make an ideal political couple. Liang's decision to break up with Ru Yan and marry Jiang Xiaoli implies that he completely abandons his dream to pursue his true self in the private realm and begins to wholeheartedly embrace the Party nature. No longer trapped between Ru Yan and the Party – nor torn by the conflict between his "human" nature and his Party nature – his mind seems to regain its unity and peace, as indicated by the return of the "serene confidence" on his face.[63] However, with his true self completely enshrouded by the Party nature, he becomes a "stranger" to Ru Yan.[64] At this moment, readers suddenly realize that, under the Party's political logic and ethics, it is no contradiction for a person to simultaneously be an amicable and considerate boyfriend, a seemingly dutiful yet indifferent government official, and a horrible "old crone" hidden behind the computer screen (though it is unlikely that Liang would be the person who himself surveils Ru Yan, given his high rank in the government). In the context of the political culture of Communist China, these seemingly contradictory roles can be harmoniously united in one person acting behind different masks.

What makes this novel especially unique and thought-provoking is its portrayal of the two "antagonists" – borrowing the term from the conventional terminology of literary criticism – in the novel. Completely different from the way in which many other contemporary Chinese literary works treat "antagonists," in this novel both Liang and Jiang Xiaoli are delineated as virtuous individuals. They are both good people judged by normal moral standards. By highlighting the goodness of their original nature and by juxtaposing their goodness as individual human beings with their ugliness as cunning and indifferent government officials, the novel reveals a political logic running counter to the one sanctioned by the Party in literature. It is the system that turns these originally lovable people ugly; it is the fundamental problems inherent in the one-Party system rather than the immorality or evil of individual officials that constitute the real obstacle to the well-being of the people.

For Ru Yan, seeing the true face of Liang as a self-centred politician, as well as the truth of the Party-state behind the illusively beautiful masks, makes her wake up from political numbness and political nonchalance, and helps her walk out from under the shadow of her tragic love story. At the end of the novel, readers see a happy and energetic Ru Yan once more. But this enlightened and confident Ru Yan is no longer the same naive and carefree Ru Yan that readers saw at the beginning of the novel. She has changed to a completely different person. Ironically, the regime has produced another "reluctant" dissident, if not an enemy, through its oppression.

Summary

A pioneer oppositional political novel in early twenty-first century China, *Such Is This World* explores some fundamental issues in contemporary China, questions the political legitimacy of the Communist Party-state, and presents a political logic running counter to the one sanctioned by the Party that dominates Chinese literature. Through exposure of the government's cover-up of SARS and the tremendous, horrible consequences it brings to the nation, the novel suggests that control of information and oppression of speech can be as terrifying as the SARS virus and that Communist dictatorship is the cause of China's problems and the Chinese people's spiritual crisis. Through the depiction of different images of intellectuals, the novel demonstrates the profound and far-reaching impact of the Tiananmen Massacre upon the Chinese intelligentsia as well as the division and moral degeneration of Chinese intellectuals under the dual forces of political oppression and material reward in the post-Mao era. The novel also illuminates very clearly the consistent confrontation between the oppressive Party-state and conscientious intellectuals. Through its vivid and intriguing depiction of the hypocrisy and mendacity of the Chinese bureaucracy and the split and distorted mentality of its members, the novel exposes the degeneration of the Party into a self-serving interest group, which regards the overwhelming majority of people as "outsiders" and a threat to its privileges and power. This novel may be the first book written by a writer residing in mainland China that delineates the relationship between the Party and the people as "them versus us." In this sense, *Such Is This World* can be regarded as a groundbreaking work of contemporary Chinese political fiction.

Anne-Marie Brady, in a well-regarded book on propaganda and thought control in contemporary China, convincingly demonstrates how the Chinese Party-state has upgraded its instruments and strategies of propaganda and censorship since Tiananmen, which prove to be quite successful in restoring its political legitimacy damaged by the Tiananmen Massacre under the new conditions of market economy and the widespread use of the internet.[65] Hu Fayun's novel reflects this phenomenon in a vivid and convincing way through illustrating the new mechanisms and weapons employed by the Party-state for censorship and thought control in the age of the internet. At the same time, the novel also displays how conscientious intellectuals counteract the censorship and control with the help of the internet technology. From a broad sociopolitical and intellectual perspective, a truly original and distinctive contribution of the novel to Chinese literature and thought is its exploration of the impact of the internet upon the political and ideological contention in China in the new century.

Chapter Five

The Fat Years: Social Injustice, Forced Amnesia, Distorted Mentality, and Fascism

Since the "literary explosion" in the years immediately after Mao's death,[1] few Chinese novels have made such a sensation in the Chinese intellectual world as Chan Koonchung's *The Fat Years*. Prohibited from public release on the mainland, the book has spread rapidly among mainland readers through the internet and other underground channels,[2] and immediately conquered the Chinese intellectual world. The impact of this novel on Chinese intellectuals has proved so tremendous that some even claim, according to Paul Mooney's account,[3] that the novel changes not only their way of defining friends but also their view of the world. Given the magnitude of the sensation that the novel triggered among Chinese intellectuals, it is only natural to find that it has quickly made waves in English-speaking media as well.[4] Unlike the craze for *Wolf Totem*, whose chauvinist and social Darwinist discourses have evoked worries and fears in readers who cherish the values of freedom, democracy, justice, and equality, the popularity of this novel among intellectuals brings us optimism and hope for China's future.

The novel, published in Hong Kong in 2009, is set against the surreal background of the "near future," the year 2013, when China reaches the peak of its power and prosperity, becoming the only superpower in the world. At that time, many US enterprises, Starbucks for example, have been purchased by and merged into China's giant, transnational companies. It is a golden age for China. Feeling blessed by being born into the best country on earth, the whole nation's people, except for a few, are all intoxicated with happiness. No one, except for the few unhappy souls, notices that a month-long period is missing from the memory of the entire population. This tiny group of unhappy souls who still remember that lost month try painstakingly to uncover the truth about it; they eventually succeed after many setbacks and hardships. The secret behind the lost month shocks all of them and makes them see the truth of China's fat years.

The novel is divided into two parts. Part one mainly introduces the central characters, focusing on their personal experiences and fate in the ever-changing political climate. The employment of multiple first-person narrators in this part helps project the mindset and inner world of each character. Part two is narrated from the conventional third-person perspective along two lines. While Fang Caodi, a male main character and one of the few people with memory of the terrifying lost month, searches for a potential witness to the lost month, another male main character, the Taiwanese writer Old Chen, tries to find his true love. The two lines converge on the female protagonist Little Xi, who turns out to be the common target of the two men's quest. During their long journey across half of China's territory in search of Little Xi, the true face of China, with all its astonishing darkness behind its dazzling material prosperity, unfolds before the two men. The story climaxes in the scene where the truth-seekers kidnap a high-ranking Chinese official named He Dongsheng, an incumbent Politburo member and a "national leader," and force him to tell the truth about the lost month. After learning the truth that the Party-state manipulates not only the state's political and economic affairs but also the people's memory, mentality, and spiritual world, the characters eventually see the true face of this "prosperous, powerful, and happy" China. At the end of the novel, it is hinted that Old Chen and Little Xi plan to escape the country permanently.

The final section of the novel, which accounts for more than one fifth of the novel's length and is composed almost exclusively of He Dongsheng's explanation and analysis of China's guiding principles and its national and international policies, deserves special attention. Despite being labelled "Epilogue," the section is actually the most important part of the novel from both stylistic and thematic perspectives. Technically, through He's explanation of the truth about the lost month, the section reveals the outcome of the truth-seekers' search and completes the plot line of the novel. By providing a space for all the main characters to act on the same stage together, the epilogue also serves to bind the multidirectional narrative threads in the previous parts into a unified structure. Thematically, this section, which represents the Party's monopolistic voice, along with the plentiful comments made by Old Chen on the Chinese political system and the current situation, helps highlight the political nature of the novel. Most importantly, this concluding part, as we will discuss later, constitutes the key to understanding the main themes of the novel. He's lengthy talk to some extent can be read as a summary of the political ideas conveyed in the novel. His detailed and in-depth explanation of what took place in the lost month exposes the bloody, cunning, and exploitive strategies employed by the Party-state to create the so-called Chinese economic "miracle," the fascist nature of its national policy, and the colonialist nature of its international policy. His talk also reveals the secret behind China's collective amnesia and sheds light on the future that the Chinese model would lead the nation to. In some way, we can say that the epilogue is a crystallization of the ideology expressed in the novel.

What makes the novel unique is that it represents the first Orwellian Chinese political novel.[5] It obviously inherits "the 'classic' tradition of dystopian writing" in world political fiction as founded by Huxley, Orwell, and some others.[6] It not only exposes the tremendous darkness behind the Chinese economic "miracle" – the predation of the underprivileged by the predatory state and the tiny group of ruling elites, the collusion of powerful business interest groups and local governments, the abuse of power on the part of government agents, the collective amnesia and mental distortion of China's younger generations, and so on – but also questions the morality and political legitimacy of the Chinese model and challenges the fundamental principles of the Chinese Party-state. The novel indicates that the Chinese model of development has already led the nation on the path to fascism, though it is only in the primitive stage. Rather than regarding the Chinese model as a remedy for the alleged corruption of modern civilization as represented by Western-style democracy, Chan Koonchung suggests that the Chinese model itself is a potentially lethal disease that will bring a horrible catastrophe not only to the Chinese people but also to the entire human civilization. In this sense, the novel can be read both as the pathology of the Chinese model of development and as an apocalyptic allegory of the modern nation-state out of its people's control.

If *Nineteen Eighty-Four* portrays a "model of a totalitarian state in its 'pure' or 'essential' form"[7] as well as "the bareness of terror,"[8] *The Fat Years* depicts the evil and terror of a totalitarian state cloaked in an illusory, beautiful veil of prosperity and happiness. The world of *The Fat Years* to a large extent can be seen as a hybrid of *Brave New World* and *Nineteen Eighty-Four*, where a totalitarian regime combines technological control and terror to build a world of conformity, homogeneity, and obedience.[9] The fictional world created by Chan Koonchung is in essence a dystopia with an intoxicating utopian aura.[10]

Fake Paradise: Darkness behind the Chinese "Miracle"

In her brief yet incisive and insightful preface to its English edition, Julia Lovell commends the novel, along with many other merits, for "its unusual honesty" in reflecting "contemporary Chinese reality."[11]

Chaohua Wang, in her reading of the novel, also points to its "numerous references to contemporary events."[12] Lovell's and Wang's observations prove to be accurate and convincing, as the novel indeed displays remarkable authenticity and audacity in exposing the enormous darkness of the Chinese political system and society, often hidden behind the dazzling material prosperity.

The so-called Chinese model of development, dubbed "developmental autocracy" or "crony capitalism" by Minxin Pei,[13] is presented in the novel as an aggregate of controversies, paradoxes, and self-contradictions. A minor character named Zhuang Zizhong, a founder of the leading Chinese intellectual journal *Dushu* (Reading), summarizes the character of the Chinese political system as comprising the following ten major features:

> a one-party democratic dictatorship; the rule of law with social stability as the most important element; an authoritarian government that governs for the people; a state-controlled market economy; fair competition guaranteed by state-owned enterprises; scientific development with unique Chinese characteristics; a self-centered harmonious foreign policy; a multi-ethnic republic ruled by one sovereign ethnic group of Han Chinese; post-Westernism and post-universalism as the nation's chief world views; the restoration of Chinese national culture as the world's unrivalled leader.[14]

As readers might easily discern, almost all of the ten features are combinations of two incompatible elements such as "democratic" and "one-Party dictatorship," "authoritarian" and "for the people," "multiethical republic" and "one sovereign ethnic group," and so on. The self-contradictory nature of those combinations suggests that these features are merely political rhetoric for propaganda purposes, and they cannot actually exist in reality. In real life, for example, there can never be such a thing as "a democratic one-Party dictatorship," because one-Party dictatorship and democracy are opposites; as such, there is no possibility for a one-Party dictatorship to be democratic, though dictatorship in reality does indeed often act in the name of the people, claiming to represent the interests of the people. By the same token, it is impossible for an authoritarian regime to subject its own will and interests to the people. Likewise, a country where one single ethnic group claims absolute superiority over all others has no chance of being a true multi-ethnic republic.

Paradoxes and contradictions in the system and politics inevitably cause real troubles in society. In the novel, Chan presents a naturalistic picture of the disastrous consequences that the Chinese model has brought to China with "journalistic immediacy."[15] First, one of the most serious problems inherent in the Chinese model, as exposed in the novel and seen in real life, is its predatory nature. The astonishingly rapid accumulation of tremendous wealth on the part of the Party-state and a tiny minority of privileged people is actually achieved by preying on the underprivileged and the poor, especially the peasants and grassroots urban workers. The novel depicts this phenomenon in many places. In one case, for example, readers witness how Zhang Dou, a peasant's son from Henan province, is kidnapped at a railway station when he is only thirteen years old, sold to a "black brick kiln" in Shanxi province, and forced to labour as a child slave there. He tries to run away and is rescued by some strangers on the road, who take him to the local Labour Bureau. Shockingly enough, shortly after being rescued, he is sold again to another illegal brick kiln – this time not by any human traffickers but by the Labour Bureau itself. Here, the depiction of how a government department can be as vicious as real criminals makes the predatory and inhumane nature of the Chinese system especially clear.[16] Zhang Dou is not emancipated until several years later when the many illegal brick kilns in the area are exposed by the national media. He and many other child labourers – most of them the same age and background as him – are finally saved.[17] Clearly, Zhang Dou's experience is a powerful example showing that the Chinese style of primitive accumulation of capital is made possible by ruthless exploitation and inhumane abuse of the underprivileged.[18] Another salient case revealing the predatory nature of the Chinese model of development in the novel is the story of how a powerful business interest group colludes with a local township government to seize peasants' land by tricks and violence in Henan province.[19] This case is typical of the "collusion between business people and government officials [to] infringe the rights and well-being of the common people."[20] One of the most shocking pictures in the novel portrays how the lethal pollution from a state-owned chemical factory pushes a little village in Hebei province, which is not far away from the prosperous capital city of the nation, to the brink of extinction.[21] Later on, it is discovered that this factory is the very plant used by the government to make the chemical that is put into drinking water and other beverages to control people's moods and memory. This act is an explicit embodiment of state oppression and state predation.

What makes the novel unique is that all these events, however despairing and horrible, are not imagined but taken from real stories occurring in today's China that once made headlines in the mainland Chinese media. Through these terrifying yet realistic pictures, Chan Koonchung reveals the grim truth that the prosperity of today's China is built on the tears, blood, and even lives of the underprivileged and on the predation of future generations. As mentioned earlier, the predatory nature of the Chinese model and of the Party-state has been well studied by Minxin Pei's highly acclaimed research on the social transition in contemporary China.[22] Their predatory nature inevitably puts into question the morality and political legitimacy of the so-called Chinese model, a theme on which I shall elaborate in the last section of the chapter.

A second shadow darkening the Chinese model that the novel exposes is the collusion among varied elite groups – political, economic, and intellectual – to monopolize state power, control the society, and manipulate the people to maximize their own interests.[23] In both aforementioned cases of Zhang Dou and the forced land seizure, the vicious joined hands of the "business and bureaucratic interest groups" are already unveiled.[24] However, the most powerful case in the novel that demonstrates the collusion of interest groups is the SS Study Group. This so-called study group is an organization composed of elites in all important sectors of the society; it is also a network to connect these highly influential people in the nation. Wei Guo, the youngest member of the group, explains:

> The SS Study Group brings together political and business circles. Its formal members include government officials of vice-ministerial rank, army officers of major-general rank, directors of major state-owned enterprises, chairmen of sovereign funds, and leaders of China's top-100 private businesses, as well as a few professors and institutional heads from the Chinese Academy of Social Sciences and key universities. In fact, our network of connection extends all the way up to the Heavenly Court.[25]

The description not only provides a brief yet clear sketch of the collaboration of China's elites from all fields but also divulges the message that this network of elites is connected directly to the highest leadership. The most powerful and influential figure and the true leader of the study group is Big Brother Crewcut (*bancuntou dage* 板寸头大哥),[26] a giant whose power and influence spread across several fields:

> Ban Cuntou is a genuine Red aristocrat. On the surface, he is supposed to be an investor in overseas projects, but in the point of fact he is intimately connected with all of the legitimate and illegitimate activities of the Party, the government and the military establishment. He is, as we say, able to "communicate with Heaven itself," and I believe he will eventually become one of our nation's heads of state. Everyone in the group is well connected, but they all exhibit reverence and fear when talking to big brother Ban Cuntou.[27]

It is clear that Big Brother Crewcut himself is a crystallization and symbol of the intricate and intertwined network of China's elites in all fields. The fact that the three most powerful and wealthy people in the novel – Big Brother Crewcut, the business magnate Jian Lin, and the kidnapped national leader He Dongsheng – are cousins reinforces the sense of the intertwined connection among the ruling elites in China.

It is not clear in the novel what exactly this group does or what consequence their activity would bring to China. However, judging by the group's name – which readily reminds readers of the Nazi SS group – and by all the evidence scattered throughout the novel, it can be safely inferred that what it does is definitely not for the common good of the Chinese people. First, in both Zhang Dou's case and the aforementioned forced land seizure case, powerful businessmen and government officials collude to infringe the rights and well-being of the unprivileged for their own interests. Both cases hint at the malicious nature of the collaboration between businessmen and government officials and among other elites in China today. Second, the group indoctrinates the philosophy of hatred and fascism under the guise of patriotism and nationalism, which will inevitably poison the hearts of its followers and distort their mentality. The pernicious effect of the indoctrination is clearly reflected in the mentality and behaviour of Wei Guo and the gang of "iron-blooded loyal braves" led by him.[28] I shall return to this topic and elaborate on it in more detail later. Third, the nature of the group is also reflected by the moral character of its members. Wei Guo, a self-proclaimed patriot and nationalist, for example, is actually a fascist. He does not hesitate to report and persecute his own mother, whom he regards as a nuisance to the Party and an obstacle to his political career. Big Brother Crewcut, the "highly revered" leader of the group, takes the opportunity to rape Little Xi when she asks him for help with the reopening of her restaurant. All these facts – the predatory nature of collusive interest groups in general, the terrifying doctrine of the group, and the despicable character of its members – provide readers with good reasons to question the real purposes of the group and its impact on society, despite the sublimity of its self-proclaimed mission. Given that the group is composed either of Party members or those closely associated with the Party, the depiction of this group also testifies to Minxin Pei's observation that the Party has already turned into a "self-serving ruling elite," "a huge entrenched interest group," as dubbed by the deposed former general secretary of the Chinese Communist Party, Zhao Ziyang.[29]

A third dark aspect of the Chinese model exposed in the novel is the massive and unrestrained abuse of power on the part of the arbitrary and corrupt bureaucracy, and the tremendous social injustice it brings to China. In the novel, the regime's abuse of power is displayed in many aspects of social life, but it is most evidently epitomized in its surveillance over and persecution of its own people. As demonstrated by the miserable life experience of Little Xi, a victim of and witness to the regime's abuse of power, the Party-state not only uses public resources to spy on and persecute its real or imagined enemies and political dissidents but also puts under surveillance innocent people who only want to stay away from the regime but harbour no intention to confront or sabotage it. The experience of Wei Guo, an official informer for both public and state security units, also provides solid evidence of the abuse of power on the part of the state, though in a way completely different from Little Xi's case. As Wei Guo testifies, the Party-state finances college students to watch their professors and to report anyone "promoting the Western system of values or liberalism in class."[30] The surveillance proves so widespread that, according to He Dongsheng, "even the Party and national leaders are afraid they're being watched."[31] In response to Old Chen's question about whether there are bad people among the customers of their family's restaurant who would have a bad influence upon him, Wei Guo declares proudly and confidently that "everything is under the Party's and the government's control; they know everything."[32] This description readily reminds readers of the omnipresent eyes of Big Brother in *Nineteen Eighty-Four* and the horrible slogan on the poster that reads "Big Brother is watching you." It also affirms the fact that a one-Party dictatorial state is necessarily a police state.

Another notorious form of abuse of power presented in the novel is the extreme arbitrariness, absurdity, and inhumanity of the Chinese judicial system, which is exemplified by both Little Xi's and Fang Caodi's experiences. In 1983, when Little Xi had just graduated from law school, she was assigned a job as a legal clerk-secretary in a county-level court under the Beijing jurisdiction. That year, the government launched a crackdown on "spiritual pollution" and crime. Her work experience in the legal system proved so frightening and despairing that she quit the job very quickly. According to Little Xi, the legal procedure during the crackdown proceeded in this way:

In order to process cases rapidly the Public Security Bureau, the Prosecutor's Office and the Legal Division each assigned two people. All of us worked in an office of the Public Security Bureau. The arrest, the investigation, the decision and the sentencing all took place practically at the same time ... In every case, big or small, the accused was given the death sentence, and not one of the crimes involved murder. Robbery received a death sentence, petty theft received a death sentence, swindling received a death sentence, and no one paid any attention at all when the accused produced solid exculpatory evidence.[33]

Even worse, the novel also suggests that the authority even sets a quota of executions – how many people must be sentenced to the death penalty – for each court during the crackdown. Such a legal system is truly shocking and horrifying.

Little Xi is not the only witness to the extreme arbitrariness, absurdity, and inhumanity of the Chinese judicial system. Fang Caodi goes through a similar experience, only in a different role at a different time in a different location. During the "missing" month, Fang travelled in Guangdong province to sightsee. He did not know another crackdown campaign was launched until he was kicked out of the hotel and told by the hotel manager that this eviction was an order from the government. He hid in a peasant's house for a couple of days before the peasant turned him in. It turns out that the structure of the judicial personnel and the legal process for his trial were exactly the same as Little Xi witnessed during the 1983 crackdown. "There was a six-person joint hearing in an office of that Public Security Bureau. There were two Public Security police, two prosecutors, and two judges."[34] Also, the arrest, the investigation, the decision, and the sentencing all took place at the same time. Fang was charged with spying and sentenced to the death penalty based on the sole fact that he carried an American passport. He luckily escaped execution because a young female judge saved him, as Little Xi did for many accused during the 1983 crackdown. Despite the fierce opposition from all her colleagues, the young female judge insisted that Fang was innocent. She told her co-workers: "It is not a crime for a Chinese person to carry an American passport in China – and that's according to our own Chinese law."[35] Although Fang's tragic story came to a happy ending by pure luck, it does not deny the absurdity and inhumanity of the Chinese legal system. By juxtaposing Little Xi's and Fang's experiences – two events of the same nature that take place at different times and in different locations – the novel underscores the universality and longevity of the abuse of power on the part of the Chinese legal system.

The abuse of power on the part of the Chinese Party-state is also displayed in many other aspects of life. In one place, for example, the novel exposes how Chinese military men, taking advantage of the privileges and power they enjoy in the country, treat ordinary people's lives as nothing. "In rural areas, army vehicles sped around like crazy and often ran into people. If civilians were killed or injured, they just had to accept their fate."[36] By depicting the tragic experience of a small Christian church in Henan province, a church named "Grain Fallen on Ground Does Not Die," the novel also reveals how the Party-state suppresses people's freedom of belief by imprisoning and persecuting religious leaders and imposing all kinds of restrictions on churches.

Apart from the aforementioned dark phenomena, the novel also casts a quick glance at some other pressing problems facing today's China, such as the rapidly widening gap between urban and rural areas and between rich and poor, the increasingly intensified confrontation between ordinary people and officials and interest groups, the steadily deteriorating living environment caused by air and water pollution, and other issues. Moreover, the novel stands out as the first in Chinese literature to discuss all the major political movements launched by the Party in an explicitly critical way. This discussion almost amounts to an all-round negation of the Party-state. In this sense, the novel represents the pathology of the Party-state's and the Chinese model's darkness.

Falsified History and Forced Amnesia

Milan Kundera claims that "the struggle of men against power is the struggle of memory against forgetting."[37] Only a person like Kundera, who had personal experience of living in a totalitarian regime and witnessed what a crucial role that manipulation of memory and distortion of history play in political control, can fully understand the meaning of this statement. Indeed, our knowledge and memory of the past never function merely as a recording of, or a path to, our past; instead, they are always closely associated with and even determine our identities. Paul Connerton points out:

> Our past history is an important source of our conception of ourselves; our self-knowledge, our conception of our own character and potentials, is to a large extent determined by the way in which we view our own past actions. There is, then, an important connection between the concept of personal identity and various backward-looking mental states ... Through memories of this kind, persons have a special access to facts about their own past histories and their own identities.[38]

It is precisely out of the awareness of the crucial role memory plays in the formation of personal identity that all oppressive regimes use forced memory or forced amnesia as a tool to control their people's mentality. In *Nineteen Eighty-Four*, readers witness the powerful and horrible "memory holes,"[39] whose sole purpose is to destroy the historical records that are incompatible with the reality of today.

Aldous Huxley explains the extreme importance of the control of truth and memory for totalitarian rule as well as the logic and mechanism of the control. He argues: "A really efficient totalitarian state would be one in which the all-powerful executive of political bosses and their army of managers control a population of slaves who do not have to be coerced, because they love their servitude."[40] He adds: "The love of servitude cannot be established except as the result of a deep, personal revolution in human minds and bodies."[41] Huxley believes that the most effective way to make this "deep, personal revolution" is to lower the "iron curtain" between people and certain facts and arguments regarded as "undesirable" by the ruler to shape people's world view and mentality through propaganda. As he points out, "the greatest triumphs of propaganda have been accomplished, not by doing something, but by refraining from doing. Great is truth, but still greater, from a practical point of view, is silence about truth."[42] Control of truth and memory through propaganda, according to Huxley, is the most effective way for a totalitarian regime to control people's minds and to maintain its rule.

Like Huxley, Orwell, and Kundera, contemporary Chinese writers also understand profoundly the relationship between the control of memory and totalitarian domination. As a result, exposure of the Party-state's manipulation of historical truth and collective memory, and its disastrous consequences, constitutes a pronounced theme shared by many contemporary Chinese literary works, including, as discussed earlier, Hu Fayun's *Such Is This World*. *The Fat Years* also inherits this theme. In the novel, Chan's critical reflection on the Party-state's manipulation of history and memory is performed through the main characters' investigation of the "lost" month, which symbolizes the collective amnesia of the nation. In tracing the causes of the amnesia, the novel points to three factors: the Party-state's dictatorship, Chinese intellectuals' abandonment of their role as a social conscience and their complicity with the Party-state, and political acquiescence and political indifference on the part of ordinary Chinese people.

Fang Caodi, the most steadfast and resilient truth-seeker in the novel, travels around the entire country in search of historical evidence to prove the existence of the "lost" month. One day, when he goes to a friend's apartment for a visit, he finds an old copy of the popular liberal newspaper *Southern Weekly* from that "lost" month under a pile of junk in front of a store within the apartment building. When he compares this printed version of the newspaper with the online version, he discovers a huge discrepancy: an article critical of the crackdown that took place in the "lost" month – substantial evidence of the month's existence – which appears in the printed version, is deleted and re-placed by an article attacking Western universal values in the online version. In this way, the record of that missing month is completely erased. With this finding, Fang goes to the library to look up the daily and weekly newspapers of that year, only to discover that now the library only has the online versions, and it is no longer possible to read the printed versions. Besides, the online reports of the month are completely different from what he experienced and witnessed during that period of time; thus, the horrifying month has completely disappeared from the historical records constructed by the state propaganda machine. Fang finally realizes that nothing about the true state of things can be found from the "officially doctored books" in China, because all those books are nothing but "a pack of lies."[43]

Fang Caodi then passes on what he found about the "lost" month to Old Chen, but the writer does not believe him at first. Confused and annoyed by Fang's repeated assertions, Old Chen decides to go to the biggest online bookstores in China to check things out for himself in an attempt to shut Fang's mouth in the future. What he finds there, how-ever, comes as a huge shock to him: the real situation with regard to the cover-up and distortion of history in China is actually even worse than what Fang described. During the entire process of his web search, Old Chen does not find a single book on the various political movements in Communist China, except for two history books "authorized by gov-ernment in the last two years":

> In all the bookstores and even on their websites, where they claimed to stock every book in the world, of all the thousands of titles listed, Old Chen could not find one single book that might explain the true facts about contemporary Chinese history ... [T]here is a profusion of books everywhere, so many they knock you over, but the true facts are still being suppressed.[44]

Old Chen discovers that not only have topics like the Tiananmen Mas-sacre been banned; even the few items that come up on the Cultural Revolution – a topic still allowed to be discussed to a limited degree – are terrifying: "just a load of nostalgic guff for an adolescence spent in the brilliant sunshine of the glorious past. The few items that discussed the history of the Cultural Revolution were only simplistic officially sanitized versions." The result makes Old Chen feel "aghast."[45] Like Fang Caodi, he also eventually comes to the realization that "history had been re-written and the true facts had been air-brushed away."[46] Now he begins to understand the major reason for the "collective and selective amnesia": the people have no way to know the historical truth. He is also aware that the writing of official history in China is no different than "lying with one's eyes wide open, squinting to deliberately alter reality, distorting the true facts of history without the least scruple and nakedly falsifying the records."[47]

Fang Caodi's and Old Chen's findings both prove that the Chinese Party-state plays the dominant role in the distortion of history and in the formation of the collective amnesia in today's China. Near the end of the novel, the national leader He Dongsheng confesses to the truth-seekers that the state "totally rewrote the history of those twenty-eight days."[48] In the novel, the Party-state's manipulation of history and control of the nation's mentality are highlighted by a surreal and symbolic depiction of the government treating China's drinking water and other beverages with a chemical that can change people's moods. It is the ultimate cause of the entire nation's intoxication with the feeling of happiness. This depiction readily reminds readers of Aldous Huxley's *Brave New World*, where the government of the World State uses soma to control people's moods, to make them forget the grim reality they face, and to eradicate their desire for historical truth. It seems that the Chinese totalitarian regime in *The Fat Years* synthesizes the strategies employed by the governments in both *Brave New World* and *Nineteen Eighty-Four* – blending technological devices and government surveillance, secret police, and state terror – for the most effective way to control society and people's feelings and thoughts.

In addition to condemning the Party-state, Chan Koonchung also implicitly criticizes Chinese intellectuals for abandoning their role as a social conscience and for their complicity with the Party-state in distorting the historical truth. In response to Old Chen's question of whether "the intellectuals today are genuinely willing to be reconciled with the Communist Party," Zhuang Zizhong, a founder of the journal *Reading*, repudiates this inquiry as a pseudo question. He tells Old Chen: "The question should be, is the *Party* willing to be reconciled with the intellectuals?"[49] He asserts that "receiving positive recognition from the Party" is the greatest achievement for both the journal and for himself as an intellectual.[50] As made very clear by Zhuang's statement, Chinese intellectuals, completely giving up their independent and critical stance towards the Party-state and the Promethean role they used to play in Chinese society in the 1980s, are more than willing in the new century to submit to the Party and serve as its mouthpieces.

In the novel, Chan Koonchung subtly discloses the secret behind the intellectuals' unexpected submission to the Party since the advent of the new century. It turns out that Chinese intellectuals are bought off by the Party with material gains and high social status. In Zhuang's case, to reward his effort and achievement in leading the once critical and rebellious magazine to accept the Party's ideology, the government not only provides him with a new car and a driver but national leaders also visit him and pay tribute to him during the Spring Festival – the highest honour that a Chinese intellectual can receive from the government. Now a nationally renowned and highly respected personage, Zhuang gets for himself a new wife, who is much younger than he is and whose main duty is to look after him. The scholarly career of Hu Yan, a senior research fellow at the prestigious Chinese Academy of Social Sciences, represents another typical case of how Chinese intellectuals are bought off by the Party-state. In the 1980s and 1990s, when Hu Yan conducted research on problems of the Chinese countryside and peasants, she not only could not get any public funding but also was chastised and suppressed by the government for addressing these politically sensitive issues. After entering the new century, however, everything is different. Not only have governments at all levels changed their attitude towards both the intellectuals in general and the experts on peasantry studies in particular, but the research on peasantry, agriculture, and the countryside has also become a highly popular and respected subject. As a result, now Hu not only receives abundant funding from the government but also becomes a consultant in decision-making for government at all levels. Now that she is a big beneficiary of the government's new policy and generosity, she no longer stands out as a troublemaker and a critic of the government. Instead, she becomes a supporter of the government and a model intellectual in the eyes of the Party.[51] Judging by the fact that she accepts what is said in *People's Daily* – the Party's official newspaper and most powerful mouthpiece – as absolute truth,[52] as well as by her comments on the current situation in China's countryside, it is not difficult to infer that the conclusions she draws from her "research" are no more than explanations or extensions of the Party's policies or official statements disguised as scholarly findings. Obviously, like Zhuang, she has also bought into the system. Given that history in Communist China is written by intellectuals like Zhuang and Hu, it can be imagined what kind of history the country could have. The images of intellectuals as presented here might remind readers of the intellectuals in Kundera's *Unbearable Lightness of Being*,[53] who are also forced to keep silent in the face of Communist dictatorship. Unfortunately and sadly, in contrast to Kundera's characters, who often maintain a rebellious heart behind their superficial submission, the intellectuals in Chan's novel display an incredible docility before oppression, a willingness to submit, and a love for their servitude.

The depiction of Zhuang and Hu readily remind us of another intellectual portrayed in *Such Is This World*, Maozi, who is also bought off by the Party-state with material gain, social status, and fame after the Tiananmen Massacre. The life experience of these intellectuals testifies to the success of the Party-state's policy of co-opting the intellectuals after Tiananmen. It once again confirms Minxin Pei's observation that China's economic prosperity grants the Party-state "more material resources to strengthen [its] repressive capacity and co-opt potential opposition groups, especially counterelites."[54] As he argues, "the CCP's [Chinese Communist Party's] efforts to co-opt the intelligentsia and the private entrepreneurs – the former being the leading opposition group in the 1980s and the latter a likely challenger to the Party's power in the future – were highly successful in the 1990s mainly because the rapid growth gave the CCP the economic means of political co-optation."[55]

Apart from the dictatorial Party-state and the subservient intellectuals, Chan Koonchung, as Yan Lianke does in *Lenin's Kisses*, also blames ordinary Chinese people for their acquiescence and indifference in the face of the distortion of history by the Party-state. Like the submissive intellectuals, ordinary Chinese people also serve as accomplices in creating the collective amnesia. As the "national leader" He Dongsheng points out, the Central Propaganda Department did indeed do a lot of work to cover up the truth of the "lost" month, but it is the Chinese people themselves who should take the major responsibility for the amnesia because they chose to forget in the first place. He argues: "If the Chinese people themselves had not already wanted to forget, we could not have forced them to do so. The Chinese people voluntarily gave themselves a large dose of amnesia medicine."[56] He also explains why Chinese people do not want to remember all those terrible things now: "people couldn't stand to remember those hard times, and everyone was too busy making and spending money."[57] Moreover, now "everybody was living very well and very few people had any interest in recalling the Cultural Revolution and June 1989, so those memories just naturally faded away."[58] He provides a detailed account of how that terrifying month is completely erased from people's memory. Taking advantage of the Chinese people's new psychology of desire for material satisfaction and sensuous pleasure, and their rejection of the past pain and terror, the government forbids the media to discuss that terrifying "lost" month. And "when someone in or outside the country mentioned those events, we simply filtered them out. Very soon the new version of things became the only available version."[59] It turns out that "no one objected to this distortion of reality, and practically no one even noticed it."[60] As a result, the memory of that horrible month has been completely erased from people's minds:

> And then something unimaginable happened that to this day I still cannot fathom: more and more people genuinely forgot these twenty-eight days, and it was not just temporary memory loss, but they absolutely could not remember that time, just as though the whole country had unconsciously erased some painful childhood trauma.[61]

This forgetting is how the "collective and selective amnesia" comes into being in the nation. Old Chen, in his analysis of the role that ordinary Chinese people played in the amnesia, arrives at a similar conclusion: "Most people don't care about the truth" because "the price of maintaining a firm commitment to truth is too great. Besides that, the true facts are often painful to recall, and who doesn't prefer pleasure to pain?"[62] Also, as Old Chen observes, Chinese people now are highly satisfied with the status quo – they have enjoyed "90 percent freedom" already, and that is more than enough for them. "The vast majority of the population cannot even handle 90 percent freedom; they think it's too much. Aren't they already complaining about information overload and being entertained to death?"[63] Most importantly, the Chinese people care much more about their self-interests in the here and now than about grand and remote missions like democracy and freedom. For them, it does not make much difference whether the power of the government is given to it by the people or the people's freedom is given to them by the government.[64] Both He Dongsheng's and Old Chen's observations testify to Julia Lovell's judgment of the Chinese collective amnesia. As she argues, "much of the urban population seems to have tacitly agreed to forget past political violence, and to try to take advantage of the fat times of the here-and-now."[65] She believes that amnesia results from "the marriage of mass acquiescence and violent political intimidation."[66]

Ironically and intriguingly, in the epilogue of the novel, it is suggested that there possibly exists another kind of amnesia – the one inflicted on the ruler by the oppressed. According to the "live or die together" agreement, in order to come out of the room alive and later climb up the ladder in officialdom, the "national leader" He Dongsheng must tell the truth of the "lost" month and keep silent about what happens on that night forever. The underprivileged and seemingly impotent truth-seekers eventually manage to impose amnesia upon the powerful national leader. This description implies that the collective amnesia inflicted on the people by the Party-state will ultimately end in vain, and the oppressors will taste what they have done to the oppressed one day.

Mental Distortion and Spiritual Agony

Because history and our memory of it, as Paul Connerton points out, are ultimately related to and, to a large extent, determine our mentality and identity,[67] falsification of history and manipulation of memory will inevitably bring disastrous consequences to people's spiritual world. Yuan Weishi 袁伟时, an established historian and outspoken Chinese intellectual, in an article that can be said to have caused an earthquake in the Chinese political and intellectual world, fiercely criticizes the Party-sanctioned history textbooks for falsifying historical truth. He denounces such a history education as "wolf milk" (*langnai* 狼奶), at whose core is a philosophy of hatred and cruelty. He claims all Chinese people under the Communist domination grow up nurtured on this kind of "wolf milk."[68] Indeed, as elaborated in chapter 1, in order to control people's thought and to re-establish its political legitimacy after the Tiananmen Massacre, the Chinese Party-state systematically sponsored and implemented programs such as the "national studies fever" and the "patriotic education campaign." These programs aimed to indoctrinate a selective and distorted history education into the minds of the younger generations so as to shape their values and world view, which has proved quite successful from the Party's point of view. In *The Fat Years*, Chan Koonchung provides a vivid and convincing presentation of the horrible consequences that falsified history and distorted memory bring to the Chinese nation.

Falsified history and forced amnesia, as presented in the novel, bring dual disastrous consequences to China. On the one hand, for the overwhelming majority of Chinese people, who are either deceived by or willing to accept the Party's propaganda, falsified history and distorted memory lead them to develop a distorted personality and mentality: "love of their servitude," the willing submission to the Party-state's deception and oppression. On the other hand, for a tiny minority of awakening and conscientious Chinese people, who see through the nature of the "wolf milk" and reject it, distorted history and forced amnesia will unavoidably arouse spiritual agony and existential perplexity in them and at the same time will provoke the spirit of rebellion in their hearts. In the novel, whereas the mindset and behaviour of Wei Guo, Little Xi's only son, are best illustrative of the first phenomenon, Little Xi herself represents the second type of person, which her experiences, feelings, and thoughts best demonstrate.

Though Wei Guo is a minor character in the novel, his portrayal bears tremendous ideological significance. His thoughts, speeches, and behaviour clearly illustrate the distorted mentality and values of China's younger generations, who were brought up on the Communist education of history in the post-Mao era, where the political follies and atrocities committed by the Party-state are either completely filtered out or subject to "sanitized interpretations" and the image of a "great, glorious, and correct" Party leading the nation to an unprecedented "miracle" amid a global economic crisis is deeply implanted in their minds. According to Little Xi, Wei Guo was born a person of vicious nature:

> Ever since he was born, he has frightened me. He had a face like a little angel, but he lied, ingratiated himself with his teachers, ingratiated himself with anyone who could do him any good, and bullied anyone weaker than he was. His character was just naturally cruel. OK, so he was like that from childhood. Now he writes letters informing on his classmates, getting them into troubles with the authorities and persecuting them.[69]

When he makes his first appearance in the novel, Wei Guo is already a graduate student at prestigious Peking University and the youngest member of the elite SS Study Group. He is a steadfast and wholehearted supporter of the Party, which represents absolute truth in his eyes. To show his absolute loyalty to the Party-state, he changes his original name Wei Min, which means "defend the people" and is also a homophone of "for the people," to Wei Guo, which implies "defend the (Party-)state" or "for the (Party-)state." He believes that no country on earth is as good as China. His life goal is to work for the Party's Central Propaganda Department. Rather than regarding it as an apparatus of intellectual and spiritual oppression and an enemy of freedom of speech and thought, Wei Guo considers the Central Propaganda Department a "romantic and idealistic" organization that "guides the spiritual life of the entire nation."[70] He not only voluntarily spies on his colleagues and reports every suspicious activity of theirs to the Party but also organizes other people to do so. More shockingly, considering his own mother a threat to the Party and an obstacle to his own future, he watches her closely and makes every effort to dig out her secrets and report them to the Party. The cruellest thing he does is collude with the police to send his own mother, who has no mental problems at all, to a psychiatric hospital. Obviously, this young man's view of right and wrong and of good and evil is completely upside down, and his personality and mindset are totally distorted. The image of Wei Guo once again reminds us of the children in *Nineteen Eighty-Four* who voluntarily work as spies for Big Brother. Wei Guo's story suggests that the current Chinese political system attracts and absorbs people of an evil nature and then provides the favourable soil for the evil in their hearts to grow and proliferate.

Wei Guo's life experiences also illustrate the pernicious effects of ideological indoctrination in a highly explicit and impressive way. The SS Study Group Wei Guo joins is in essence a propaganda organization whose major purpose is to spread state ideology in the name of scholarly research. At the core of this group's doctrine is a philosophy of hatred. The doctrine promotes the ideas that the "martial spirit" is the paramount virtue for human beings and that "enemies and hatred can strengthen people's martial spirit – enemies and hatred are an aphrodisiac for the marital spirit."[71] It propagates the notion that "hate is indispensable if we want to accomplish great things"[72] and, consequently, denounces "great love, universal love, and love for all mankind" as harmful for the nation.[73] It asserts that only after being charged with hatred can a nation be energized and finally achieve wealth and power. After hearing this doctrine from Professor Z in the study group, Wei Guo becomes highly stimulated and excited. He accepts it as absolute truth and immediately puts it in action. He organizes six students from Peking University and Tsing-Hua University into a group called "iron-blooded loyal braves" to practise the martial arts. To stimulate their "killing spirit" and elevate the degree of hatred in them, they watch "documentary films on the Nanjing Massacre and the Nazi extermination of Jews" and kill stray dogs to build up their courage.[74]

Though claiming to be steadfast patriots and nationalists, Wei Guo and his fellow "iron-blooded loyal braves" are actually fascists – even Communist Party leader He Dongsheng calls this group "a fascist cell."[75] Wei Guo and other "braves" are reminiscent of a real fascist group within the Kuomintang in the 1930s, the Blue Shirt Society, a semi-secret society that admired fascism and thought they were morally superior to other members of their party and all other people in the nation.[76] The "iron-blooded loyal braves" divide the country's population into different classes and openly discriminate against the people they classify as the underprivileged and the abject, especially the peasants. The only reason they beat Zhang Dou is that he is a peasant and therefore despicable. As a Tsing-Hua "brave" asserts, "peasants are a vulgar social class lower than anybody and nobody should sympathize with them."[77] Esteeming themselves "superior men with a sense of mission"[78] and political elites who shoulder the responsibility of protecting the nation, they adopt terrorist strategies to destroy facilities or people they regard as the Party-state's enemies. As the "national leader" He Dongsheng confesses, the group attempted to blow up a factory, which was erroneously assumed to be a threat to the state but actually is the very plant that produces the chemical that can control people's moods. The venture only ended up with several "braves" being killed by the state machine.[79] Wei Guo and his fellow "braves" provide a perfect example of how pernicious indoctrination can distort people's mindsets and behaviour, and bring disasters to the entire society.

With the depiction of Wei Guo, Chan Koonchung also exposes the "hypocrisy of the Chinese Communist Party"[80] and the two-facedness and split inner world of its members. Despite his repeated proclamations of commitment and loyalty to the Party and the nation, Wei Guo is not a real patriot or nationalist, not even a true fascist; for example, when he incites other "iron-blooded loyal braves" to beat Zhang Dou and to sacrifice their lives to blow up the chemical factory, he himself hides in a safe place behind the scenes. As his mother Little Xi remarks, "he is always spouting empty slogans, pretending to embrace a wonderful idealistic morality."[81] Obviously, he only pays lip service to the grand mission of serving the nation and the Party-state; what he truly cares about are his own selfish interests. As he admits, the real reason he reports his own mother is that he considers her to be an obstacle to his political career and future. What motivates Wei Guo to join the SS Study Group and to choose Professor X as his mentor is not any grand discourse or noble mission promoted by Professor X but rather his belief that the professor has "the best future prospects" and "would go the furthest in the shortest period of time."[82] Clearly, Wei Guo's motive is completely selfish. In essence, he is an opportunist, a schemer, and "an absolute and sophisticated egoist" as defined by Qian Liqun, a well-known liberal intellectual and highly regarded professor at Peking University.[83] Qian claims:

> Our education, especially that kind of pragmatic, utilitarian, nihilistic education, only produces people whom I call "absolute and sophisticated egoists." Here, "absolute" refers to the fact that self-interest is the sole, absolute, and direct drive behind their speeches and actions; for them, doing something for others is simply an investment. What does "sophisticated" mean here? These people have high intelligence and a good upbringing, and everything they do is reasonable, legal, and flawless. They are surprisingly worldly wise, mature, and clever; they pretend to be loyal and know how to adapt and perform, and how to utilize the power of the system to achieve their own goals.[84]

An "absolute, sophisticated egoist," Wei Guo reminds us of Adolf Eichmann as observed by Hannah Arendt. The notorious Nazi war criminal, according to Arendt, is not fanatic, eccentric, or intelligent at all; he is actually just a normal average person. His behaviour is motivated less by "grand" ideological inspiration than by secular considerations such as promotion, social status, and personal gain.[85] The depictions of Wei Guo and Adolf Eichmann both reveal the hypocrisy and mendacity of the mentality of absolute egoists disguised as steadfast believers of an ideology. They provide perfect examples to illustrate Arendt's notion of "the banality of evil." I will return to this topic for a detailed elaboration in the next chapter.

Little Xi represents someone completely different from Wei Guo and his fellow "iron-blooded loyal braves." She belongs to the generation of Chinese intellectuals who were "baptized in the Enlightenment values such as Reason, Liberty, Democracy, Truth and Human Rights,"[86] which prevailed within the Chinese intelligentsia in the 1980s and were still highly influential among the liberal intellectuals in the 1990s. She and Fang Caodi, as the narrator comments, are "representatives of that extremely difficult-to-describe Chinese style of idealism."[87] "She is willing to endure the greatest suffering, hardship and personal humiliation as long as it brings her closer to the truth."[88] Although born into an orthodox "revolutionary" family and growing up nurtured on the Communist "wolf milk," she sees the true face of the Party-state and all its propaganda when she works as a secretary for a local court. Shocked and horrified by the unbelievable arbitrariness and inhumanity of the Chinese system of "justice," she quickly quits her job. She then opens a small restaurant with her mother, which becomes a salon for liberal intellectuals in the 1980s and the late 1990s, a few years after Tiananmen. In the process of interacting with those intellectuals, she also becomes "an obscure but genuine public intellectual."[89]

After the advent of the twenty-first century, when the overwhelming majority of Chinese intellectuals had been bought into the system, enjoying their newly gained wealth, privilege, and fame with satisfaction, Little Xi continues her resistance:

> In the last two years, though, when the intellectuals appeased the government or were "harmonized" away, Little Xi rose up in opposition and threw herself into solitary combat. Without a backward glance, she argued strongly for truth and justice, expressing her opinions on the Internet.[90]

Based on her observation of the life experiences of Little Xi, Fang Caodi, and a few others, Chaohua Wang concludes that a "focus" of the novel "is on the solitary battles fought by our relatively isolated protagonists to retain the possibility of serious intellectual engagement in public life, including, but not limited to, being truthful about collective history."[91]

In a country where almost everyone is intoxicated with the feeling of happiness and complacency, it is only natural that someone like Little Xi suffers frustration, loneliness, and depression in her solitary combat. Considered a threat to the Party-state, she is put under surveillance and suffers persecution. What makes her desperate is that she finds her only son is the very person who masterminds the conspiracies and dirty tricks against her. As a result, she loses trust in everyone, except for her mother. She is seized by the feeling of alienation, anxiety, and loneliness. She is so disappointed with the world, where almost everyone tells lies, that she finds life itself is no longer worth cherishing. As she confesses to Old Chen, "I don't have anyone to talk to. I feel like there are fewer and fewer people like us ... [T]here are so few of us left that life hardly seems worth living."[92] In order to evade surveillance and persecution, she is forced to drift about all her life, becoming a stranger in her own country. Little Xi's feeling epitomizes the desperate inner world of a conscientious individual under a dictatorial regime.

A country where historical truth is covered up or distorted, and where its people suffer either mental distortion or spiritual agony, is inevitably an abnormal and absurd world, where everything is upside down. As Little Dong, one of Old Chen's close female friends, complains, "today, a normal person doesn't remember ... [T]hose of us who remember are the abnormal ones."[93] Here people lose trust in each other and are "wary" of each other.[94] The fact that Miaomiao, originally a conscientious and brave journalist dedicated to exposing the corruption of the bureaucracy and the cruelty of the society, is forced to resign from her post and finally becomes insane serves the best to illustrate the absurdity and abnormity of the society. The tenuous love story between Old Chen and Little Xi and the oppression of the church also prove that the dictatorship of the Party-state is the sole source of the people's unhappiness and of the spiritual crisis suffered by the entire nation.

"Fascism? We Are Only in Its Early Stages!"

Apart from exposing the darkness of the Chinese model and tracing the reasons for the enormous social injustice, historical manipulation, collective amnesia, and mental distortion in China, the novel also raises serious philosophical questions regarding the Chinese model. Given that the darkness of the Chinese model has already been explored by authors of anticorruption fiction, officialdom fiction, and some other genres, the philosophical questioning of the Chinese model can be regarded as the most original contribution the novel has made to Chinese literature and thought.

Chan Koonchung conducts his questioning mainly in the final section of the novel, which is composed almost exclusively of the "national leader" He Dongsheng's explanation about the truth of the "lost" month and his analysis of China's domestic and international policies and their underlying principles. One question targets the morality and political legitimacy of the regime's rule in China. As He confesses, in order to carry out its grand economic rescue plan, the Party-state adopts Machiavellian-style strategies to rule the country and treats its people as an uncivilized and irrational mob in the Hobbesian sense. According to He's account, at the beginning of the "lost" month, when the news of economic recession in Western countries came to China, the regime deliberately held back, watching the country gradually plunge into chaos without taking any action. Moreover, the regime even encouraged and fanned rumours about the Western economic recession and the upcoming calamity in China to evoke panic and terror in the country. The government deliberately did nothing so as to create anarchy and chaos in the country, because they believed that "the people fear chaos more than they fear dictatorship"[95] and that "only a major crisis would induce the Chinese people to accept willingly a huge government dictatorship."[96] Clearly, the regime did not really care about the people's interests; its only concern was power – how to continue its dictatorship. "The machinery of state was waiting for the people of the entire nation once again to voluntarily and wholeheartedly give themselves into the care of the Leviathan."[97] The regime deliberately "terrorizes" its people to accentuate its significance for the country and to underscore its political legitimacy. According to He, the ability to maintain social stability is considered by the Party-state to be a major source of political legitimacy for its rule in the country.

Right at the brink of complete anarchy across the country, the Party-state, taking advantage of people's panic and fear of chaos and their desire for order and peace, sent out armies to control first the country's big cities and then the entire country. In order to establish absolute authority and power over the people, the regime carried out another "crackdown campaign," which once again claimed countless innocent lives and brought new bloodshed and injustice to China. Fang Caodi, as mentioned earlier, was almost executed in the crackdown merely for having an American passport. Finally, the entire country was silenced and tamed by terror. Then the government used its dictatorship to forcefully implement a set of five new policies, many of which violated people's freedom and rights, to create an economic "miracle" in the nation. It turns out that the Chinese "golden age" was actually achieved by cunning, deception, bloodshed, and terror, which is the very reason the Party-state works so painstakingly to try to erase this truth from the records of history and from people's memory.

Here several questions naturally arise: Is it morally and politically legitimate for a state, which claims to be founded on "people's sovereignty" or "people's democracy," to treat its people merely as slaves or a mob in the Hobbesian sense? Is a political system normal and sound if it values merely economic success and national interests while ignoring human rights and individual freedom? Also, as presented in the novel and seen in real life, the success of the Chinese miracle is achieved through preying on the underprivileged and the poor – the working class and the peasants, which are the nation's leading classes according to the country's constitution – and through heavy pollution of soil, water, and air. Is it then morally and politically legitimate if the economic boom benefits only the state machine and a minority of the privileged while victimizing the majority of the underprivileged and future generations?

Another question raised in the novel concerns international relations. As He Dongsheng explains, the Chinese government adopts sheer utilitarianism, vulgar materialism, and the notion of the absolute superiority of the Chinese nation over others as its guiding principles with regard to international relations. When the Chinese government deals with African countries, for example, it is only interested in those countries' natural resources; it never cares about whether those countries' governments commit genocide or violate human rights; nor does it care about local people's interests or those countries' environments. Fang Caodi's personal experiences testify to this mindset:

When Chinese enterprises worked on major infrastructure projects in Africa, they hired only Chinese workers; they did not employ local workers and didn't help reduce the high levels of local unemployment. Cheap Chinese products flooded the African markets and ruined those few manufacturing industries still in existence there. The Chinese were no different from the former European colonists. They colluded with corrupt local ruling elite to exploit Africa's natural resources, and they didn't help the African people with any long-lasting economic development that could be of genuine assistance.[98]

What is presented in the novel has been proved by journalistic investigations. In an article for *New York Times*, Brook Larmer takes as an example China's involvement in the economy of Namibia, one of the poor yet resource-rich African countries. He provides a detailed account and an incisive analysis of how the Chinese government and

Chinese companies, driven by both economic and political purposes, do business in the country at the cost of the soundness of the country's political system, its people's welfare, and the environment. Even worse, the Chinese also committed many crimes in the country. According to Larmer's description, in many Namibians' eyes, what the Chinese are doing to the country is no more than a "new form of colonialism":

> China's no-strings financing ... unlike Western aid, is not conditional on such fine points: human rights, clean government, or fiscal restraint ... For some Namibians, however, the flood of Chinese loans and investments doesn't look so much like freedom as it does a new form of colonialism. The infrastructure is welcome, but as projects made possible by loans – financed by the Chinese – they have saddled the economy with debt and done little to alleviate the nearly 30 percent unemployment rate. Over the last few months, moreover, a series of scandals involving Chinese nationals – including tax evasion, money-laundering, and poaching endangered wildlife – has soured locals on a foreign presence that can seem largely extractive: pulling uranium, timber, rhino horns, and profits out the country without benefiting a population that, because of apartheid's legacy, ranks among the most unequal economically in the world.[99]

Given what Chinese businessmen and officials have done to their own people, their own land, and their own environment, it can be imagined how they would treat other countries. It is common knowledge that discourses of anti-imperialism and anti-colonialism are a crucial part of Chinese Communist ideology to justify Communist rule in China, and they constitute an important source for the moral superiority and political legitimacy of the Chinese Party-state.[100] Naturally, a truly serious question emerges. If a party-state that bases its moral superiority and political legitimacy on discourses of anti-imperialism and anti-colonialism behaves exactly like the old imperialists and colonialists, perhaps even worse in some ways, how can it maintain the credibility of its ideology and the source of its moral superiority and political legitimacy?

Towards the end of the novel, there is a highly meaningful scene. When the truth-seekers accuse the Chinese regime of implementing fascism and using the powerful state machine and national resources to suppress its people, He Dongsheng, to their great surprise, does not deny it at all; instead, he calmly affirms it as truth. He tells his captors that, both in the Party and in society, "real fascism already has a firm hold in China."[101] As mentioned earlier, he considers the "iron-blooded loyal braves" fascists. He further explains: "Even if we are fascist . . . we are only in the early stages of fascism now. You still haven't tasted the full flavor of violent fascist despotism."[102] He suggests that "the Chinese-style fascist dictatorship made up of a combination of collective nationalism, populism, statism and Chinese traditionalism" could be upgraded to a much more advanced form, and as such it would be much more horrible.[103] He also indicates that, if the few Party leaders who harbour "true fascist ambitions" come to power, "not only China but the whole world would be in for terrible trouble."[104] At this point, we reach the most profound question posed by the author through his presentation of the Chinese model. What are the consequences if a superpower is completely out of its people's control? In some sense, all the presentations in the entire novel can be said to target this one single question.

This question is certainly not a pseudo or fantastic one. It is a very realistic issue, given how more and more people all around the world eulogize the Chinese model. An article in *Christian Science Monitor*, for example, claims that, in the twenty-first century, competition between political systems will take the form of "consumer democracy against capable governance with too little democratic accountability."[105] In some ways, the parallel of democracy and the dictatorial yet "capable" system itself can be construed as an affirmation of the latter. In light of this mode of thinking, democracy – the system that puts people's basic rights and interests at the centre of political life – would not matter in the social life of humanity. The only thing that matters will be the "capability" of a government. In the novel, the "national leader" He Dongsheng identifies the ability to "accomplish big things that democratic systems are unable to accomplish" as the paramount advantage and the most important source of political legitimacy for the "Chinese model of one-party rule."[106]

What kind of "big things" is an almighty government capable of doing? Countless historical facts have shown that a powerful modern nation-state, if out of its people's control, as Zygmunt Bauman's study of modernity and the Holocaust convincingly demonstrates, is often capable of doing "such big things" as "triggering acts of social cannibalism on an undreamed-of scale."[107] According to Bauman, the Holocaust reveals the potential of a powerful, centralized state to perpetrate crimes unimaginable in the past, with all its tremendous "capability" of ideation, of transforming its ideology into practical policy, and of commanding a "huge, efficient bureaucratic apparatus."[108] In other words, a modern nation-state could become a formidable destructive force if it is out of its people's control. The root cause is the universally worshipped notion of the absolute superiority of the nation-state in modern times. As George M. Kren and Leon Rappoport point out, "within certain limits set by political and military power considerations, the modern state may do anything it wishes to those under its control. There is no moral-ethical limit which the state cannot transcend if it wishes to do so, because there is no moral-ethical power higher than the state."[109] The absolute authority possessed by the nation-state, with the support of modern technologies, makes it very easy to shirk off all the checks intended to confine it and to slip into totalitarianism, a system that, according to Hannah Arendt, is more horrible than ancient tyranny.[110] This perception is especially true in a country like China, where the Party-state has absolute power over its people and regards the survival of the regime to be its paramount goal. In this sense, the novel can be read as an apocalyptic allegory of both the Chinese model and a modern nation-state out of its people's control.

Summary

The first Orwellian-style Chinese political novel, *The Fat Years*, which has changed the way that Chinese define political fiction, is a groundbreaking work. It presents a truly critical and in-depth reflection on the Chinese model of development, especially concerning the real and potential negative consequences that it could bring about.

The novel first can be read, from a sociopolitical perspective, as a realistic presentation of the shocking darkness behind the dazzling economic miracle created by the Chinese model. As presented in the novel and seen in reality as well, the predation of the underprivileged majority by the tiny minority of people who hold political power, the rise of varied interest groups and their collusion with the state power, and the nationwide corruption and abuse of power on the part of the massive bureaucracy are among the most serious problems facing today's China. The novel also proposes that China's younger generations suffer from the consequences of collective amnesia and the historical distortion imposed by the Party-state. In tracing the reasons for the amnesia and historical distortion, apart from pointing the finger at the Party for its deceptive propaganda and manipulation of historical truth, the author also criticizes Chinese intellectuals for abandoning their role as a "social conscience" and their critical spirit, and ordinary Chinese people for their acquiescence and indifference before the state machine.

The novel can also be read, from a philosophical perspective, as an allegory of the modern nation-state. Taking China as a case study, by questioning the morality and political legitimacy of the Chinese model of development, the novel is intended to lead us to the potential catastrophes that a modern nation-state may bring about if it is out of its people's control. In this sense, this novel also represents a philosophical reflection on the fundamental principle of the modern nation-state and a warning against blind belief in its absolute superiority.

The novel displays profound continuities in motif and theme with other novels under consideration. It shares with *Such Is This World*, for example, the theme of exposing the collective amnesia imposed upon the Chinese people by the dictatorial Party-state, the division of the Chinese intelligentsia after Tiananmen, and the moral depravity of Chinese intellectuals under the lure of the Party's rewards. Like *Lenin's Kisses*, this novel also targets the cruelty and absurdity behind the Chinese economic "miracle" and points to its disastrous consequences and unsustainable future. It also joins *Wolf Totem* in presenting and reflecting on the fascist tendency, nurtured on extreme nationalist and social Darwinist propaganda, which exists in politics, society, and the people's minds in contemporary China. Unlike Jiang Rong, who holds a basically positive attitude towards this fascist tendency based on his extreme nationalist mindset, Chan Koonchung shows his unambiguous condemnation of the trend towards fascism through his depiction of the devastating consequences it would bring to both the Chinese nation and the entire world.

Chapter Six

The Seventh Day: Dystopian Wasteland versus Modern Peach Blossom Spring

In contemporary Chinese literary circles, few writers are more concerned with the miserable life of ordinary Chinese people under Communist domination than Yu Hua. His novel *The Seventh Day* represents his evolving effort on this theme. Yu Hua authored four full-length novels before the publication of *The Seventh Day*. In all those novels, depiction of the unbearable misery and suffering inflicted upon ordinary Chinese people by the inhumane Communist regime is the dominant theme.[1] *The Seventh Day* inherits the legacy of critical realism and the "sweeping historical vision" of these novels,[2] but transcends them by incorporating a utopian dimension and symbolic and allegorical elements, and consequently elevates his critical reflection on the Chinese model to a higher, philosophical level. The novel not only exposes the enormous social injustice, spiritual bankruptcy, and all-round moral depravity in today's China with journalistic immediacy and accuracy but also paints an intoxicating picture of an ideal society full of justice, love, and happiness, which represents Yu Hua's vision of the path that China should take.

The Seventh Day is narrated by a newly dead man named Yang Fei, who falls all the way from a company section head to a wretched person in the human world, recounting his experience in the afterworld during the first seven days following his death. The surrealistic technique allows him to see two totally different worlds: the world of the living and the world of the dead. The two worlds make a sharp contrast on both "the level of surface manifestation" and "the deeper narrative level."[3] The discursive profundity and artistic originality of the novel lie mainly in the contrast between the two worlds. Whereas the human world epitomizes today's China, seized by the bloody predation of the underprivileged by the privileged, the cover-up of truth by the state, the destruction of positive human relations and feelings, and the callous indifference towards others' suffering among people, the world of the dead symbolizes a utopia, an imaginary world of natural beauty, equality, justice, and love, where people are free of oppression, exploitation, and the shackle of desires, enjoying dignity and happiness. Most importantly, in this beautiful utopia, all truth that was covered up in the bleak human world comes to light, and justice reigns. What makes the structure of the novel especially original and the thought of the novel especially provocative is that the beautiful utopian world is built exactly of the qualities and values that are absent, lost, or destroyed in the human world: truth, justice, mutual understanding and care, love, and happiness. As such, the creation of the dreamland itself constitutes a fierce criticism of a materialistic, soulless China, which has turned into a moral and spiritual wasteland under political dictatorship, state predation, and stark hedonism. By demonstrating that the Chinese model of development destroys the inner world of the Chinese people and brings spiritual bankruptcy to the nation, the novel questions the morality and political legitimacy of the Chinese model.

Bloody Predation and Deceptive Propaganda

The primitive accumulation of capital in the West was a history of blood and tears, but it is not necessarily more bloody and horrifying than the "Chinese model of development" in the post-Mao era. Due to the absence of the rule of law and the deprivation of people's right of political participation by the regime, the predation on the underprivileged by local governments in collusion with interest groups in the Chinese-style crony capitalism proceeds in an extremely brutal and frenzied way. In *The Seventh Day*, through the stories of Yang Fei and those related to him, almost all of whom struggle at the bottom of society leading miserable lives, Yu Hua provides a panorama of today's China with all its cruelty and absurdity. His exposure of the bloody and predatory nature of the Chinese model centres mainly on "forced demolition," the "mouse tribe," and abuse of power on the part of government officials – some hallmark social phenomena in post-Mao China highly illuminative of the nature of the Chinese model.

In a country where the government monopolizes almost all the land, capital, and other important resources, it is only natural that the real estate industry becomes a field where state predation is performed in an extremely cruel and unrestrained way. As a result, forced demolition, along with many other incredibly brutal forms of destroying ordinary people's properties and seizing their land with violence, almost becomes an everyday scene in post-Mao China, especially during the early stage of the Chinese-style market economy. Yu Hua devotes a whole chapter to dealing with this phenomenon. The Chinese-style forced demolition, as presented in the novel and commonly seen in real life, is performed in many horrible and shocking ways. Some people find their houses gone after they come back from shopping at grocery stores.[4] Others even go through "terror" in the process, as evidenced by the experience of a family one night "when they were woken from sleep by huge blasts, their house swaying back and forth as though in an earthquake; only when they rushed out in panic did they see bulldozers and excavators destroying their housing complex."[5] The experience of two young lovers is even more shocking. One night, right in the process of their lovemaking, several fierce-looking men suddenly break into their house, tie them up inside their comforter, and throw them into a vehicle waiting outside. The car drives around the city the whole night. Only at dawn does the car return them to their place of departure, and only then do they find that their house has already been flattened. The couple are so horrified by the experience that they break up immediately, with the man losing his sexual ability permanently.[6] The most tragic and horrifying story of forced demolition presented in the novel is a married couple who are buried alive in the rubble when their house is destroyed while they are sleeping, leaving their young daughter alone in the world. It happens in the early morning, when the couple, who are both ordinary workers, have just come back home after getting off the night shift. After sending their daughter to school, they go to bed and fall asleep. "In their dreams, they heard a loudspeaker outside delivering one warning after another, but they were just too tired to wake up properly ... They were shaken awake only when the building began to sway violently amid clamorous din."[7] They try to escape, but it is too late, and both of them are buried alive in the rubble. These stories presented here are merely a few examples of countless cases of forced demolition that occurred in real life during the making of the Chinese economic "miracle," most of which are actually more bloody and shocking than portrayed here.[8]

Another social phenomenon featured in great detail in the novel is the life of the so-called "mouse tribe" (*shuzu* 鼠族). Like forced demolition, the emergence of the population collectively dubbed "mouse tribe" or "ant tribe" (*yizu* 蚁族) is also a signature social event highly indicative of the nature and consequences of the Chinese model. As in many countries during their modernization, the Chinese "economic miracle" in the post-Mao era also proceeds along with rapid urbanization and large-scale migration of the population. Being forced – or choosing, in some cases – to leave their rural homeland, those unfortunate peasants have to drift about in the city to make a living there. As mentioned in chapter 1, due to the many discriminatory policies issued by the city governments, these rural migrants become second-class city residents. Unfortunately, vast numbers of peasants are not the only victims of the "Chinese miracle." There are a large number of urban residents who, prey to the incredibly high house prices, unemployment, unaffordable medical, educational expenses, and so on, also join the ranks of the downtrodden. Undoubtedly, almost all members of the "mouse tribe" in big cities are those wretched people who come either from the countryside or from small cities. These second-class residents struggle on the margins of big cities, doing the hardest, most dangerous, and worst paid jobs, suffering all kinds of discrimination, bullying, and humiliation. They usually live in large groups in basements or underground accommodation complexes converted from abandoned air-raid shelters built in the Mao era, separated from their neighbours only by pieces of cloth. They are called the "mouse tribe" or "ant tribe" because they, like those petty animals, emerge from their "caves" to toil for food in the daytime and return to their "caves" only for sleep at night, not knowing where the next meal will come from and having no hope and no future. This portrayal is an honest and naturalistic depiction of the lives and fate of the people who struggle for a living on the margins of the city.

In the novel, the story of Mouse Girl and her boyfriend, Wu Chao, epitomizes the life of the "mouse tribe." Like all other people of this group, they both leave their hometowns to make a living in a big city. They first work as hairwashers at a salon and then as servers at a restaurant. They both work very hard, dreaming that one day they would own a small business. The young man is very smart and talented; at both places, his work is highly praised by the managers, and he has opportunities for promotion. But each time, his hope is shattered. If his failure in the first job is mainly due to personal reasons, the second occasion is strong evidence of class discrimination and social injustice. After quitting the salon jobs, they begin to work in a restaurant. While the young man serves the large dining room downstairs and is shortly promoted to captain, the girl works in an upstairs private room serving mainly businessmen and government officials. One day this pretty girl is sexually assaulted by a bunch of drunken guests. Refusing to accept the abuse and humiliation of his girlfriend, the outraged young man barges into the room and starts a fight with them. Outnumbered, he ends up being badly beaten, with his face "covered in blood."[9] Even though they are the victims of bullying, the manager does not stand up for them; instead, he curses them for offending the privileged guests and fires them. Given how these two humble country people struggle helplessly in a highly discriminative and hostile urban environment, the outcome is predictable. After the two short-lived, failed work experiences, they have difficulty finding jobs. They are in such an impoverished condition that sometimes they have to beg for food in the street. After experiencing poverty, humiliation, and discrimination, both of them eventually end their young lives in tragic ways. Mouse Girl takes her own life by jumping off the highest building in the city, due to the feeling of being deceived by her boyfriend (who had given her a knock-off iPhone as a birthday gift but claimed it was a real one). The young man dies from infection in a medical operation performed by a veterinary surgeon to cut out one of his kidneys, which he has sold through an underground channel for money to buy a burial space for Mouse Girl. Both their lives and deaths turn out to be tragedies: this story is an epitome of the real living conditions of a vast underclass within the Chinese model.

While in the events of forced demolition and the "mouse tribe" the predatory, dictatorial political power functions merely as an evil "invisible hand" behind all those atrocities and tragedies, in other cases it emerges from the background and looms large, revealing itself explicitly as the major cause for the victimization of the underprivileged in contemporary China. The novel depicts several cases that demonstrate how abuse of power perpetrated by corrupt government apparatuses and officials turns predation on ordinary people into an everyday routine, ruining people's happiness and lives, and producing countless tragedies in the country. The Tan Family Eatery is an example of the victimization of ordinary people by official corruption and state predation. The small restaurant, run by a man named Tan Jiaxin and his family, is very popular. Given that "there was a regular flow of customers and business seemed to be booming" in the restaurant,[10] the narrator assumes that they must make good money. He is surprised to learn that the restaurant actually does not make any money at all, because their "expenditures exceeded their income."[11] It turns out that many government officials from varied departments, including public security, emergency services, sanitation, and the commerce and tax bureau, "regularly come and eat extravagant meals" but pay little or nothing.[12] Those corrupt officials also make up all kinds of excuses to extort the Tans.[13] Despite their strong indignation, Tan Jiaxin and his family have to keep silent, because they understand very well that, for ordinary Chinese, "nobody dares to offend government people."[14] This knowledge is why Tan always looks worried and depressed. The hard work of this family not only does not bring them wealth and happiness but instead pushes them into debt, which demonstrates very clearly how unchecked public power can prey on ordinary people.

Whereas the nightmarish experience of the Tan Family Eatery exposes how a government that claims to represent the interests of the people actually turns into an exploitive apparatus in the hands of its corrupt agents, two other cases illuminate how a legal system, which is attached to and controlled by the state machine, degenerates into a source of injustice itself. The first story concerns a young male who is arrested by the police for disguising as a woman and working as a prostitute. In the process of interrogation, a policeman deliberately kicks him in his groin and crushes his testicles. After being released from police custody, he spends the following three years protesting the abuse and seeking justice. But all his protests and petitions end in vain. In complete despair, he decides to take justice into his own hands. The story ends with the man sneaking into the police station, killing the policeman and heavily injuring three others with a long knife. He is executed for the crime six months later.

The other story is about a man who is wrongly executed for a murder that he did not commit. The story is very simple. A man marries a woman who has mental problems. One day the woman suddenly disappears. Coincidently, a few days later, the police find an "already decomposed and unrecognizable" female corpse that is similar to the missing woman in height.[15] With the assistance of modern human identification technologies, it would not be hard to determine whether it is the woman or not. But the police do not bother to carry out any investigations, because they, like the woman's family, are "convinced" that the man killed his wife.[16] So they arrest the man and torture him to force a confession. The victim himself relates:

> The police strung me up and beat me, insisting I confess, beating me till I was shitting and pissing in my pants. My hands were tied tightly for two whole days and four of my fingers went black – I'd never be able to use them again, I was told. Later, they strung me up by my feet instead, with my head pointing down ... I thought I'd be better off dead, so I admitted the crime.[17]

Convicted by his own "confession," he is subsequently executed. No one, except his family, cares whether he was wronged or not, until six months later his missing wife suddenly returns home. But it is too late. The government gives his family 500,000 yuan as compensation; but there are no apologies to him and his family or punishment of the policemen for their crime – that is the ultimate outcome of this unbelievable tragedy. The horrible experiences of these ordinary Chinese people in both cases demonstrate very clearly how far the abuse of power by an unaccountable government can go and how terrible its consequences can be.

All these events distress us, indeed, but more distressing is the cover-up by the state machine. Exposure of the cover-up of truth by the Party-state and the mass media it controls constitutes a pronounced motif running through the novel. At the very beginning of the novel, Yu Hua paints a bleak and eerie picture of a "barren and murky" city shrouded in a "thick fog," where the boundaries between day and night, morning and evening are erased.[18] Amid the murky figures and ghostly buildings come "the sounds of collapsing masonry – one huge crash after another" – and "cars crashing into each other."[19] This gloomy picture not only serves to reflect the heavy pollution and environmental crisis facing today's China but also, and more importantly, symbolizes the sociopolitical reality under a one-Party dictatorship, where all the darkness, ugliness, and absurdity in society are covered up with a veil of deceptive and distorted propaganda. In the novel, Yu Hua provides plenty of vivid accounts revealing how the Chinese state machine, along with the media and the intellectuals, who are reduced to propaganda tools for the Party, painstakingly covers up the wrongdoings and evils committed by the government.

As mentioned earlier, there are many notorious cases of horrifying forced demolitions. Outraged by the extreme brutality and greed of the real estate companies and the local government, victims of forced demolitions and their supporters organize a peaceful protest on the square in front of the city government headquarters. The government, however, instead of responding to these protesters' appeal and bringing justice to them, dispatches a group of people to the square, who disguise themselves as protesters, smash the glass windows of the government buildings, and provoke violence among the crowd, creating an excuse for the police to suppress the protest. After the end of the brazen suppression, the government holds a conference, denouncing the protest as a social disturbance created by "a small group of troublemakers."[20] At the conference, the spokesman for the city government "strenuously denies" the story of a couple being buried in the rubble during the demolitions as pure rumour and declares that those responsible for fabricating it are now in custody.[21]

Surprisingly, yet understandably in the Chinese context, the media and the intellectuals, faced with the government's shameless acts, do not stand up for the truth but instead sheepishly submit to the oppressive state machine. Echoing the government's claims, they provide utterly distorted and deceptive coverage of the event to demonize the victims in order to justify and glorify the government. As a consequence, the just and peaceful protest is portrayed by the state-controlled propaganda machine as a violent social disturbance and the victims as troublemakers deserving only condemnation:

> A female reporter was interviewing some people in the street, who all expressed outrage at the reckless behavior of those who had vandalized the government headquarters. Then a professor appeared on the screen ... He talked with slick fluency, first condemning the violence that afternoon, then emphasizing how the people needed to trust and understand and support the government.[22]

Here the truth is turned upside down; right and wrong are confused, clearly and explicitly exposing the shameless face of the media and the intellectuals and their despicable role as accomplices of the government.

In the novel, the cover-up of forced demolitions and of people's protest is not an isolated case. There are many other moments in the novel revealing how the government, in collusion with the media, produces false reports on events regarding life-and-death issues of ordinary people. For example, just as they lie about the tragic death of the couple buried alive in the rubble during a forced demolition, the government and the media also conceal from the public the real number of casualties of a deadly fire accident. They also trample on the dignity of humanity by treating dead babies as trash, and then make every effort to hide this atrocious scandal. Just as the city is always shrouded in a murky fog, the truth of all important social events is covered up in the human world.

Destruction of Sanctified Human Feelings

In addition to exposing the predatory and bloody nature of the Chinese model and the cover-up of truth by the Party-state and the media, the novel also examines the noxious impact of the Chinese model of development upon the spiritual world of the Chinese people. In fact, reflection on the enormous, irreparable damage that this model of development does to the spiritual life of the nation is the most significant contribution that the novel makes to contemporary Chinese literature and thought.

According to Yu Hua, one of the most disastrous consequences that the Chinese model of development has brought to society is that state predation works together with vulgar materialism to destroy positive human relations and feelings, turning the country into a heartless and soulless place. Here it is worth noting that Yu Hua's exposure of the destruction of positive human relations and feelings by the Chinese model does not proceed in a direct way. He takes a detour by first accentuating the precious and crucial role that secular human feelings play in Chinese society and then showing the inevitable destruction of these positive human feelings in a cold and hopeless society. In this way, the sickness and absurdity of the society and the disastrous impact of the developmental model upon the spiritual world are projected.

In the novel, Yu Hua portrays three main types of positive human relations: familial affection, as exemplified by the relationship between Yang Fei and his adoptive father Yang Jinbiao; romantic love, as represented by the relationship between Mouse Girl and her boyfriend Wu Chao, and between Yang Fei and his ex-wife Li Qing; and communal care and support, as indicated by the lifelong friendship between Yang Jinbiao and his fellow worker and neighbour Hao Qiangsheng and his wife Li Yuezhen. These human relations and secular feelings are portrayed as so sublime that they seem to be endowed with religious solemnity. For many of the characters in the novel, maintaining and fostering the most cherished human relations and feelings is the ultimate goal and meaning of life, and some even die for it. Yang Jinbiao's life experiences illustrate most clearly the sanctified nature of human relations in Chinese society.

Yang is a switchman working for the state railway department. One night at work, the twenty-one-year-old man suddenly hears a few feeble sobs between two rails; he moves quickly enough to rescue the crying baby before a train races past with a deafening roar. Refusing to send the baby boy away, he raises him single-handedly under extremely difficult conditions. This event is how the unmarried and inexperienced young man suddenly becomes a father. Having a little boy with him, which is considered a huge burden by many girls, he has difficulty finding a girlfriend. However, due to the unwavering matchmaking effort by warm-hearted Li Yuezhen, he finally dates a girl and falls in love with her. The girl seems also to love him and agrees to marry him under the condition that he give up the boy and send him to an orphanage. After a long time of hesitation and painful inner struggle, the young man, though extremely reluctant, decides to surrender to his girlfriend's will. He takes a morning train with his son to a nearby city, puts the four-year-old boy on the smooth surface of a big rock by the side of a place that he thinks is an orphanage but is actually a kindergarten, and then goes home. He goes to the marriage registry office with his girlfriend the next day. Right before they are granted the marriage certificates, the young man, tortured by the feeling of unbearable sin, suddenly changes his mind and decides to give up this romantic love. He rushes back by train to the city where he left his son behind the day before, and takes the boy home. This decision changes his entire life forever. After that, as the son testifies, "my father simply devoted himself to raising me, without entertaining any further romantic aspirations. I was his everything."[23] The term "devoted" and the statement that the son is "everything" to the father explicitly demonstrate the quasi-religious nature of the fatherly affection. The sanctity of the father's love for his son is made even clearer later: the father remains unmarried all his life for the sake of his son, and he spends the last moment in his life by the very rock where he once left the boy behind, repenting his "sin" of thinking to abandon his son.

In the novel, many other characters also show quasi-religious devotion and self-sacrifice for love, be it familial or romantic. Yang Fei, raised by his selfless adoptive father, repays his father with equally deep love and self-sacrifice. In order to cure his fatally ill father, he sells their house to cover his father's medical expenses and quits his well-paid job to take care of his father. He devotes almost everything he has to saving his father's life. After his dying father leaves home in order to release him from the huge burden, he never gives up the effort to look for him. He continues his search in the afterworld and eventually succeeds. By virtue of both realistic and surrealistic literary techniques, the quasi-religious nature of Yang Fei's love for his father is made very clear here. Similar to his affection for his father, Yang's love for his ex-wife also reveals a strong sanctity. Though it is his ex-wife who betrays and divorces him, Yang does not hate her and still loves her deeply, even after their divorce. He maintains his loyalty to her and never touches any other woman for the rest of his life. Even his death is directly related to his love for her. He is so absorbed in reading a story in a local newspaper reporting her dramatic life and tragic death that he completely ignores the lethal fire that eventually devours him. Mouse Girl and her boyfriend Wu Chao, despite their frequent quarrels caused by their dire living conditions, treat love with a quasi-religious faith. Mouse Girl commits suicide because she feels deceived and betrayed by her loved one, which conversely proves how deeply she cares about his feelings for her. Wu Chao, in turn, dies for her when he sells a kidney through illegal channels for money to buy a burial plot for her and gets infected with a fatal disease. For all these characters, love seems not merely a secular human feeling but also a faith, a quasi-religious belief, and death becomes a necessary rite or sacrifice to it. In the novel, the sanctified nature of secular human feelings is also heightened by the symbolic portrayal of Li Yuezhen, the woman who feeds baby Yang Fei with her breasts and treats him as her own son during her lifetime, who becomes the eternal mother for Yang and twenty-seven dead babies in the afterworld. Here it should be emphasized that Yu Hua's depiction of the sanctification of secular human feelings in Chinese society does not spring from his imagination; rather, it is compatible with the grand Chinese cultural tradition.[24]

From an intellectual perspective, what makes Yu Hua's treatment of human relations and feelings unique and provocative lies less in his sanctification of them than in his exposure of their tragic outcomes in a cold, hopeless society. Here three of Yu Hua's observations are especially thought-provoking. First, despite the selfless and sublime nature of all these positive human relations and feelings, as clearly demonstrated by the experience of the two Yangs and that of Mouse Girl and her boyfriend, they seem to bring more suffering than happiness to the characters in the human world. In the case of the two Yangs, whereas the father's selfless love for his son ruins his own potential marriage and his whole life, the son's love for and repayment to his father completely impoverish him and consequently destroy his future. In the case of Mouse Girl and Wu Chao, their deep love for each other only leads both of them to tragic deaths. Paradoxically and sadly, it seems that these positive human relations and feelings turn into weapons against the characters themselves. Second, despite the tremendous value and sanctity of these positive human relations and feelings, none of them is able to survive in society, and all of them come to a sudden and tragic end, caused by the characters' accidental death in almost all cases. By indicating that positive human relations and feelings bring only tragedy and harm to people and eventually are unable to survive in the society, Yu Hua subtly points the finger at the sickness and absurdity of the society itself. The logic is very simple: if positive human relations or human feelings are not able to survive in a society, it means that the society lacks the necessary soil and atmosphere for human goodness to grow; therefore there must be something wrong with the society. Third, by contrasting the goodness of human relations – mutual care, support, and friendliness among colleagues and neighbours – among the older generation (Yang Fei's father's generation) with the callous indifference and even hostility among the younger generation (Yang Fei's generation), the novel also draws a vague yet visible trajectory of the moral degradation in contemporary Chinese society.

The fact that the tragic death of most of his characters is closely related to poverty and social inequality serves to reinforce Yu Hua's perception that the sickness of the society is the root cause of the destruction of positive human values. Yang Jinbiao's life-and-death experience, for instance, is an explicit and powerful embodiment of social inequality. Although he works all his life for the national railway department, he receives little or no support from the state when he is in grave difficulties. During the last days in his life when he is fatally sick, he can rely on nobody but himself and his son for help. As mentioned earlier, in order to cover the medical expenses, they have to sell their house, and his son also has to quit his job to take care of him at the hospital. To release his son from the huge financial burden and to save his son's life and future, he chooses to leave home quietly and finally dies a miserable death in a foreign land. It is evident that the state's predatory policy – regarding people merely as working machines while providing little or no welfare and security for their health and old age – plays a crucial role in the tragedy of Yang Jinbiao's death.

Mouse Girl and her boyfriend are two other examples of the victimization of the underprivileged by poverty and social inequality. Mouse Girl dreams of having an iPhone, but she is simply unable to turn her dream into reality no matter how hard she works. To please her, her equally poor boyfriend gives her a knockoff iPhone as a birthday gift but claims it is a real one, which becomes the fuse leading to her eventual suicide. Her boyfriend Wu Chao's story projects the desperate condition of the underprivileged caused by social inequality even more explicitly: he has to trade his life for a burial place for Mouse Girl, which implies that the life of this underprivileged yet hardworking and resourceful young man is no more valuable than a tiny burial spot. In the novel, the most powerful and shocking evidence showing that the Chinese government tramples human values and human dignity is the way the state-owned hospital authorities treat twenty-seven dead babies: they refer to them as "medical refuse" and dump them into a river in the same way as they dispose of trash.[25] Through his vivid and impressive presentation of these tragic cases, Yu Hua drives home the message that Chinese society is seriously sick. Given that the Chinese Party-state still controls all the important aspects of Chinese society, Yu Hua's criticism of the Chinese system and the Chinese model becomes explicit.

In addition to the problems rooted in the system, Yu Hua believes that hedonism or vulgar materialism, a principle inherent in the Chinese Communist project, also constitutes a major cause of the erosion and destruction of beautiful human relations and feelings. In the case of Mouse Girl's tragedy, for instance, even though social inequality and social injustice are primarily responsible for her miserable life and death, she herself is also to blame. As mentioned earlier, the tragedy of

Mouse Girl and her boyfriend originates from her desire for an iPhone. Given their dire conditions (sometimes they do not even have enough food), that desire is obviously unrealistic and excessive. After discovering that the iPhone given to her by her boyfriend as a birthday gift is a knockoff, she becomes furious and desperate, which eventually leads to her suicide. Here the influence of vulgar materialism upon her mindset is obvious. This conclusion is also supported by her admiration of a girlfriend of hers who purchases all kinds of luxuries through working as a prostitute, and she even expresses the intention to become a prostitute herself. Obviously, pursuit of excessive material satisfaction becomes a fateful temptation for Mouse Girl.

Yang Fei's marriage with his ex-wife, Li Qing, ends for similar reasons. Although the couple love each other, have well-paid jobs, and live a comfortable life, the woman is not satisfied. A chance encounter with an ambitious young man, who has just come back to China from the United States with a PhD and a grand business blueprint, ignites the woman's desire for secular success and material satisfaction. After a period of consideration and hesitation, she finally makes her decision to break up with Yang and join the young man. Their company turns out to be very successful in the beginning, and the woman becomes a highly influential personage in the field of business, enjoying the enormous feeling of satisfaction brought to her by wealth and fame. Unfortunately, her time of glory and pride does not last. Years later, their company is investigated by the government for involvement in illegal activities and potential crimes. While her husband flees furtively, abandoning her, she eventually commits suicide in her bathroom. Obviously, in this woman's eyes, material success counts much more than love, though pursuit of wealth eventually leads her on a path to death. When examining Yang Fei's failed marriage with Li Qing, Li Yuezhen unambiguously blames the woman for the failure, as she is convinced that Li Qing is a "gold digger." Taking Li Qing as an example, she deplores the situation in today's China, where "you get more respect if you're a whore than if you're poor."[26] Here her comments actually point to the dominant influence of hedonism and vulgar materialism upon the mentality, morality, and behaviour of Chinese people.

To sum up, in the novel, Yu Hua identifies two factors – the sickness of Chinese society due to social inequality and social injustice caused by state predation; and the prevalence of vulgar materialism – as the major causes of the destruction of positive human relations and feelings. Because state predation and vulgar materialism are two defining features of the Chinese model, Yu Hua's presentation amounts to a fierce criticism of the Chinese model itself.

Banality of Evil: Callous Indifference and Moral Corruption

In the face of a society where positive human relations and feelings cannot survive, readers are bound to ask: What does this kind of society look like? If there are no good human relations and human feelings in it, then what can we find there? These are questions Yu Hua attempts to answer in the novel. In answering these questions, he portrays a despairing picture of the social reality of today's China.

After all positive human relations and feelings are destroyed, as presented in the novel, only a spiritual wasteland is left behind, where people, absorbed with their self-interests and the greed for material satisfaction, show no sympathy, no care, and no support for each other. They display callous indifference towards the suffering of others, except for their family and friends. Even their affection for their loved ones, however, as discussed in the previous section, seems excessive and somewhat distorted. To some extent, the excessiveness of the affection among family members and friends might serve as a psychological compensation for being treated with coldness by other people. More surprisingly, here people even tend to entertain themselves with the suffering of others. In the novel, three occasions demonstrate in an explicit way the moral callousness of Chinese society and the corruption of people's inner worlds.

The first moment is Mouse Girl's suicide. As mentioned earlier, Mouse Girl long dreams of having an iPhone. To please her, her boyfriend Wu Chao gives her a knockoff as a birthday gift but claims it is authentic. Later on, Mouse Girl finds out the truth. Considering Wu's gift-giving to be deceptive and disloyal, she gets extremely furious. She tries every possible means to summon her boyfriend, but in vain. It turns out that Wu's father has suddenly become seriously ill, and Wu has had to go back to the countryside and stays there to look after him. With the service of Wu's cell phone suspended due to his failure to pay the fees and without internet access in the backward countryside, Wu has no way to contact Mouse Girl. But Mouse Girl knows nothing about all these complications. Consumed by fury and despair, she announces online that she wants to die and makes public the time and place of her planned suicide.

Expectedly yet sadly, the news instantly creates a wave on the internet. Netizens respond to her plan with great enthusiasm. Among the massive "encouraging" responses, not even a single one tries to persuade her to give up the idea of suicide. Almost all of them provide "constructive" suggestions of how to carry out the suicide in a more "comfortable" and sensational way. And "two residents asked her not to die just outside their front door, for this would bring them bad luck."[27] After many rounds of discussion with the netizens, Mouse Girl finally decides to jump from the tallest building in the city, which would certainly make the event sensational enough. "This time no netizen opposed her plan – indeed, some praised this as an excellent choice, saying that before dying she could enjoy the stunning view."[28]

On the day of her scheduled suicide, while Mouse Girl is standing high up on the skyscraper facing death, "a huge crowd" gathers in front of the building to witness – or precisely, to enjoy – this spectacular moment. Though the glare of sunlight makes these spectators feel uncomfortable, they do not mind at all; they are "craning their necks and then lowering their heads and rubbing their eyes, before looking up once more" at the skyscraper. "Petty tradesmen and street vendors arrived on the scene, squeezing in and out among the throng," selling various kinds of commodities, "all knockoff versions of name brands." A very considerate vendor is selling sunglasses on the scene, which would help the spectators to "focus more intently on the tiny figure high up on the Pengfei Tower" and thus be able to enjoy the scene more comfortably.[29] Here, we do not discern even a trace of sympathy, care, or sorrow for the pitiful girl; instead, we witness a shocking and desperate scene, as we did in reading *Lenin's Kisses*, where the excited crowd turns a heart-breaking human tragedy into a carnival. From Mouse Girl's confession in the afterworld, we learn that she did not really want to jump from the tower; she took that extreme step just to force her boyfriend to show up. The cruelty and cold-heartedness of those spectators, displayed in their excitement and joy over her suicide, appear to have put her in complete despair and pushed her into the abyss of death.

The second occasion in the novel that reveals how people entertain themselves with the suffering of others occurs at Yang Fei's workplace. Li Qing, Yang's ex-wife and the prettiest woman in the company, has many suitors before she starts a relationship with Yang. One day an avid suitor suddenly kneels down before her and woos her, surrounded by a crowd of fellow workers, but is rejected coldly by the woman. Seeing this scene, all his co-workers simply cannot conceal their excitement and joy. "The next day the poor man didn't show up for work. The office rang with peals of laughter." His co-workers are so eager to enjoy his embarrassment and disgrace that "his absence was a disappointing moment, as though life suddenly had lost a lot of its interest."[30] The man quits his job that afternoon. Feeling too embarrassed to face his co-workers, he does not go to the office to collect his stuff. He places quite a few phone calls requesting one of them to collect his things and send them to him downstairs, but no one is willing to help. Finally,

Yang Fei lends him a hand. The callousness of his co-workers towards the pitiful man really surprises Yang and makes him feel chilly: "He had worked for the company for five years, but in the end his coworkers treated him no differently from a stranger in the street."[31] The excitement and joy continue in the office even after the poor man leaves:

> That day our office – all ten thousand square feet of it – was overflowing with cheerful spirits. I had been working there for a couple of years, and this was the first time I had seen so many people in such a good mood. They recalled the scene of him kneeling down on the floor and remembered other ridiculous things he had done in the past, such as how he had once been robbed when walking in a park.[32]

It is truly shocking to see that a man's misery – even his horrible experience of being robbed – becomes a source of joy for his fellow workers. As occurs in Mouse Girl's suicide, here once again we witness how people entertain themselves with another's suffering in a callous way.

The third moment in the novel illuminating the moral depravity of ordinary Chinese people is embodied by the behaviour of the parents of murdered policeman Zhang. After Zhang's death, his parents continuously demand that the government award him the title of "martyr," but their petition is repeatedly rejected. The couple does not quit. For over ten years, they keep fighting with the government on this matter, which causes the government a lot of trouble, especially on politically important occasions. To stop their petitioning, the government at first takes harsh, punitive measures, but all of them have little effect. Then the government changes its tactics. Instead of using suppressive means, it begins to adopt the strategy of buying them off. Afterward, on every politically sensitive occasion, rather than detaining or threatening the couple, the government sends people to escort them on sightseeing excursions all around the country. As a result, "every year, the parents ended up enjoying the kind of expense account tourism that only Party leaders normally get to enjoy."[33] The government is rumoured to have spent a million yuan on them for this purpose in the past ten years. Under the government's policy of buying them off, the couple's original intention to seek justice for their son eventually gives way to the satisfaction of their own disgraceful desires. This story is a plain example of moral depravity on the part of ordinary Chinese people. It is also solid evidence that the moral and spiritual crisis in today's China is not limited to officialdom but actually permeates every corner of the society. And it makes very clear that not only the ruling elites but also ordinary Chinese people are responsible for this grave, all-round national crisis.

To explain the callous indifference of Chinese people towards the suffering of others and the corruption of their hearts, Hannah Arendt's notion of the "banality of evil" provides us with a highly useful perspective,[34] though this concept itself seems "banal" because of its familiarity. Radically differing from the conventional view that the notorious Nazi war criminal Adolf Eichmann was a highly fanatic, intelligent, and ardent believer in fascism, Arendt insists that he was actually just an average, normal person and that his behaviour was motivated less by "grand" ideological beliefs than by secular considerations such as desire for promotion and pursuit of high social status. Rather than possessing original thought, according to Arendt, Eichmann is actually characterized by the extreme normalcy, mediocracy, and even "stupidity" of his thought and behaviour. It was his "banality" rather than his uniqueness that led him to horrendous evil. Amos Elon summarizes for Arendt:

> [Arendt] insisted that only good has any depth. Good can be radical; evil can never be radical, it can only be extreme, for it possesses neither depth nor any demonic dimension yet – and this is its horror! – it can spread like a fungus over the surface of the earth and lay waste the entire world. Evil comes from a failure to think. It defies thought for as soon as thought tries to engage itself with evil and examine the premises and principles from which it originates, it is frustrated because it finds nothing there. That is the banality of evil.[35]

Arendt's notion that evil generates from failure to think and from mundane motivations logically leads to the conclusion that ideological conformity and social homogeneity as a result of thought control and the effort to cater to the people's mundane desires cannot give rise to virtue in society; on the contrary, they provide a breeding ground for evil to grow and proliferate. All the three aforementioned occasions clearly demonstrate that the evil in people – entertaining themselves with others' suffering and the corruption of their hearts – stems from mundane considerations: the pursuit of stimuli and excitement, jealousy, or the attempt to gain petty advantages at the cost of the common good. The first two occasions, in which everyone in an excited crowd goes with the flow without even thinking of right and wrong, also testify to Arendt's insight that evil comes from the inability to think.

In the novel's search for causes of the severe moral depravity and spiritual crisis facing China today, the media are particularly singled out for criticism. This focus is only natural, given how crucial a role the media play in a modern society. In a sound society, the media are expected to construct a healthy public sphere for society, to keep people informed, and to speak to power; they are supposed to be a positive force in advocating for truth, justice, and fairness. In Communist China, however, the media as a whole are reduced to a mouthpiece for the Party-state, an accomplice of the regime in suppressing truth, justice, and freedom, though, as suggested in the novel and seen in real life, not all individual journalists lose their sense of morality and courage as truth-seekers and critics of power.

As presented in the novel, the media in China have been distorted into a pernicious force for generating and spreading moral depravity, a source of China's moral crisis, as many journalists lose their sympathy for the weak and the underprivileged as well as their sense of right and wrong. In the previous discussions, we have already mentioned how the media collude with the government to cover up the horrible truth of forced demolition. In their coverage of Mouse Girl's suicide, the media once again reveal their ugliness through their loss of the basic sense of right and wrong. Rather than taking Mouse Girl's suicide and the couple's misery as a case of social injustice to investigate its causes, the media engage in voyeurism, treating it as a juicy story of a failed love affair by focusing only on the details of the couple's personal history and even their most private matters. The media are certainly more interested in exhibiting and consuming the misery of the pitiful couple to entertain the apathetic masses than in seeking truth and justice for them, and there is not even a trace of sympathy and sorrow for the miserable couple that can be discerned in the coverage. The same thing happens in the media reports about the tragic story of Li, the male prostitute who killed the policeman Zhang Gang. Once again, the media show themselves to be a part of moral depravity in today's China. Instead of treating the story as a serious social event to investigate the causes and mechanisms of social injustice, the Chinese media are only interested in Li's body and the real or imagined sexual skills he employed to entertain other males. Once again, we witness the depravity and brazenness of the media: they are more eager to cater to readers' voyeurism than to seek truth and justice. In sum, lack of sympathy for the underprivileged, lack of conscience, morality, and courage as social critics and truth-seekers, and vulgarization of their mentality are some of the most serious symptoms revealing the corruption of the Chinese media.

Peach Blossom Spring: Utopia of Truth, Love, and Happiness

The construction of the utopia, the world of the dead, is the most brilliant and original part of the novel, both artistically and discursively. There are thus two worlds that exist in the novel: the human world and the world of the dead. Whereas the former represents present-day China, the latter stands for Yu Hua's vision of an ideal society. The two worlds constitute a sharp antithesis in many ways. Whereas the human world is dominated by predation, deception, callous indifference, and tragedy, the world of the dead is an enchanting place ruled by truth, love, care, and happiness – those positive qualities that are absent, lost, or destroyed in the human world. Ironically and paradoxically, whereas the world of the living is shrouded in a deathly atmosphere, the world of the dead is full of the vitality and hope of life. Obviously, Yu Hua builds a utopia based on the reality of today's China but moving in the opposite direction. As Yiju Huang, in her reading of the novel, incisively points out, "the land of the unburied evinces a utopian impulse, which must be understood in connection with the dystopian vision of the mundane world."[36] Through the contrast between the two worlds, Yu Hua elevates his presentation of the Chinese model from the level of phenomenal description to the level of philosophical reflection. By constructing a utopia composed of those essential values that are absent, lost, or destroyed in the human world, Yu Hua attempts to reflect on the fundamental problems of the Chinese model, not only on its specific flaws.

In the novel, the world of the dead, dubbed the "land of the unburied," is the homeland for those dead people who cannot afford burial spots. It is an unspoiled land of intoxicating natural beauty and freedom, where human beings and nature coexist peacefully and harmoniously, and where good prevails while evil is eradicated:

> Steams flowing, grass covering the ground, trees in luxuriant growth, with fruit hanging from their branches and heart-shaped leaves that fluttered to a heartbeat rhythm. And people – some fully fleshed, many just bones – were strolling at leisure, back and forth.
>
> The tree leaves there will beckon you, the rocks will smile to you, the river will greet you. There's no poverty here and no riches; there's no sorrow and pain; no grievances and no hate … Here everyone finds equality in death.[37]

In addition to all these beautiful phenomena, there is also eternal life here. Obviously, this beautiful, free, peaceful, and equal dreamland symbolizes an ideal society.

This land of the dead differs fundamentally from the human world in every aspect. The first thing that makes this new land appealing is the recovery of truth. The truth of things covered up by the deceptive state propaganda machine in the world of the living comes to light here. In this dreamland, those significant events whose nature is completely distorted or falsified in the human world – what happens to the couple buried alive in the rubble during the forced demolition, the real number of causalities in that fatal fire accident, what truly happened to Li Yuezhen and the twenty-seven dead babies inside the hospital morgue, the real cause for Mouse Girl's suicide, and so on – all emerge from behind the "iron curtain" and reveal their true face. The cause for this fundamental change turns out to be very simple: people of the "land of the unburied" have freedom of speech, a basic human right taken away by the government in the human world. Having the right to speak for themselves, the people in this dreamland can freely tell their own stories and recount what they experienced and witnessed back in the human world. Free from the distortion, falsification, or cover-up by the deceptive state propaganda machine, truth can be recovered easily in this dreamland.

Along with the retrieval of human rights and the rediscovery of truth comes the recovery of human dignity and the true human self. In sharp contrast to the human world, where the twenty-seven dead babies are treated as "medical refuse" and dumped into a river, in this dreamland, they are happy angels who are cared for by their eternal mother Li Yuezhen and all other people. Mouse Girl, who suffers poverty, humiliation, and misery in the world of the living, now enjoys praise, admiration, and respect from everyone. With human rights and human dignity recovered, every individual finds a true self and true identity as well as the feeling of belonging in this new land. Yang Fei's remarks express this feeling explicitly: "I felt that I was a tree transplanted back to its native forest, a drop of water returning to the river, a mote of dust returning to the earth."[38]

Completely different from the human world, where people care only about their family and friends while treating others with callous indifference and even cruelty, in the "land of the unburied," people treat others with care, friendliness, and warmth. As an old skeleton remarks, "people over there make distinctions between family and strangers ... but there are no such demarcations here."[39] In this new land, every newcomer is welcomed warmly, and everyone can always rely on others for solace, support, and help. Those beautiful emotional bonds pull all the people together, turning the land into a united and amicable community and a home for everyone. The friendliness and unity of the community can be seen everywhere in the novel, but these qualities are most conspicuously crystallized in the scene of people helping Mouse Girl and seeing her off in unison to her resting place.

After Wu Chao sells his kidney and purchases a burial spot for Mouse Girl with the money he earns at the cost of his life, Mouse Girl finally has her resting place; she becomes the first one to leave "the land of the unburied." Upon the good news, everyone is happy for her, and everyone comes to congratulate her. Subsequently, the entire community mobilizes to help her in preparation for her departure. Two people who used to work in a clothing factory in the human world take over her unfinished funeral dress and complete it for her. All come out to fetch water from the river to bathe her. In response to Mouse Girl's grateful remarks that "many" people helped her with her funeral bath, a skeleton politely corrects her by emphasizing that "not many of us – but all of us" had offered helping hands. He also stresses: "Here we're good to everyone."[40] After everything is ready, all the people accompany Mouse Girl to the funeral parlour. Here as well as on many other occasions in the novel, the narrator repeatedly uses the term "in unison" to underscore the unity and intimacy of the people in the "land of the unburied." By comparing this scenario with what occurs "there" in the departed human world, a fundamental difference between the two places is revealed: whereas people are "isolated individuals" and "lonely orphans"[41] under the superficial covering of political conformity and social homogeneity in the human world, people in the "land of the unburied" are independent individuals who enjoy full freedom and dignity, yet are united under the common principles of love, care, and equality. There is a harmonious unity of individual rights and the common goals of the community there. Because of the harmony and unity, people in this dreamland always treat each other like family, and as such they "no longer [feel] lonely and abandoned."[42]

Because of the love, care, mutual understanding, and support, hatred – the dominant feeling in the human world – disappears in the dreamland, since this pernicious feeling is completely eradicated from people's hearts. Mouse Girl does not harbour a grudge towards her boyfriend any more after arriving in this new land; now all she has in her heart are regrets for her immature thoughts and silly behaviour in the past and her gratitude to Wu Chao. The man who was wrongly executed as the result of the police's abuse of power now forgives his in-laws, who played a crucial role in his victimization and execution, and expresses a sincere understanding of their feelings and actions at that time. The murdered policeman Zhang Gang and his murderer, the male prostitute surnamed Li – two fierce enemies back then in the human world – now become good friends, "close as brothers,"[43] who play chess together all the time. As the narrator comments, "the grudge between them had not crossed the frontier between life and death. Enmity had been sealed off in that departed world."[44] Getting rid of hatred and anger, they have only "smiles of understanding" on their faces.[45] What they have in this new land is "the history of their happy chess playing and the history of their happy arguments."[46]

Happiness is not a feeling particular to Zhang and Li. It is the dominant state of mind and inner experience of everyone in this new land. Liberated from inequality, injustice, evil, and the feeling of hatred commonly seen in the human world, happiness fills everyone's heart in the dreamland. Mouse Girl and Wu Chao are happy, as the misunderstanding between them is eventually clarified, and now their hearts are full of gratitude to and love for each other and all other people. Being the eternal mother of the twenty-seven angelic babies, Li Yuezhen is happy. The babies are also happy under Li Yuezhen's care; they are either sleeping soundly on huge heart-shaped tree leaves or singing like nightingales all the time. Even on the face of the wrongly executed man, there is a "smile" of happiness. "His smile was not a mobile expression of feeling as much as a light breeze wafting from his vacant eyes and empty mouth."[47] His happiness comes from his heart. Among all these cases, the change of people's state of mind in this new land is demonstrated most conspicuously by Tan Jianxin, the owner of the Tan Family Eatery. When Yang Fei meets with Tan again for the first time in the new land, he sees a completely different Tan who is "no longer with a frown on his face but wreathed in smiles."[48] Although he does exactly the same job in the new place, Tan no longer sighs, worries, or complains as he did in the departed human world; instead, he now has "a happy expression on his face, an expression I had never seen in that departed world."[49] During the entire period of time when Yang dines at the restaurant, all he sees is a Tan who is constantly "beaming, chuckling, and laughing."[50] Happiness flows out from the bottom of Tan's heart like water out of a well.

Change in mood is an explicit indication of change in world view. As Robert Solomon and Martin Heidegger point out, mood is a primordial way that human beings view and attune to the world.[51] Change in people's world view may result from change in people themselves, change in the world, or both. In the novel, Yu Hua suggests that the change in mood and world view of people in the "land of the unburied" is caused by the change of the world: people are the same people, but the place in which they are now living is completely different from the one where they used to live. In response to Yang Fei's question of why the restaurant is able to open so quickly here, Tan Jiaxin tells him that it is because there is no predatory government, no corrupt officials, and no exploitation.[52] The customers, in the midst of "laughter and good cheer," also praise the food here for its "fresh, delicious, and healthy" quality, which contrasts sharply with "those defective food items so pervasive in the departed world."[53] Tan's and his customers' remarks all point to some significant differences between the two worlds, but they do not touch the crux of the issue.

The essential difference between these two worlds derives from their difference in guiding principles. Whereas the departed old world is dominated by vulgar materialism, where people value only material gain and take pursuit of wealth as the ultimate goal in life but overlook the value of spiritual dimension in people's lives, the people in this new world cherish spiritual satisfaction and regard happiness as the highest goal and the ultimate meaning of life. The essential difference in guiding principles leads to fundamental differences in every aspect of life in the two worlds: whereas commodity fetishism gives rise to greed, corruption, predation, and inequality in the human world, pursuit of spiritual satisfaction makes people break away from material shackles and embrace positive human bonds – mutual understanding, care, and love – and eventually leads them to happiness in "the land of the unburied." In this beautiful new world, the significance of material is reduced to a minimum – people do not even have flesh on their bodies. As indicated explicitly by the Tan Family Eatery business, where "paying the bill was simply an exchange of words, with no action involved,"[54] work does not serve as a means to make money anymore here, but becomes a way to serve others with one's expertise and abilities, an intrinsic need for human beings to endow their lives with meaning, a source of happiness. Simply put, here people work not for material gain but for spiritual satisfaction and the happiness derived from helping others. Yu Hua's notion that happiness comes from giving rather than taking, from spiritual satisfaction rather than material gain, and from serving others rather than satisfying one's own selfish desires obviously constitutes a fierce criticism of the money fetishism and the utilitarian world view that prevail over China today.

Yu Hua's blueprint of an ideal society contains these elements: truth, universal love and care, mutual understanding, social equality, spiritual satisfaction and happiness, as well as an unspoiled land of great beauty; all of them are values absent from today's China. In tracing the intellectual origins of the novel, we find that Yu Hua resorts to multiple sources, mainly China's own traditions, both ancient and modern. Despite the ostensible allusion of its title to the Bible, the dreamland constructed in the novel is not a paradise dominated by divine power; instead, it is a utopia that resembles the Peach Blossom Spring portrayed by Tao Yuanming: a peaceful, friendly, and isolated human world where people and nature coexist in harmony without any divine power involved.[55] In addition to the Tao Yuanming–style

Taoist utopian elements based on "effortless effort,"[56] there is also the notion of social equality with minimum material needs, which is reminiscent of both Confucian egalitarianism[57] and Maoist ascetic socialism.[58] The notion that work is an intrinsic human need endowing life with meaning, rather than serving merely as a means for living, reflects a basic Marxist principle, whereas the ideas of freedom and universal love are core values of modern liberalism. Obviously, Yu Hua's social ideal is a mixture of multiple intellectual sources.

Summary

The Seventh Day could be regarded as a representative work of subaltern literature. In the novel, Yu Hua aims at dual goals: to criticize the darkness and cruelty of the Chinese model of development and to articulate his image of an ideal society. Through presentations of forced demolition, the life of the "mouse tribe," abuse of power on the part of government officials, and other prominent social phenomena characteristic of the Chinese model of development, Yu Hua exposes the predatory and bloody nature of the model as well as the tremendous social inequality and social injustice it has caused. By showing how positive human relations and human feelings are unable to survive in Chinese society and how the dictatorial Party-state destroys the Chinese public sphere through control of the mass media and the intelligentsia, Yu Hua points out that the Chinese model of development with its vulgar materialism and pure utilitarianism has brought a grave moral and spiritual crisis to the nation. In addition to the dictatorial government and the submissive mass media, ordinary people are also a target of Yu Hua's criticism. Through his vivid and provocative depiction of the cold-hearted callousness and cruelty of ordinary Chinese people towards others' suffering, Yu Hua convinces readers that ordinary people play a significant role in the moral and spiritual crisis in China today and that they serve as an accomplice in their own victimization. Here we see a profound thematic continuity between this novel and *Lenin's Kisses*.

What distinguishes this novel from others discussed in the book is that all the other novels only expose the darkness of present-day China, whereas this novel goes one step further to shed light on the path China should take in the future. By portraying a beautiful, free, and equal world of the dead, Yu Hua creates a blueprint for an ideal society. Yu Hua's dreamland is full of the positive values that are absent, lost, or destroyed in the human world: truth, mutual understanding and care, love, and happiness. Rather than treating people as strangers with callous indifference and even cruelty, in the dreamland, people treat all others as family. As such, there is a harmonious unity of individual rights and the common goals of community in this new land. In sharp contrast to the ugly and dark human world, which is dominated by vulgar materialism while overlooking the significance of the spiritual dimension in life, the new world is guided by the principle of spiritual satisfaction and happiness. Here, hatred disappears; happiness prevails. Work no longer serves as a means for living but becomes an intrinsic need for human beings to help others and to seek meaning in life. Yu Hua's imagining of an ideal society draws inspiration from a mixture of intellectual sources: the Tao Yuanming–style vision of the Peach Blossom Spring, the Taoist notion of "effortless effort" of governance, Confucian egalitarianism, Maoist ascetic socialism, Marxism, and modern liberalism.

Limits of Transgression and Mechanisms of Counter-Censorship

In discussing oppositional political novels in a country where strict censorship of the press and cultural products is a consistent policy, the following questions are unavoidable: How are those literary works that contain highly subversive messages able to evade censorship? What discursive and narrative strategies do those writers employ to circumvent the censorship under such politically oppressive circumstances? These questions, and the answers to them, are highly significant, because they can shed light on the fundamental mechanisms of censorship, self-censorship, counter-censorship, and the relationship between literature and politics in a dictatorial Party-state.

To answer these questions, we first need to take a look at the workings of censorship and its impact on literature in society. Censorship as a form of power, according to the Foucauldian formulation, is not a one-directional process of the censor imposing restrictions on the censored, with the censored passively submitting to the censor, but a dialectical interaction between the two. While the government or other authorities can enforce regulations or restrictions on writers and literary products, writers can also take counter-measures to evade censorship and achieve their subversive goals. As Nicole Moore points out, "literature and censorship have been dialectical forms of culture, each actively defining the other in an ongoing, agonistic engagement."[1] His edited volume, which focuses on the interaction of censorship and literature from a global view, provides insightful and inspiring case studies of censorship that take place in different countries during different periods of time.[2] These studies not only confirm the universality of the dialectical relationship between censorship and literature but also reveal the differences in expressive form of the relationship caused by geopolitical and temporal disparities.

In the Chinese context, due to the ubiquity and severity of censorship under Communist domination, the oppressive effect of censorship upon writers and literature is more conspicuous and more serious than in democratic countries, where the right to freedom of speech is protected by law and public power is regulated by law. As historical experience in the Soviet Union, the Eastern European socialist bloc, and Communist China has proved, the most serious consequence of long-term, strict censorship is that it imposes self-censorship upon people and turns them into their own censors. This finding reminds us of Foucault's conceptualization of a panoptic carceral society, where an individual simultaneously plays the roles of both the subject and the object of surveillance, becoming "the principle of his own subjection."[3] This duality is exactly the case in contemporary China, where long-lasting, consistent, and strict censorship implemented by the Party-state instils self-censorship in Chinese writers, who internalize the Party's requirements and restrictions, and take them as the principles to guide and discipline their thought and literary creation. As a consequence, they become their own guards and prisoners simultaneously.

Julia Lovell, in her comments on contemporary Chinese literature, points to a "tacit consensus" reached by Chinese writers with regard to literary creation: "not to write about politics."[4] This "consensus" to some extent can be read as Chinese writers' conscious submission to the Party's demand that literature cannot "openly attack the Party and leadership or call for a new system of government," a red line drawn by the Party-state in the post-Mao era.[5] In the Chinese context, when it comes to writing about politics in literature, criticism of the Party and the system is unavoidable, given how the dictatorship of the Party and the predatory system are the ultimate reasons for injustice and inequality in the country. In this sense, the "consensus" is actually an indication of Chinese writers' abandonment of their role as critics of power and their spontaneous submission to the Party's will. As such, the "consensus" serves as a good example of the dynamics of censorship and self-censorship, and the interaction between them.

Jeffrey Kinkley, in his study of the relationship of anticorruption novels, politics, and critical realism in contemporary Chinese literature, calls attention to a "universal contradiction" between "the existence of corruption and a happy ending" in anticorruption novels,[6] where justice always wins in the end, "even if that achievement probably seems unrealistic to most readers when intellectually considered."[7] This contradiction is actually quite easy to explain in the Chinese context if one grasps the ideological guideline for anticorruption fiction set by the Party. As elaborated in the introduction, in accord with the Party's ideological rules for literature, anticorruption fiction places stress on "anti" rather than on "corruption." The ultimate political message that an anticorruption novel attempts to convey is that, however rampant the official corruption is, the Party always has the ability to destroy it. Accordingly, the happy ending of the ultimate triumph of justice as commonly seen in the novels of this genre is a necessary and indispensable part of the narrative pattern, in conformity with the ideological guideline prescribed by the Party. This scenario is another example of the workings of self-censorship in contemporary China, showing how writers willingly submit to the political and ideological guidelines set by the Party and materialize them in the process of literary creation on both thematic and technical levels.

The negative impact of censorship and self-censorship is also clearly reflected in the political novels discussed in the present study, although these novels are supposed to be oppositional. Despite the audacity, scope, and depth of these novels' exposure of the darkness of the Chinese model and their questioning of the fundamental principles of the Chinese Party-state, the discursive limitations or restrictions in these novels imposed by the authors themselves are obvious. These ideological limitations are displayed in different ways in different individual works. The main purpose of *Wolf Totem*, for instance, is to promote the mainstream political discourses and state ideology of nationalism and social Darwinism. Paradoxically, however, the historical facts presented, based on the author's real life experience on the Mongolian grassland during the Cultural Revolution, *objectively and unconsciously* subvert the social Darwinist and nationalist discourses that the author openly advocates in the novel, thereby adding a paradoxical character and critical edge. Certainly, the ideological "opposition" contained in the novel is not the author's major concern. In *Such Is This World*, the political theme is deeply hidden beneath the plot line of a love story. The most important and subversive messages conveyed in the novel – that the Party turns into a self-serving interest group which oppresses the people, and that the people and the Party take different sides, forming the paradigm of "them versus us" – is deliberately concealed under a thick covering of personal affairs, used to explain the reason for the break-up of the couple. *The Seventh Day* largely avoids direct depictions of the workings of the oppressive and predatory state power, though exposure of the predatory nature of the Party-state is a major theme in the novel. Through the employment of techniques such as fantasy, farce, and melodrama; through presentation of the grotesque and the supernatural; and through the creation of a utopia, the novel creates a surreal and metaphysical aura as a protective artistic veil. *Lenin's Kisses* adopts a similar approach to the sociopolitical reality in contemporary China. Although the novel unambiguously targets the absurdity and cruelty of the Chinese model, and all the presentations in the novel are based on the reality of today's China, it deliberately adopts the technique of "mythorealism" – incorporating the elements of fantasy, farce, legend, surrealism, magical realism, and other such techniques into conventional realism – to disguise fact as non-fact and consequently to hide and decrease its realistic and critical character. Obviously, these novels' criticism of the Chinese political system and exposure of the darkness of the Chinese model are rather restrained, tactful, and subtle.

We say that the political messages conveyed in these novels are "original and provocative" only in the sense that it is the first time these messages appear in literary works created by writers currently residing in mainland China. They seem "original" only for mainland Chinese writers and readers. Beyond China's borders, these messages, even the most sensitive and critical ones – those exposing the predatory, deceptive, and hypocritical nature of the Party-state and its fascist tendency; those directly presenting the horror of the Tiananmen Massacre and its disastrous impact upon the intelligentsia and the society; those questioning the morality and political legitimacy of the Chinese system and the Chinese model; and the like – are nothing new for scholars of Chinese studies in Hong Kong, Taiwan, and overseas. They are also familiar motifs in literary works by Chinese writers in exile, such as Gao Xingjian, Ma Jian, and Ha Jin.

Readers might notice that, in discussing the discursive limitations of these "oppositional" political novels, *The Fat Years* has not been mentioned. This omission is not neglect or a mistake. Instead, it is because this novel is an exception to the aforementioned alleged limitations. Of course, like all literary works, this novel is not perfect, and it also has weaknesses or limitations. For instance, some may argue that the novel imitates *Nineteen Eighty-Four* to an excessive degree and that a few characters in the novel are portrayed merely as mouthpieces for ideas rather than as real people. But those possible weaknesses largely result from the author's limited imaginative capacity as a writer and are not consciously imposed by him as a result of self-censorship. The fact that *The Fat Years* is able to avoid many limitations as commonly seen in Chinese political fiction can, to a large extent, be ascribed to the author's special status as a non-Chinese resident, which provides him the much-needed geographical distance, political safety, and financial independence that mainland Chinese writers lack. Of the five novels discussed here, *The Fat Years* is the only one that was not published in mainland China. As such, it is the only novel that was able to escape political censorship. As suggested by Julia Lovell's account of her meeting with Chan Koonchung in a Beijing restaurant after the publication of *The Fat Years*, during which they could freely discuss the novel and politics in today's China,[8] it seems that the publication of the novel did not substantially affect Chan's life in Beijing. That would be impossible for a mainland Chinese writer. Of course, a novel like *The Fat Years* has no chance of being published in mainland China in the first place. This observation conversely demonstrates how decisive a role political censorship and self-censorship have played in contemporary Chinese literature.

For all the discursive limitations imposed by censorship and self-censorship, the highly subversive nature of these oppositional Chinese political novels, their remarkable contributions to Chinese literature and thought, and the courage and intelligence of these writers in creating them are undeniable. Here the question naturally re-emerges: how do these writers manage to circumvent the censorship and reach their subversive goals under such highly oppressive and dangerous political circumstances? As discussed in the introduction, the external environment – the marketization of cultural products, the wide spread of the internet, and globalization – is certainly a positive factor for these writers, because it provides them more channels, means, and resources to circumvent censorship. But a more significant and decisive factor is the writers' own determination and decision – how they employ varied narrative strategies and techniques to penetrate the censorship and successfully convey their subversive messages to the readers. The crux of the issue is the strategies and devices they adopt in the creation of their literary works. Here I feel it necessary to quickly point out that, despite my fondness of and familiarity with modern narratology,[9] in this section I shall not engage in a detailed elaboration of the specific literary techniques that the writers adopt in their novels. Instead, I will focus only on the guiding principles and strategies employed by these writers to conduct their subversion for a brief discussion from a grand narrative perspective.

The fundamental challenge that the writer faces in creating a political novel is how to deal with the relation between aesthetics and ideology. In Western society, where writers enjoy freedom of speech and autonomy of creation, a political novelist only needs to figure out a way to express the political ideas or ideology in an artistic and impressive manner in order to reconcile the aesthetic and political values in the novel. In the Chinese context, however, a political novelist must do more than that. One additional challenge that a Chinese political novelist faces is how to effectively wrap or conceal those subversive political messages in an artistic veil so that the messages, as well as the novel itself, are able to escape the censors. Whereas a Western political novelist arranges the artistic aspects of the novel in a way to highlight the political ideas or ideology contained in it, the Chinese counterpart has to use all kinds of artistic techniques and devices to hide the subversive political messages deep within the narrative structure in order to reduce their visibility. Thus, a Chinese political novelist faces dual and seemingly contradictory challenges – that is, he or she must find a way to convey those subversive political ideas *both effectively and safely* under the condition of strict censorship. Oftentimes Chinese writers' effort to "wrap, hide, or conceal" their subversive messages in their novels is no more than a symbolic pose or studied gesture to show their respect for the Party's regulations, which in turn provides a ready pretext for the censor to give them the green light. This strategy is a special kind of "mutual understanding" between writers and (conscientious) censors, and also a good example of the complex, dialectical relation between literature and censorship in contemporary China.

Lynda Ng, in a highly insightful study of the impact of censorship upon contemporary Chinese literature, points to a significant strategy that Chinese writers use to counteract censorship. As she argues, contemporary Chinese writers tend to present "elusive truths" by deliberately "exaggerating the fictive elements" in their literary works, because "casting off the mantle of fiction and engaging openly with the truth" in literature is too dangerous for writers under Communist domination.[10] Taking Mo Yan and Yan Lianke as two examples, she demonstrates how contemporary Chinese writers employ varied literary techniques and devices to disguise truth as fiction in order to evade censorship. She comments: "In both cases any criticisms of the government or society are made under the cover of satire, and the exaggerated style of Mo Yan's magical realism or Yan Lianke's 'mythical realism' allows clear lines to be drawn between fictive and non-fictive forms of discourse, even if the distinction between truth and fiction within those discourses is less clear."[11] Howard Goldblatt emphasizes that contemporary Chinese writers have to adopt varied modernist and avant-garde literary techniques and devices, including "opaque language, self-reflective and disjoined narrative," surrealism, allegory, and so on, not only to produce certain artistic effects but also to weave an aesthetic veil to obscure or conceal the subversiveness of the political ideas contained in their works.[12] Jeffrey Kinkley also reminds us of Chinese novelists' "celebrated use of magical realism, fantasy, allegory, and burlesque [to] help them evade censorship."[13] Indeed, to wrap or conceal the highly subversive political messages in an artistic veil woven with varied literary techniques and devices is the most significant strategy that writers of oppositional Chinese political novels use to counteract censorship. It is also the guiding principle for their treatment of the relation between political ideas and aesthetics in their works – a defining component in a political novel. Georg Lukács emphasizes the notion of ideology as "the formative principle underlying the style of a given piece of writing."[14] Political novelists in contemporary China push the ideological significance of the form of a literary work to an extreme. As mentioned earlier, contemporary Chinese writers have to consciously conduct self-censorship under political pressure. Self-censorship, however, does not necessarily mean sheepishly containing one's own thought to fit in with the Party's ideology or regulations; it could also mean making use of wisdom and resources to counteract censorship. In this way, self-censorship can turn into a disguised form of counter-censorship.

From the dialectical perspective of self-censorship and counter-censorship, the alleged "discursive limitations" of these political novels can also be construed as narrative strategies deliberately employed by the writers to counteract censorship. In *Wolf Totem*, for instance, despite the loudness of his voice in promoting social Darwinist and nationalist discourses on the surface, Jiang Rong quietly presents abundant evidence, based on his personal experience and observation, laying bare the disastrous consequences that Communist domination has brought to Mongols and their culture. More importantly, by treating the protagonist raising a wolf cub as a political allegory, where a member of the dominant ethnic group enslaves an animal regarded by an ethnic minority as their totem, Jiang subtly compares this episode to the lives and fate of China's ethnic minorities under Communist domination. Consequently, he subverts the social Darwinist and nationalist discourses that he painstakingly propagates throughout the novel. Clearly, allegory and paradox are two major narrative strategies employed by the author to reach his goals of subversion. In *Such Is This World*, Hu Fayun adeptly wraps the core of the novel as a political fable in the cloak of a love affair and disguises the most significant political message the novel tries to convey – that the Party has already turned into a self-serving interest group and taken the opposite side from the people – as the excuse for the break-up of the female protagonist and the high-ranking government official. By treating the Chinese government's handling of the SARS epidemic as an epitome of the Communist rule over China in general and by playing with symbolism and allegory, the novel furtively leads readers to the realization that Communist domination itself is a fatal disease. Obviously, clever manipulation of the plot line and employment of symbolism and allegory are the dominant strategy adopted by Hu Fayun to circumvent censorship.

Compared with these two writers, Yu Hua's manoeuvre is even subtler and more innovative. In *The Seventh Day*, Yu Hua creates two worlds – the world of the living and the world of the dead. Whereas the former represents today's China with all its absurdity and cruelty, the latter stands for an ideal society, a utopia dominated by the positive human values of truth, mutual understanding, love, and equality. By constructing his ideal society with exactly the same fundamental human values that are absent, lost, or destroyed in present-day China, Yu Hua subtly hints at the dystopian and destructive nature of the current system and thus unequivocally criticizes the Chinese model for destroying positive human values and turning the country into a spiritual wasteland. The most powerful instruments used by Yu Hua to camouflage his subversive discourses are the innovative design of the novel's structure – the construction of two worlds antithetical in fundamental principles and values – and the employment of surrealism.

In writing *Lenin's Kisses*, the guiding principle Yan Lianke adopts to evade censorship, as Lynda Ng incisively points out, is to disguise reality in the novel as pure fiction. The most significant narrative strategy he employs is what he dubs "mythorealism" – that is, to incorporate farce, fantasy, legend, folk tales, magical realism, surrealism, and hyperbole into conventional realism – to deliberately obscure or cover up the realistic nature of the events presented in the novel. There is plenty of evidence in the novel showing that sometimes Yan Lianke weaves the protective political veil at the cost of discursive profundity and artistic appeal. To be sure, veiling the critical edge of his novel by adding some farcical, fantastic, and popular and modernist elements to his literary text is the most important strategy employed by Yan Lianke in this and his other novels for political camouflage. In the Orwellian-style political novel *The Fat Years*, Chan Koonchung does not, as Orwell did before, depict a horrible totalitarian dystopia in its naked state; instead, he conceals the dreadful picture of a fascist Party-state behind a beautiful image of a wealthy and powerful utopia, where everyone is intoxicated with the feeling of enormous happiness and enjoys 90 per cent freedom. The adoption of the science fiction form in this novel adds an imaginative and "elusive" aura to it, which serves as an artistic veil to obscure the fierce attack on the Chinese model.

From a technical perspective, the relation between ideas and aesthetics in a political novel is mainly displayed in the tension between the "immediacy and closeness" of human experience and the "generality and inclusiveness" of ideas or ideology.[15] To release the tension, according to Irving Howe, a political novelist should adopt the "psychology and politics of 'one more step'" – starting from the real human experience and then moving one step forward to describe the imaginary "reality" as presented in the novel.[16] The ideas or ideology will derive from and be expressed in the logicality between the real human experience and the fictional "reality," and the distance of "one step" is where political ideas or ideology comes from in a political novel. Taking this concept as a point of departure, Howe emphasizes that, to create a good political novel, the author should take only "one more step," not further. As he argues, what makes *Nineteen Eighty-Four* such a good political novel lies in exactly that, in presenting the terrifying fictional world under the complete control of Big Brother, Orwell usually takes only one step forward from the social and political reality of the time he lives in.[17] Likewise, when readers occasionally find a "fact" in his novel incredible, it is because Orwell makes a "mistake of taking more than 'one step' and thereby [breaks] the tie between the world we know and the world he imagines."[18] According to Howe's logic, it might be inferred that, for a writer of political novels, presenting something that cannot be induced from real life or treating the "reality" presented in a political novel from a non-political perspective obviously can be counted as "going too far."

In opposition to Irving Howe's conceptualization, Chinese political novelists oftentimes deliberately take more than one step to obscure, conceal, or cover up the similarity, continuity, or logicality between the sociopolitical reality in Communist China and their imaginary political worlds to evade censorship. In *Such Is This World*, for instance, on many occasions the narrator deliberately interprets the process of the female protagonist's political enlightenment from an existential, value-neutral perspective to dilute the political overtones of the novel. In *The Seventh Day*, by focusing on the two extreme existential phenomena of being human – life and death – Yu Hua wittingly adds a metaphysical aura to the politically oriented fictional world he paints. In *Wolf Totem*, Jiang Rong intentionally examines a serious ethnic problem caused by political dictatorship mainly from a cultural, intellectual perspective – an approach that might be ascribed to the influence of the May Fourth legacy but is certainly also motivated by the need to circumvent censorship. In *Lenin's Kisses*, as just discussed, Yan Lianke deliberately disguises the reality presented in the novel as farce and myth, thereby obscuring the tie between the sociopolitical reality of today's China and what is presented in his fictional world, and concealing the seriousness of the critical edge of the novel.

As discussed in the introduction, one major reason these oppositional political novels are allowed to emerge in the Chinese literary circles is the marginalization of "serious" literature under the influence of commercialization and the rapid rise of popular internet literature in China. From the effort of the authors of these oppositional novels, we discern a paradoxical and absurd situation similar to that Sisyphus faces as depicted by Albert Camus. Taking advantage of the limited freedom and autonomy resulting from the marginalization of their status in society, Chinese writers attempt to exert some influence upon a society where knowledge and "serious" literature have lost their hold on the general public. Given the sociopolitical reality in contemporary China, the Chinese political novel has a long way to go.

Notes

Introduction: Rise of Oppositional Chinese Political Novels

1 Howe, *Politics and the Novel*, 17.
2 Kinkley, *Corruption and Realism*, 15.
3 Yeh, *Chinese Political Novel*, 72–99.
4 Catherine Vance Yeh argues: "Chinese poetry and drama also had a long and rich tradition of using literary means to discuss political issues and even confront the powers-that-be. From the seventeenth century, this potential was also seen in the novel." See Yeh, *Chinese Political Novel*, 1. Jeffrey Kinkley claims that late Qing fiction of condemnation, along with May Fourth literature, is the origin of China's "classical tradition of realism," of which "speaking truth to power" and "political implications" are pronounced features. See Kinkley, *Corruption and Realism*, 154–60.
5 Plaks, *Chinese Narrative*, 311. See also Idema and Haft, "The Central Tradition," 42.
6 Yu and Huters, "The Imaginative Universe," 2.
7 Yeh, *Chinese Political Novel*, 350.
8 Howe, *Politics and the Novel*, 19.
9 Lin Yü-sheng, in his highly acclaimed book on May Fourth radical antitraditionalism, points to the intertwined relationship between the imperial political system and the Confucian value system in traditional China. As he argues, in traditional China the sociopolitical order and the cultural-moral order were bound together by the universal kingship into a unified one. Consequently, the breakdown of the sociopolitical order as a result of the collapse of the universal kingship inevitably undermined and eventually destroyed the cultural-moral order, bringing about a serious cultural and spiritual crisis. See Y. Lin, *Crisis of Chinese Consciousness*.
10 Chang, "New Confucianism," 276–83.
11 Reynolds, *China 1891–1912*.

12 Schwartz, *In Search of Wealth and Power*. See also Levenson, *Liang Ch'i-Ch'ao*.

13 Pusey, *China and Charles Darwin*.

14 Zarrow, *Anarchism and Chinese Political Culture*.

15 Yeh, *Chinese Political Novel*, 14.

16 D.D. Wang, *Fin-de-siècle Splendor*, 2–3. See also J. Wang, *Merry Laughter and Angry Curses*, 157.

17 Y. Lin, *Crisis of Chinese Consciousness*, 26–39.

18 For a more detailed analysis of Chinese intellectuals' changing mode of thinking from the late Qing "self-strengthening movement" to the May Fourth period, see Y. Lin, *Crisis of Chinese Consciousness*, 38–9.

19 Tsi-an Hsia, in a book on China's leftist literature, discusses the tremendous influence of Lu Xun upon later Chinese writers. As he points out, prior to the publication of Mao's famous Yan'an talks on literature and arts in 1942, "the popularity of Lu Hsün's satirical style" brought up a "brood of imitators," and "there even appeared a magazine called *Lu Hsün feng* or *In Imitation of Lu Hsün*" after his death. See Hsia, *Gate of Darkness*, 239.

20 Xiao Hong's *Shengsi chang* 生死场 (The field of life and death), Xiao Jun's *Bayue de xiangcun* 八月的乡村 (Village in August), and Ye Zi's *Fengshou* 丰收 (The harvest), for example, were all published in 1935 by Nuli She 奴隶社 (The slave society) under Lu Xun's sponsorship. All these works fall into the category of critical realism.

21 For a detailed and in-depth analysis of the influence of Mao's Yan'an talks on Chinese literature and thought, see Denton, "Literature and Politics," 224–30.

22 Hsia, *Gate of Darkness*, 234–62.

23 Dai, *Wang Shiwei and "Wild Lilies."*

24 Michael S. Duke argues that scar literature represents the return of critical realism in China. For a detailed discussion on this topic, see his "Introduction" in *Contemporary Chinese Literature*, 1–5. For a detailed and in-depth discussion on scar literature, see Duke, *Blooming and Contending*. See also Link, *Uses of Literature*.

25 Scholars argue that root-seeking literature represents the revival of the cultural approach to literature in China. For a detailed discussion on this topic, see Duke, "Reinventing China." See also Li, "Searching for Roots."

26 For a detailed discussion of Chinese avant-garde fiction, see Z. Yu, *Chinese Avant-garde Fiction*.

27 Yan Jianbin 阎建滨, "Shengcun zhi lei yu xinyang zhi qing."

28 For a detailed and in-depth discussion on the topic, see Gong, *Uneven Modernity*, chapter 3.

29 Kinkley, *Corruption and Realism*.

30 This tendency is best demonstrated by the drastic change in both theme and style of the fiction of the three leading Chinese avant-garde writers, Yu Hua, Su Tong, and Ge Fei. See Z. Yu, *Chinese Avant-garde Fiction*, 4.

31 According to Jeffrey Kinkley's study, anticorruption fiction emerged in Chinese literary circles in 1995, reached its peak in 2000, and faded away after 2002. Roughly, this genre flourished during the Jiang Zemin period and ended when Hu Jintao took office. See Kinkley, *Corruption and Realism*, 14–18.

32 For a detailed account of the varied forms of corruption and its spread in China, see Kinkley, *Corruption and Realism*, 3–10.

33 Y. Yan, *Individualization of Chinese Society*.

34 Y. Yan, xvi.

35 For all his high evaluation of the thematic significance of anticorruption novels in exposing the political problems in contemporary China, Jeffrey Kinkley admits that these novels do not dare to touch the "fundamental concerns of Chinese readers," such as their desire for democracy, political and civil rights, freedom to form groups, freedom to be well-informed, and so on, let alone their resentment of the one-Party dictatorship. See Kinkley, *Corruption and Realism*, 7.

36 The nature of anticorruption fiction as a supportive force to the Party-state is clearly reflected by the Party's attitude towards it and its authors. In a regime well-known for strict censorship, anticorruption novels and their TV adaptions have been praised by the Party-state as representative artistic works of the "main melody" (*zhu xuanlü* 主旋律) – a term adopted to refer to cultural productions that propagate state ideology and government policies in contemporary China. Zhang Ping 张平, a mediocre writer but a major practitioner of anticorruption fiction, was promoted to vice chairman of the Party-controlled Association of Chinese Writers after Jiang Zemin, then the Chinese Communist Party's general secretary, praised his anticorruption novels and TV adaptions. Zhang's novel *Jueze* 抉择 (Choice) even won a Mao Dun prize – the most prestigious literary prize in China. For more information about the phenomenon, see Kinkley, *Corruption and Realism*, 19.

37 Although 1990s anticorruption fiction and late Qing fiction of condemnation share the theme of exposing the darkness of the Chinese bureaucracy and official corruption, they are essentially different in their purposes and functions. Whereas the latter aimed to "delegitimize the Qing rule," the former serves as a supportive force for the Party's rule. See J. Wang, *Merry Laughter and Angry Curses*, 17.

38 For a brief yet insightful analysis of the negative consequences of the Chinese model in the twenty-first century, see Perry, "Growing Pains."

39 Kahn and Yardley, "As China Roars."

40 For a comprehensive study of China's social protests and riots since the 1990s, see O'Brien, *Popular Protest in China*.

41 For a detailed and in-depth analysis of the moral and spiritual crisis in post-Mao China, see Ci, *Moral China*.

42 Apter, "Discourse as Power," 198.

43 Apter, 193–200.

44 For a detailed and incisive analysis of Maoist voluntarism, see Meisner, *Marxism, Maoism, and Utopianism*, 60–2.

45 Lovell, "Preface," in *The Fat Years*, 13.

46 Pei, *China's Trapped Transition*, 19–20.

47 For a detailed analysis of the division of the Chinese intelligentsia and the debate between Chinese liberals and the New Left in the 1990s, see Wang and Lu, "Introduction: China and New Left Critique." See also Xu Jilin 许纪霖, "Qimeng de ziwo wajie."

48 G. Yang, *Power of the Internet in China*, 210.

49 G. Yang, 210.

50 Y. Yan, *Individualization of Chinese Society*, xvi.

51 For a detailed explanation of the phrase and its historical origins, see Bandurski, "Musings on a CCP Buzzword."

52 For a detailed and in-depth analysis of the tightened political control over society under Xi Jinping, see Economy, *The Third Revolution*. In her book, the author points to some significant strategies adopted by Xi to reinforce the control of the state over society: "the dramatic concentration of authority under his personal leadership; the intensified penetration of society by the state; the creation of a virtual wall of regulations and restriction that more tightly controls the flow of ideas, culture, and capital into and out of the country." Economy, 10.

53 Kinkley, *Corruption and Realism*, 150.

54 Kraus, *The Party and the Arty in China*, vii.

55 Kong, *Consuming Literature*, 8.

56 Kong, 2.

57 See Ng, "China's Elusive Truths," 237.

58 See Yu Hua 余华, "How My Books Have Roamed the World."

59 G. Yang, *Power of the Internet in China*, 1.

60 G. Yang, 209.

61 M. Jiang, "Authoritarian Deliberation on Chinese Internet."

62 Roberts, *Censored*, 8–9.

63 Huang Zhaohui 黄兆晖, "*Ruyan@sars.come.*"

64 For a detailed account of the entire process of the publication and circulation of the novel, see A.E. Clark's preface to the novel's English edition; Clark, "Preface," i–iii.

65 Eberlein, "China 2013."

66 After the publication of *The Fat Years*, Chan Koonchung published two
other novels, *Luoming* 裸命 (The unbearable dreamworld of Champa the
driver) and *Jianfeng er nian: Xin Zhonguo wuyou shi* 建丰二年：新中国乌
有史 (The second year of Jianfeng: An alternative history of new China).
Whereas the former portrays the injustice and oppression that Tibetan
people suffer under Communist domination, narrated in the form of an
educated young Tibetan man's sexual fantasies, the latter imagines what
would have happened in China if the Chinese Communist Party had lost
to the Kuomintang in 1949. For a review of the first book, see Du Ting
杜婷, "Chan Koonchung tan *Luoming*." See also Whitehead, "Author
Chan Koonchung Finds Humor." For more information about the second
book, see an interview with Chan Koonchung by Di Yufei 荻雨菲, "Chan
Koonchung."

67 Hu Fayun published another novel to expose the cruelty and absurdity
of the Cultural Revolution. See Hu Fayun 胡发云, *Midong* 迷冬 (Misty
winters).

68 For a detailed and in-depth analysis of Chinese internet literature, see
Hockx, *Internet Literature in China*. Putting it in the broad context of
"postsocialist" Chinese culture, Hockx examines the ways that internet
literature has brought about literary innovations and challenged the
established publishing system in today's China. As he argues, although
internet literature challenges and undermines the influence of existing
"serious" literature, "its practices, sites, and terminologies rapidly became part of serious literary discourse." Hockx, x.

69 Some mainland Chinese literary critics distinguish between "subaltern
literature" and "migrant workers' literature" (*dagong wenxue* 打工文学).
The two genres share the theme of exposing the miserable lives of the
people struggling at the bottom of society in present-day China, but they
differ in the subject of creation. Whereas the former is often created by
well-established professional writers, the latter is largely authored by
amateur writers who are migrant workers themselves and whose works
are often based on their personal life experiences. I prefer to employ the
term "subaltern literature" to cover both genres, because they both focus
on the misery of the ordinary people at the grassroots level in today's
China.

70 For a detailed and in-depth analysis of China's subaltern literature, see
Zhong, "*Internationale* as Specter." See also Li Yunlei 李云雷, "The Rise
of 'Subaltern Literature.'" Zhao Dongmei 赵冬梅, a mainland Chinese
critic, identifies three keywords in subaltern literature. They are *zhimian*
直面 (to confront directly), *dangxia* 当下 (the here and now), and *kunian*
苦难 (suffering). According to Zhao, the defining feature of Chinese subaltern literature in the twenty-first century is that it "directly confronts"

the "suffering" of ordinary people in the "here and now" of present-day China. See Zhao Dongmei 赵冬梅, "You diceng wenxue de ji ge guanjianci tanqi."

71 See Wang and Lu, "Introduction: China and New Left Critique." See also Li Yunlei 李云雷 and Shi Tianqiang 石天强, "Diceng wenxue: Yizhong xinde wenxue xiangxiang?"

72 Julia Lovell and Jeffrey Kinkley both mention the political taboos prescribed by the Party-state. These taboos include issues of political reform, human-rights abuse against critics of the regime, ethnic tensions (especially in Xinjiang and Tibet), widespread censorship, desire for democracy, political and civil rights, freedom to form groups, freedom to be well-informed, and the like. Of course, criticism of the Chinese one-Party system and of the Party itself is the biggest taboo in Communist China. See Lovell, "Preface," 14; and Kinkley, *Corruption and Realism*, 7.

73 Howe, *Politics and the Novel*, 17.

74 Kinkley, *Chinese Justice, the Fiction*; and *Visions of Dystopia*.

75 For a critical introduction of Chan Koonchung's life experience and career, see C. Wang, "Dreamers and Nightmares," 28.

1. Destruction of Communist Myths

1 Howe, *Politics and the Novel*, 238.

2 All ideologies, according to Hannah Arendt, share three defining features: the claim to total explanation, the independence of all experience, and the strategy to reduce thought to logical deduction. Arendt argues that totalitarian ideology goes even further, because it no longer appeals primarily to the "idea" of the ideology but rather to the "logical process which could be developed from it." She insists that the power and effectiveness of a totalitarian ideology come from "its inherent logicality" – the "ice cold reasoning" and the "irresistible force of logic." Here Arendt actually emphasizes the imaginary and arbitrary nature of totalitarian ideology. See Arendt, *Origins of Totalitarianism*, 470–2. Clifford Geertz also points to the "ideologization of ideology" in recent centuries, characterized by its deliberate "overselectivity" and "distortion" of certain "aspects of social reality." See Geertz, *Interpretation of Cultures*, 193–9.

3 Van de Ven, "Emergence of the Text-Centered Party."

4 Van de Ven. See also Apter, "Discourse as Power."

5 Apter, 201.

6 Apter, 203.

7 S. Zhao, *Nation-State by Construction*, 209.

8 Dai, *Wang Shiwei and "Wild Lilies."*

9 For a detailed account and an in-depth analysis of the *"Bitter Love* incident,"* see Duke, *Blooming and Contending*, 123–48.

10 B. Liu, *People or Monsters?*

11 Pei, *China's Trapped Transition*.

12 Pei, 30.

13 Pei, 29–30.

14 Pei, *China's Crony Capitalism*, 23.

15 In post-Mao China, a large portion of workers are *mingong* 民工 or "peasant workers," people who come from the countryside to work in the city. Due to the notorious household registration system (*hukou dengji zhidu* 户口登记制度) and the discriminatory regulations and practices associated with it, a "peasant worker" has to pay various extra fees to get a "temporary residence certificate" and work permit in order to work in the city. Moreover, according to Sun Liping's study, many cities implement discriminatory policies against "peasant workers." Both Beijing and Shanghai, for instance, have regulations to prohibit "peasant workers" from doing certain jobs, which, needless to say, are relatively easy and well-paid and reserved only for urban residents. See Sun Liping 孙立平, "Quanli shiheng."

16 According to Minxin Pei, "collusive corruption by elites" is "the heart and soul of crony capitalism" in the Chinese model of development. See Pei, *China's Crony Capitalism*, 23.

17 The Chinese mining industry is so dangerous that some even compare it to the battlefield. Some other industries are equally dangerous, though for different reasons. For example, in the Shenzhen factory of Foxconn Technology Group, fourteen workers died an "abnormal death" in the year 2010 – most committing suicide by jumping off tall buildings – due to the unbearable pressure of work. See Tam, "Foxconn Factories Are Labor Camps."

18 Since the 1980s, when China's economy began to take off, each year there were a large number of protests and riots caused by underpaid or unpaid wages all around China. A notorious case took place in Taiyuan, the capital city of Shanxi province, on 13 December 2014: A female "peasant worker" from Henan province had a fight with her employer, who refused to pay her full wages on time. Later on she was detained by the local police because of this incident and tortured to death in the police station. See J. Wu, "Rural Woman 'Beaten to Death.'"

19 Sudworth, "Counting the Cost."

20 *Pindie* 拼爹 literally means "to compare daddies" (to see who is powerful and wealthy and who is not). This term is coined by Chinese people to refer, in a satirical and critical tone, to the phenomenon that younger generations of Chinese in today's China take advantage of their family

background – their parents' or even grandparents' wealth, power, and privilege – to achieve success in society, rather than relying on their own abilities and efforts. This phenomenon is an explicit reflection of both the widespread social inequality and injustice and the prevailing social atmosphere of moral nihilism and utilitarianism in present-day China.

21 Sun Liping 孙立平, "Women zai kaishi mianlin yige duanlie de shehui?" See also Sun Liping 孙立平, "Quanli shiheng."

22 Pei, *China's Trapped Transition*, 43.

23 Pei, 188.

24 O'Brien, *Popular Protest in China*.

25 For a detailed and incisive account of the Party's changed attitude towards the intellectuals, see Fewsmith, *China since Tiananmen*, 11–12.

26 Pei, *China's Trapped Transition*, 89.

27 For a detailed and inspiring account of the transformation of the Chinese intelligentsia from the late 1970s to the end of the twentieth century, see Xu Jilin 许纪霖, "The Fate of an Enlightenment." See also Y. Zhang, "No Forbidden Zone in Reading?" For a detailed and thoughtful analysis of the transformation of the Chinese intelligentsia after Tiananmen, see Fewsmith, *China since Tiananmen*, 12–13.

28 For a detailed and insightful discussion of the division of the Chinese intelligentsia since the 1990s and the debates between liberals and the New Left, the two dominant and contending intellectual groups after Tiananmen, see Xu Jilin, Liu Qing, Luo Gang, and Xue Yi, "In Search of a 'Third Way.'"

29 For a highly incisive analysis of the division of the Chinese intelligentsia since the 1990s, the rise of the "New Left" and its debate with the Chinese liberals, see Wang and Lu, "Introduction: China and New Left Critique," ix–xvi.

30 Barmé, *In the Red*, 333.

31 Chen Sihe 陈思和, *Zhongguo xinwenxue zhengtiguan*, 98–106.

32 Gan Yang 甘阳, "Ziyouzhuyi?" 85.

33 S. Zhao, *Nation-State by Construction*, 209.

34 Apter, "Discourse as Power," 202.

35 Apter, 202.

36 Bianco, "Peasant Responses."

37 S. Zhao, *Nation-State by Construction*, 210.

38 S. Zhao, 210–11.

39 S. Zhao, 213.

40 S. Zhao, 209.

41 Fewsmith, *China since Tiananmen*, 13.

42 For a detailed and incisive analysis of "patriotic education campaign," see S. Zhao, "State-Led Nationalism." See also Z. Wang, "National

Humiliation." For an incisive analysis of the intrinsic relation between the "national studies fever," the "patriotic education campaign," nationalism, and their influence upon the Chinese intelligentsia and the general public, see Lei Yi 雷颐, "'Guoxue re.'"

43 For a detailed description and analysis of the "national studies fever," see Dong Enlin 董恩林, "Dalu 'guoxue re' xianzhuang."
44 S. Zhao, "State-Led Nationalism," 287–302; and *Nation-State by Construction*, 209–15. Z. Wang, "National Humiliation," 783–806.
45 Lei Yi 雷颐, "'Guoxue re,'" 9; S. Zhao, *Nation-State by Construction*, 213–16; Z. Wang, "National Humiliation," 790–2.
46 Z. Wang, "National Humiliation," 790–2.
47 Anderlini, "Patriotic Education."
48 Anderlini.
49 Lei Yi 雷颐, "'Guoxue re,'" 6–8.
50 Dong Enlin 董恩林, "Dalu 'guoxue re' xianzhuang," 33–41.
51 X. Zhang, *Chinese Modernism*, 42–54.
52 Lei Yi 雷颐, "'Guoxue re,'" 12 (my translation).
53 Lei Yi 雷颐, 12.
54 Lei Yi 雷颐, 12.
55 Dong Enlin 董恩林, "Dalu 'guoxue re' xianzhuang," 34.
56 For an insightful analysis of the mechanism and logic that the Chinese Party-state has employed to manipulate nationalism for its own purpose and of the relationship between state nationalism and popular nationalism, see Johansson, *Libidinal Economy of China*, 11–17.
57 For a detailed and profound analysis of the origins, features, and impact of populist nationalism in contemporary China, see B. Xu, "Chinese Populist Nationalism."
58 Carrico, "The New Nationalism."
59 Carrico.
60 For a detailed account and in-depth analysis of extreme nationalism in today's China, see Deng and Lin, "Nationalism Takes a Dark Turn."
61 Anderlini, "Patriotic Education."
62 For an insightful analysis of the reasons for China's younger generation's support of the government, see Luqiu, "Why Is China's Younger Generation More Pro-Government?"
63 See Zhu Xueqin 朱学勤, "Wusi yilai de liang ge jingshen 'binzao.'"
64 Oakeshott, *Rationalism in Politics*, 61.
65 Oakeshott, 63.
66 Oakeshott, 66.
67 Oakeshott, 66.
68 Oakeshott, 70.
69 Oakeshott, 69.

70 Oakeshott, 69.
71 For detailed and in-depth analyses on radical antitraditionalism in modern China, see Y. Lin, *Crisis of Chinese Consciousness*. See also L.O. Lee, *Voices from the Iron House*.
72 As mentioned earlier, studies by Guobin Yang, Rebecca MacKinnon, and Margaret E. Roberts all indicate the impossibility and inability of the Chinese government to completely control the information on the internet. See G. Yang, *Power of the Internet in China*; MacKinnon, *Consent of the Networked*; and Roberts, *Censored*.
73 Pusey, *China and Charles Darwin*, 241.
74 See Pusey, *China and Charles Darwin*; *Lu Xun and Evolution*.
75 Mao Zedong 毛泽东, *Quotations from Mao Tse Tung*.
76 Z. Wang, "National Humiliation."
77 Ci, *Dialect of the Chinese Revolution*, 8–16.
78 Ci, 8–16.
79 Elegant, "China's Me Generation."
80 Fewsmith, *China since Tiananmen*, 1–2.
81 Gramsci, "The Formation of the Intellectuals," 118.
82 Lovell, "Preface," 13–15.

2. *Wolf Totem*: Paradoxical Eulogy to a Culture

1 Goldblatt, "Translator's Note," in *Wolf Totem*, viii.
2 Choy, "Review of *Wolf Totem*."
3 Wasserstrom, "The Fur Is Flying."
4 H. Lee, "Lord of the Wolves?"
5 Seymour Chatman, in his well-known book on narrative in fiction and film, argues that any work, fiction or film, can be read both on "the level of surface manifestation" and on the "deeper narrative level." See Chatman, *Story and Discourse*, 41.
6 Jiang Rong 姜戎, *Wolf Totem*, 61.
7 Jiang Rong, 246.
8 Jiang Rong, 7.
9 Jiang Rong, 358.
10 Jiang Rong, 96.
11 Jiang Rong, 458.
12 Jiang Rong, 229–30.
13 Jiang Rong, 289.
14 Jiang Rong, 462.
15 Jiang Rong, 462.
16 Jiang Rong, 16.
17 Jiang Rong, 383.

18 Jiang Rong, 384.

19 Jiang Rong, 67.

20 Jiang Rong, 94.

21 Jiang Rong, 314.

22 Jiang Rong, 63.

23 Jiang Rong, 63.

24 Jiang Rong, 125.

25 Jiang Rong, 125.

26 According to Benjamin Schwartz, "correlative cosmology" as a world view and mode of thinking is not unique to traditional Chinese culture but exists in most "primitive" societies in human history. See Schwartz, *The World of Thought*, 351.

27 Jiang Rong 姜戎, *Wolf Totem*, 45.

28 Jiang Rong, 57.

29 Jiang Rong, 55.

30 Jiang Rong, 55.

31 Schwartz, *The World of Thought*, 370–1.

32 Jiang Rong 姜戎, *Wolf Totem*, 1.

33 Jiang Rong, 170.

34 Choy, "Review of *Wolf Totem*."

35 Lu Xun 鲁迅, *The Real Story of Ah-Q*, 17.

36 Jiang Rong 姜戎, *Wolf Totem*, 162.

37 Jiang Rong, 318.

38 Jiang Rong, 361.

39 Jiang Rong, 269.

40 Jiang Rong, 377.

41 Jiang Rong, 377.

42 Jiang Rong, 377.

43 Jiang Rong, 350.

44 Jiang Rong, 304.

45 Jiang Rong, 304.

46 Jiang Rong, 99.

47 Jiang Rong, 377.

48 Jiang Rong, 218.

49 Jiang Rong, 98.

50 Jiang Rong, 98.

51 Jiang Rong, 98.

52 Jiang Rong, 57.

53 Jiang Rong, 218.

54 Jiang Rong, 303.

55 Wolfgang Kubin, for example, believes that the novel reminds people of Hitler's fascist Germany. See Yun Yetui 云也退, "Gu Bin." Haiyan Lee,

Linda Jaivin, and Howard Y.F. Choy also share Kubin's view. See H. Lee, "The Lord of the Wolves?"; Jaivin, "Review of *Wolf Totem*"; Choy, "Review of *Wolf Totem*." Ling Cangzhou 凌沧州 refers to *Wolf Totem* as a Nazi ghost and fascist virus. See Ling Cangzhou 凌沧州, "Nacui youling yu Faxisi bingdu." Zhang Hong 张闳 also argues that at the core of *Wolf Totem* are the worship of the law of the jungle, the notion of the superiority of profit, and fascism. See Zhang Hong 张闳, "Zhongshan lang de zhanyu."

56 Jiang Rong 姜戎, *Wolf Totem*, 305.
57 Jiang Rong, 303.
58 Jiang Rong, 377.
59 Jiang Rong, 44.
60 Jiang Rong, 57.
61 Jiang Rong, 54.
62 Jiang Rong, 257.
63 Jiang Rong, 55.
64 Jiang Rong, 255.
65 Jiang Rong, 477.
66 Jiang Rong, 507.
67 Jiang Rong, 508.
68 Jiang Rong, 524.
69 Jiang Rong, 524.
70 Jiang Rong, 509.
71 Jiang Rong, 165.
72 Jiang Rong, 174.
73 Jiang Rong, 269.
74 Jiang Rong, 266.
75 H. Lee, "The Lord of the Wolves?"
76 Jiang Rong 姜戎, *Wolf Totem*, 384.
77 Jiang Rong, 385.
78 Jiang Rong, 389.
79 Jiang Rong, 389.
80 Jiang Rong, 388.
81 Jiang Rong, 501.
82 Jiang Rong, 388.
83 Jiang Rong, 495.
84 Jiang Rong, 456.
85 Goldblatt, "Translator's Note," ix.
86 For a detailed account of the different readings of the novel among mainland Chinese critics, see Cheng Yumei 程玉梅, "*Lang tuteng* de duozhong jiedu." For a survey of the reviews of the novel by scholars in the anglophone academic world, see Wasserstrom, "The Fur Is Flying."

87 H. Lee, "Lord of the Wolves?"

88 Literary critic Li Jianjun 李建军, for example, in his preface to Long Xingjian 龙行健, *Lang tuteng pipan*, describes how the dealers of *Wolf Totem*
used a tape recording to promote the novel through a loudspeaker at a
Beijing book market. See Li Jianjun 李建军, "Lang shi shuide tuteng (dai
xu)," 1. In the preface, Li Jianjun provides a detailed account of the advertising and marketing efforts to promote the novel (5–7).

89 In his book on *Wolf Totem*, Long Xingjian 龙行健 provides plenty of evidence, including surveys, online discussions, and his interviews with
ordinary readers, to demonstrate that nationalism and social Darwinist
mentality constitute the dominant drive for the popularity of the novel.
See Long Xingjian 龙行健, *Lang tuteng pipan*, 296–315. Ye Yixiang 叶奕
翔, by juxtaposing *Wolf Totem* with other popular books, including non-
fiction books that spread extreme nationalistic discourses and sentiments
such as *China Can Say No* and *China Is Unhappy*, points out that nationalism is the major driving force for the extreme popularity of *Wolf Totem*
and many other bestsellers in contemporary China. See Ye Yixiang 叶奕
翔, "Changxiaoshu yu minzu zhuyi."

90 Zhang Hong 张闳, "*Lang tuteng*: 'wenhua shifuzhe' de jingshen
shengyan."

91 Lin Xi 林希, "'Lang wenhua' yu shikuai zhexue"; and "Zai lun lang wenhua yu shikuai zhexue."

92 See Li Jianjun 李建军, "Lang shi shuide tuteng (dai xu)," 3–4. See also Lei
Da 雷达, "*Lang tuteng* zai pingjia yu wenhua fenxi."

93 Gramsci, "The Formation of the Intellectuals," 118.

94 Gramsci, 114.

95 Gramsci, 113.

96 Gramsci, 118.

97 Cheek, *The Intellectual in Modern Chinese*, xiii.

98 Cheek, xii.

99 Hamrin and Cheek, *China's Establishment Intellectuals*.

3. *Lenin's Kisses*: Absurdity, Dehumanization, and Dilemma of the Chinese Utopia

1 For a detailed introduction to Yan Lianke's writing career and an insightful analysis of his major works, see Leung, "Yan Lianke."

2 See Tao Dongfeng 陶东风, "*Shuohuo*."

3 Rojas, "Translator's Note," in *Lenin's Kisses*, vii.

4 For detailed and in-depth discussions of Yan Lianke's mythorealism,
see Sun Yu 孙郁, "Yan Lianke de 'shenshi zhuyi.'" See also Sun Yu 孙郁,
"Cong *shouhuo* dao *rixi*."

5 Yan Lianke 阎连科, *Faxian xiaoshuo*, 181.

6 Yan Lianke, 207.

7 Li and Yan Lianke, "*Enjoyment*: A New Experiment," 156.

8 See Xie, "An Age without Classics."

9 Xie.

10 Li and Yan Lianke, "*Enjoyment*: A New Experiment," 159.

11 Li and Yan Lianke, 158.

12 Yan Lianke 阎连科, *Lenin's Kisses*, 368.

13 Yan Lianke, 123.

14 Yan Lianke, 147.

15 J. Liu, "To Join the Commune?"

16 Yan Lianke 阎连科, *Lenin's Kisses*, 136.

17 Yan Lianke, 135.

18 Bianco, "Peasant Movements," 270.

19 Bianco, 270.

20 Bianco, "Peasant Responses," 178, 179.

21 For a detailed analysis of Su Tong's presentation of the Chinese revolution, see Z. Yu, *Chinese Avant-garde Fiction*, 59–60.

22 Yan Lianke 阎连科, *Lenin's Kisses*, 152.

23 Yan Lianke, 152.

24 Yan Lianke, 153–4.

25 Yan Lianke, 160.

26 Yan Lianke, 273.

27 Yan Lianke's depiction of the Great Famine has been proven by scholarly research. For instance, in his highly influential book on the Great Famine, Yang Jisheng, a courageous journalist and writer, estimates that about 36 million Chinese starved to death during the human catastrophe. He also provides numerous cases of cannibalism during the famine. See Yang Jisheng, *Tombstone*.

28 Yan Lianke 阎连科, *Lenin's Kisses*, 285.

29 Chen, "Ridiculing the Golden Age," 69.

30 Chen, 69.

31 D.D. Wang 王德威, "Geming shidai de ai yu si," 30.

32 Ci, *Dialectic of the Chinese Revolution*, 136.

33 Ci, 7.

34 Ci, 134.

35 Chen, "Ridiculing the Golden Age," 66.

36 Ci, *Dialectic of the Chinese Revolution*, 136–9.

37 Yan Lianke 阎连科, *Lenin's Kisses*, 204.

38 Yan Lianke, 203–4.

39 Yan Lianke, 203.

40 He Libo 何立波, "The Whole Story."

41 Rojas, "Time Out of Joint," 308.
42 Yan Lianke 阎连科, *Lenin's Kisses*, 184.
43 Yan Lianke, 339.
44 Yan Lianke, 476.
45 Yan Lianke, 341.
46 Yan Lianke, 342.
47 S.W. Chan, "Narrating Cancer, Disabilities, and AIDS," 186. See also Chen, "Ridiculing the Golden Age," 70.
48 S.W. Chan, "Narrating Cancer, Disabilities, and AIDS," 186.
49 S.W. Chan, 179.
50 For a detailed and in-depth analysis of Yan Lianke's presentation of the biopolitics of post-Mao China in the novel, see Cao, "Village Worlds." See also Rojas, "Time Out of Joint," 297–303.
51 Cao, "Village Worlds," 183, 187.
52 For a detailed and in-depth analysis of Lu Xun's portrayal of the cruel crowd, see L.O. Lee, *Voices from the Iron House*, 73–5.
53 For a detailed analysis of Yu Hua's "1986," and especially of the discursive continuity between the madman in this novella and the madman in Lu Xun's "Dairy of a Madman," see Z. Yu, *Chinese Avant-garde Fiction*, 190–2. For an analysis of the callousness of a crowd entertaining themselves with a person's death in Yu Hua's *The Seventh Day*, see chapter 6 of the present book.
54 Benjamin, "The Work of Art."
55 Yan Lianke 阎连科, *Lenin's Kisses*, 255.
56 Yan Lianke, 186.
57 Yan Lianke, 280–1.
58 Yan Lianke, 281.
59 Yan Lianke, 389 (italics in original).
60 J. Liu, "To Join the Commune?" 205.
61 Song, "Yan Lianke's Mythorealist Representation," 650.
62 Chen, "Ridiculing the Golden Age," 70; Rojas, "Time Out of Joint," 303, and "Speaking from the Margins," 433.
63 Chen, "Ridiculing the Golden Age," 70. "Happy" is Chen's rendition of the name of the village, *shouhuo*.
64 "Little nin" is a term used by the people of Liven to refer to a girl whose growth is stunted. See Yan Lianke 阎连科, *Lenin's Kisses*, 19.
65 For a detailed and in-depth analysis of the symptoms and reasons for the moral crisis in today's China and the potential solution to overcome it, see Ci, *Moral China*.
66 Yan Lianke 阎连科, *Lenin's Kisses*, 43.
67 Yan Lianke, 45.
68 Yan Lianke, 43.

69 Yan Lianke, 234.

70 Yan Lianke, 235.

71 Yan Lianke, 235.

72 For a detailed analysis of the integration of the sociopolitical order and the cultural-moral order in traditional Chinese culture, see Y. Lin, *Crisis of Chinese Consciousness*, 12–16.

73 Ci, *Moral China*, 21.

74 Ci, 21.

75 Yan Lianke 阎连科, *Lenin's Kisses*, 243.

76 Yan Lianke, 25.

77 Pei, "China: From Tiananmen to Neo-Stalinism," 148.

78 Weijie Song, in the aforementioned study on Yan Lianke's fiction, incisively points out that one of the remarkable accomplishments of *Lenin's Kisses* is its presentation of how the Chinese Party-state rules with "slow violence," appearing in everyday life in the forms of "demolitions, censorship, taboos, pollution, and the spread of chronic diseases," which makes a sharp contrast with "the wartime violence evidenced by corpses, wreckage, blood, or wounds." See Song, "Yan Lianke's Mythorealist Representation," 655.

79 Yan Lianke 阎连科, *Lenin's Kisses*, 441.

80 Yan Lianke, 442.

81 Yan Lianke, 230.

82 Yan Lianke, 229.

83 Huxley, Forward to *Brave New World*, xii.

84 Yan Lianke 阎连科, *Lenin's Kisses*, 263.

85 Yan Lianke, 262.

86 Yan Lianke, 262.

87 Yan Lianke, 339.

88 Gramsci, "The Formation of the Intellectuals," 118.

89 Arendt, *Origins of Totalitarianism*, 475.

90 Arendt, 474.

4. *Such Is This World@sars.come*: Dictatorship as a Fatal Disease

1 For a detailed description of the complicated process of the publication of Hu Fayun's *Such Is This World@sars.come*, see the translator A.E. Clark's preface to the English edition of the novel; Clark, "Preface."

2 In a review of the novel, Brian Bernards emphasizes that the novel bears "political implications that reach well beyond the historical moment of SARS on the global stage." See Bernards, "Review of *Such Is This World@sars.come*."

3 In an article on *Such Is This World* and Yan Lianke's *Dream of Ding Village*, Karen Thornber points out that exposure of "human and especially

bureaucratic culpability for the rapid spread of fatal diseases" is the shared theme of both novels. See Thornber, "Chinese Literary Landscapes of SARS and HIV / AIDS," 430.

4 Hu Fayun 胡发云, *Such Is This World*, 382.

5 Hu Fayun, 381.

6 Hu Fayun, 441.

7 Hu Fayun, 440.

8 Hu Fayun, 440.

9 Li Xuemei 李雪梅, "Dikang yiwang de yizhong fangshi."

10 Hu Fayun 胡发云, *Such Is This World*, 295.

11 Hu Fayun, 439 (italics in original).

12 Hu Fayun, 26.

13 Hu Fayun, 319.

14 Hu Fayun, 242.

15 Hu Fayun, 179.

16 Hu Fayun, 331.

17 Hu Fayun, 316.

18 Hu Fayun, 316.

19 Hu Fayun, 367.

20 Hu Fayun, 367–8.

21 Hu Fayun, 368.

22 Hu Fayun, 369.

23 H. Lee, "Déjà Vu."

24 Arendt, *Origins of Totalitarianism*, 475.

25 Hu Fayun 胡发云, *Such Is This World*, 231.

26 Hu Fayun, 387.

27 Hu Fayun, 314 (italics in original).

28 Hu Fayun, 256.

29 Hu Fayun, 107.

30 Hu Fayun, 213.

31 Hu Fayun, 202.

32 Hu Fayun, 202.

33 Hu Fayun, 203.

34 Hu Fayun, 196.

35 Hu Fayun, 206.

36 Hu Fayun, 206.

37 Hu Fayun, 212.

38 Hu Fayun, 214.

39 Hu Fayun, 215.

40 Hu Fayun, 217.

41 Hu Fayun, 212.

42 Hu Fayun, 196.

43 Gan Yang 甘阳, "Ziyouzhuyi: Guizu de haishi pingmin de?," 85.

44 Hu Fayun 胡发云, *Such Is This World*, 108.

45 Hu Fayun, 203–4.

46 Arendt, *Origins of Totalitarianism*, 475.

47 Shu Chong 舒崇, "Quanru Zhongguo" (my translation).

48 Zhuangzi, *Complete Works of Chuang Tzu*, chapter 10, "Cutting Open Satchels."

49 Zhuangzi, chapter 20, "Autumn Flood."

50 See Clark, "Preface," ii.

51 Hu Fayun 胡发云, *Such Is This World*, 224.

52 Hu Fayun, 239.

53 Hu Fayun, 403.

54 For an incisive analysis of the government's treatment of animals during the SARS outbreak and its political implications presented in the novel, see H. Lee, *The Stranger*, 86–92.

55 Hu Fayun 胡发云, *Such Is This World*, 403.

56 Hu Fayun, 421.

57 Hu Fayun, 422 (italics in original).

58 Hu Fayun, 422.

59 Hu Fayun, 423.

60 Hu Fayun, 423.

61 Hu Fayun, 423.

62 Hu Fayun, 426.

63 Hu Fayun, 442.

64 Hu Fayun, 442.

65 Brady, *Marketing Dictatorship*.

5. *The Fat Years*: Social Injustice, Forced Amnesia, Distorted Mentality, and Fascism

1 For a more detailed account of this literary explosion, see Link, *Uses of Literature*, 6–7.

2 As mentioned earlier, because the novel was banned in mainland China after publication, Chan Koonchung "pirated" his rights from his own publisher in Hong Kong to let Chinese mainlanders read it online for free. See Eberlein, "China 2013."

3 Mooney, "2013: Them and Us."

4 In addition to the aforementioned articles by Xujun Eberlein and Paul Mooney, see also Jaivin, "Yawning Heights"; Osnos, "The Age of Complacency?"; Z. Yu, "Questioning the Chinese Model."

5 In her preface to the English edition of the novel, Julia Lovell explicitly compares *The Fat Years* to *Nineteen Eighty-Four* and points to the similarity

of the two novels in their exposure of the logic of dictatorship. See Lovell, "Preface," in Chan Koonchung, *The Fat Years*, 18–19. Ian Johnson also claims *The Fat Years* "predicts an Orwellian future for China." See Johnson, "On the Party Circuit." Indeed, there is abundant evidence showing the inspiration of Orwell for this novel. The love story between Old Chen and Little Xi in *The Fat Years*, for instance, reminds readers of the love story between Winston Smith and Julia in *Nineteen Eight-Four*. Structurally and technically, the national leader He Dongsheng's lengthy explanation of the Party's ruling policies also leads readers to the detailed elaboration of Goldstein's theory. Moreover, readers can hardly neglect the similarity between the indoctrination of the philosophy of hatred and the manipulation of history in *The Fat Years* and the practice of Two Minutes Hate and the "memory hole" in *Nineteen Eighty-Four*, as well as the shared images of youths mentally distorted by deceptive propaganda in both novels.

6 Jeffrey Kinkley identifies "five traditions of the global dystopian novel," including the Slavic and anglophone stream, the post–October Revolution Russian and Eastern European stream, the Japanese stream, the Latin American and Caribbean stream, and the Chinese stream. He refers to the first stream, which is founded by Zamyatin, Čapek, Huxley, and Orwell, as the "classic" tradition of dystopian writing (and filming). See Kinkley, *Visions of Dystopia*, 12–17.

7 Howe, *Politics and the Novel*, 238–9.

8 Howe, 235.

9 For a detailed and incisive analysis of the thematic similarities between *The Fat Years* and *Nineteen Eighty-Four* and *Brave New World*, see Fang, "Rethinking the Orwellian Imaginary."

10 Jeffrey Kinkley in his book *Visions of Dystopia* provides a highly incisive and insightful analysis on the visions of dystopia in China's new historical novels. The book not only examines the main motifs and themes of those novels with dystopian visions that focus on China's turbulent recent history but also probes some fundamental problems facing Chinese writers and literature under Communist domination, such as the workings and mechanisms of censorship and self-censorship, the relationship between aesthetics and politics in literary works, and the strategies employed by writers for political protection, as well as other issues. Though in his discussion of those dystopian Chinese historical novels, Kinkley deliberately excludes the Orwellian-style dystopian novels created in China like *The Fat Years*, his wisdom and insight displayed in his study provide highly valuable perspectives and analytical techniques for reading this novel. See Kinkley, *Visions of Dystopia*.

11 Lovell, "Preface," 15.

12 C. Wang, "Dreamers and Nightmares," 29.

13 See Pei, *China's Trapped Transition*. See also his *China's Crony Capitalism*.

14 Chan Koonchung 陈冠中, *The Fat Years*, 146–7.

15 The term "journalistic immediacy" was coined by David Der-wei Wang to characterize the pronounced realistic feature of the late Qing "novels of exposé," a genre of broadly defined political fiction. Oppositional political novels of the early twenty-first century inherit this legacy. See D.D. Wang, *Fin-de-Siècle Splendor*, 188. See also Kinkley, *Corruption and Realism*, 151.

16 According to Minxin Pei's study, collusion between government officials and underground criminal organizations is an extreme form of "collusive corruption" in China. See Pei, *China's Crony Capitalism*, 9.

17 Chan Koonchung 陈冠中, *The Fat Years*, 76.

18 For a detailed account and incisive analysis of black kiln phenomena that took place in early twenty-first century China, see Han, "From Blood-stained Mine-shafts to Brickyard Slavery."

19 Chan Koonchung 陈冠中, *The Fat Years*, 193.

20 Chan Koonchung, 191.

21 Chan Koonchung, 180–3.

22 Pei, *China's Trapped Transition*, 7–16, 33–44.

23 As mentioned in chapter 1, the so-called Chinese model of development, according to Minxin Pei's study, which fits in with China's reality very well, is in essence "crony capitalism." "Collusive corruption by elites" is "the heart and soul of crony capitalism." See Pei, *China's Crony Capitalism*, 23.

24 Chan Koonchung 陈冠中, *The Fat Years*, 191.

25 Chan Koonchung, 84.

26 Michael S. Duke's translation of *bancuntou dage* is "Big Brother Ban Cuntou." In Chinese popular literature and films as well as in reality, *bancuntou* (crewcut) is often the hairstyle that gangsters or members of underground societies wear. I believe Chan Koonchung deliberately chose the term "Big Brother Crewcut" to name the head of the study group, both to allude to the Big Brother in *Nineteen Eighty-Four* and to hint at the quasi-underground society nature of the group.

27 Chan Koonchung 陈冠中, *The Fat Years*, 86.

28 Chan Koonchung, 90.

29 Pei, *China's Trapped Transition*, 8–9.

30 Chan Koonchung 陈冠中, *The Fat Years*, 87.

31 Chan Koonchung, 126.

32 Chan Koonchung, 44.

33 Chan Koonchung, 66.

34 Chan Koonchung, 176.

35 Chan Koonchung, 177.

36 Chan Koonchung, 68.

37 Kundera, *The Book of Laughter*, 3.
38 Connerton, *How Societies Remember*, 22.
39 Orwell, *Nineteen Eighty-Four*, 38.
40 Huxley, Forward to *Brave New World*, xii.
41 Huxley, viii.
42 Huxley, vii.
43 Chan Koonchung 陈冠中, *The Fat Years*, 155.
44 Chan Koonchung, 160.
45 Chan Koonchung, 160.
46 Chan Koonchung, 161.
47 Chan Koonchung, 161–2.
48 Chan Koonchung, 297.
49 Chan Koonchung, 158 (italics in original).
50 Chan Koonchung, 147.
51 Chan Koonchung, 165.
52 Chan Koonchung, 167.
53 Kundera, *Unbearable Lightness of Being*.
54 Pei, *China's Trapped Transition*, 19.
55 Pei, 20.
56 Chan Koonchung 陈冠中, *The Fat Years*, 297.
57 Chan Koonchung, 295.
58 Chan Koonchung, 296.
59 Chan Koonchung, 297.
60 Chan Koonchung, 297.
61 Chan Koonchung, 296.
62 Chan Koonchung, 162.
63 Chan Koonchung, 162.
64 Chan Koonchung, 163.
65 Lovell, "Preface," 13–14.
66 Lovell, 15.
67 Connerton, *How Societies Remember*, 22.
68 Yuan Weishi 袁伟时, "Xiandaihua yu lishi jiaokeshu."
69 Chan Koonchung 陈冠中, *The Fat Years*, 63–4.
70 Chan Koonchung, 44.
71 Chan Koonchung, 90.
72 Chan Koonchung, 92.
73 Chan Koonchung, 89–90.
74 Chan Koonchung, 91.
75 Chan Koonchung, 287.
76 For a detailed account and analysis of the Blue Shirts Society, see Eastman, "The Kuomintang in the 1930s."
77 Chan Koonchung 陈冠中, *The Fat Years*, 91.

78 Chan Koonchung, 84.
79 Chan Koonchung, 286.
80 Chan Koonchung, 222.
81 Chan Koonchung, 64.
82 Chan Koonchung, 84–5.
83 Qian Liqun 钱理群, "Xunzhao shiqu de 'daxue jingshen,'" 33.
84 Qian Liqun, 33–4 (my translation).
85 Arendt, *Eichmann in Jerusalem*.
86 Chan Koonchung 陈冠中, *The Fat Years*, 222.
87 Chan Koonchung, 213.
88 Chan Koonchung, 223.
89 Chan Koonchung, 223.
90 Chan Koonchung, 222.
91 C. Wang, "Dreamers and Nightmares," 30.
92 Chan Koonchung 陈冠中, *The Fat Years*, 33.
93 Chan Koonchung, 141.
94 Chan Koonchung, 103.
95 Chan Koonchung, 248.
96 Chan Koonchung, 241.
97 Chan Koonchung, 248.
98 Chan Koonchung, 279–80.
99 Larmer, "Is China the World's New Colonial Power?"
100 As mentioned earlier, according to Suisheng Zhao's study, because the Chinese Communist Party came to power through a popular, anti-imperialist war, the real source of the legitimacy of the Communist state is not Marxism but nationalism. See S. Zhao, *Nation-State by Construction*, 209.
101 Chan Koonchung 陈冠中, *The Fat Years*, 287.
102 Chan Koonchung, 283–4.
103 Chan Koonchung, 283.
104 Chan Koonchung, 284.
105 Gardels, "China vs. America."
106 Chan Koonchung 陈冠中, *The Fat Years*, 241.
107 Bauman, *Modernity and the Holocaust*, 86.
108 Bauman, 94–5.
109 Kren and Rappoport, *Holocaust and the Crisis of Human Behavior*, 130.
110 Arendt, *Origins of Totalitarianism*, 475.

6. *The Seventh Day*: Dystopian Wasteland versus Modern Peach Blossom Spring

1 For a detailed analysis of the themes of Yu Hua's novels, see Z. Yu, *Chinese Avant-garde Fiction*, 93–135.

2 Berry, "Afterword," in *To Live*, 240.
3 Chatman, *Story and Discourse*, 41.
4 Yu Hua 余华, *The Seventh Day*, 18.
5 Yu Hua, 18.
6 Yu Hua, 18.
7 Yu Hua, 22.
8 For a detailed description of forced demolitions in early twenty-first century China and people's resistance, see Cody, "China's Land Grabs."
9 Yu Hua 余华, *The Seventh Day*, 195.
10 Yu Hua, 25.
11 Yu Hua, 25.
12 Yu Hua, 25.
13 Yu Hua, 149.
14 Yu Hua, 25.
15 Yu Hua, 152.
16 Yu Hua, 153.
17 Yu Hua, 153–4.
18 Yu Hua, 3–4.
19 Yu Hua, 3–4.
20 Yu Hua, 24.
21 Yu Hua, 24.
22 Yu Hua, 26.
23 Yu Hua, 23–4.
24 It is common knowledge that ancestor worship is a defining feature of traditional Chinese culture. The essence of ancestor worship is to deify deceased human beings and sanctify human relations and human feelings. The sanctification of human relations and human feelings as presented in *The Seventh Day* reveals a profound continuity between Yu Hua and the traditional Chinese world view and values. For a detailed and insightful analysis of ancestor worship in traditional Chinese culture, see Schwartz, *The World of Thought*, 20–2.
25 Yu Hua 余华, *The Seventh Day*, 99–101.
26 Yu Hua, 46.
27 Yu Hua, 113.
28 Yu Hua, 114.
29 Yu Hua, 114.
30 Yu Hua, 33.
31 Yu Hua, 34.
32 Yu Hua, 34.
33 Yu Hua, 130.
34 Arendt, *Eichmann in Jerusalem*.
35 Elon, "Introduction," in *Eichmann in Jerusalem*, xiii.

36 Y. Huang, "Ghosts and Their Contemporary Return," 59.
37 Yu Hua 余华, *The Seventh Day*, 213.
38 Yu Hua, 156.
39 Yu Hua, 188.
40 Yu Hua, 191.
41 Yu Hua, 156.
42 Yu Hua, 156.
43 Yu Hua, 123.
44 Yu Hua, 137.
45 Yu Hua, 132.
46 Yu Hua, 136.
47 Yu Hua, 151.
48 Yu Hua, 150.
49 Yu Hua 144.
50 Yu Hua, 144–5.
51 Robert Solomon insists that mood is less a reaction to a particular object or a specific situation than a reflection of a human being's overall attitude towards and understanding of the world as a whole. He argues: "Moods are generalized emotions: An emotion focuses its attention on more-or-less particular objects and situations, whereas a mood enlarges its grasp to attend the world as a whole ... Depression, for example, is aimed at the world in general, but it is constructed upon a base of particular emotions which remains at its core, visible but no longer distinctive." See Solomon, *The Passions*, 132–3. Martin Heidegger also regards mood as a primordial way to reveal existential truth. As he points out, mood discloses *Dasein* to itself *"prior to* all cognition and volition, and *beyond* their range of disclosure" (italics in original). He also defined mood as a primordial way that human beings attune to the world. See Heidegger, *Kant and the Problem of Metaphysics*, 173, 195.
52 Yu Hua 余华, *The Seventh Day*, 149.
53 Yu Hua, 148.
54 Yu Hua, 149.
55 The Peach Blossom Spring is a fictional place portrayed in a fable written by Tao Yuanming 陶渊明, one of the most famous poets in Chinese history. It is a peaceful and beautiful small village isolated from the outside world. Later on, the Peach Blossom Spring becomes a synonym for utopia in Chinese literature. For a more detailed and insightful analysis of the political implications of Tao Yuanming's fable of the Peach Blossom Spring, see L. Zhang, "The Utopian Vision," 221–7. In this essay, Zhang emphasizes the secular and worldly nature of Tao Yuanming's utopia. As he points out, "the Peach Blossom Spring is a human community, not a land of mystical and immortal beings" (224).

56 "Effortless effort" (*wuwei* 无为) is a core concept of Taoism as represented by Laozi and Zhuangzi. On the level of moral cultivation of the individual, "effortless effort" means following the lead of intuition and human nature. On the level of governance, it means that the ruler should limit his authority and administrative capacity to the minimum. For a detailed discussion of the concept, see Creel, *What Is Taoism?*

57 Confucius claims that rulers of states and heads of noble families should not be worried over scarcity of wealth or poverty but over social inequality and social unrest. See Confucius, *The Analects*, 16:1.

58 Compared with today's China, Mao's China was indeed more equal. However, the Maoist social equality is based on poverty – everyone is equally poor – and asceticism. As Jiwei Ci convincingly points out, according to the Maoist socialist theory, the practice of asceticism in a short period of time serves as a necessary means to achieve hedonism in the long run. See Ci, *Dialect of the Chinese Revolution*, 8–16.

Epilogue: Limits of Transgression and Mechanisms of Counter-Censorship

1 Moore, *Censorship and the Limits of the Literary*, 2.
2 Moore, 2.
3 Foucault, *Discipline and Punishment*, 203.
4 Lovell, "Translator's Afterword," in *I Love Dollars*, 239.
5 Goldblatt, "Border Crossings," 215.
6 Kinkley, *Corruption and Realism*, 154.
7 Kinkley, 161.
8 Lovell, "Preface," 14–15.
9 In my book on Chinese avant-garde fiction, I have provided detailed analyses of how each of the three leading Chinese avant-garde writers, Su Tong, Yu Hua, and Ge Fei, employs varied modern narrative concepts, devices, and techniques to achieve his subversive purposes. See Z. Yu, *Chinese Avant-garde Fiction*, chapter 5.
10 Ng, "China's Elusive Truths," 238–9.
11 Ng, 239.
12 Goldblatt, "Border Crossings," 215.
13 Kinkley, *Visions of Dystopia*, xii.
14 Lukács, *Realism in Our Time*, 19.
15 Howe, *Politics and the Novel*, 20.
16 Howe, 241.
17 Howe, 240–2.
18 Howe, 247.

Bibliography

Anderlini, Jamil. "Patriotic Education Distorts China World View." *Financial Times*, 23 December 2012. https://www.ft.com/content/66430e4e-4cb0-11e2 -986e-00144feab49a.

Apter, David E. "Discourse as Power: Yan'an and the Chinese Revolution." In *New Perspectives on the Chinese Communist Revolution*, edited by Tony Saich and Hans van de Ven, 193–234. London: Routledge, 1995.

Arendt, Hannah. *Eichmann in Jerusalem: A Report on the Banality of Evil*. New York: Penguin Books, 2006.

– *The Origins of Totalitarianism*. New York: Harcourt, Brace & World, 1966.

Bandurski, David. "Musings on a CCP Buzzword That Has Everyone Stumped." *China Media Project*, 27 March 2009. https://chinamedia project.org/2009/03/27/musings-on-a-ccp-buzzword-that-has-stumped -everyone/.

Barmé, Geremie. *In the Red: On Contemporary Chinese Culture*. New York: Columbia University Press, 1999.

Bauman, Zygmunt. *Modernity and the Holocaust*. Ithaca, NY: Cornell University Press, 1991.

Benjamin, Walter. "The Work of Art in the Age of Mechanical Reproduction" (1936). Translated by Harry Zohn. *Marxists.org*. https://www.marxists.org /reference/subject/philosophy/works/ge/benjamin.htm.

Bernards, Brian. "Review of *Such Is This World@sars.come* by Hu Fayun." MCLC Resource Center, Ohio State University, August 2011. https://u.osu .edu/mclc/book-reviews/such-is-this.

Berry, Michael. "Afterword." In *To Live*, by Yu Hua, translated by Michael Berry, 237–45. New York: Anchor Books, 2003.

Bianco, Lucien. "Peasant Movements." In *The Cambridge History of China*, edited by Denis Twitchett and John K. Fairbank, 13:270–329. Cambridge: Cambridge University Press, 1983.

– "Peasant Responses to CCP Mobilization Policies, 1937–1945." In *New Perspectives on the Chinese Communist Revolution*, edited by Tony Saich and Hans van de Ven, 175–87. London: Routledge, 1995.

Brady, Anne-Marie. *Marketing Dictatorship: Propaganda and Thought Work in Contemporary China*. Lanham, MD: Rowman & Littlefield Publishers, 2010.

Cao, Xuenan. "Village Worlds: Yan Lianke's Villages and Matters of Life." *Journal of Language, Literature and Culture* 63, no. 2–3 (2016): 179–90. https://doi.org/10.1080/20512856.2016.1244917.

Carrico, Kevin. "The New Nationalism of Xi's New Era." *The Asia Dialogue*, 13 February 2020. https://theasiadialogue.com/2020/02/13/the-new-nationalism-of-xis-new-era.

Chan Koonchung 陈冠中. *The Fat Years*. Translated by Michael S. Duke. London: Doubleday, 2011.

– *Jianfeng er nian: Xin Zhongguo wuyou shi* 建丰二年：新中国乌有史 [The second year of Jianfeng: An alternative history of new China]. Hong Kong: Oxford University Press, 2016.

– *Luoming* 裸命 [Bare life; English title: The unbearable dreamworld of Champa the driver]. Taipei: Maitian chuban gongsi, 2013.

– *The Unbearable Dreamworld of Champa the Driver*. Translated by Nicky Harman. London: Doubleday, 2014.

Chan, Shelley W. "Narrating Cancer, Disabilities, and AIDS: Yan Lianke's Trilogy of Disease." In *Discourses of Disease: Writing Illness, the Mind and the Body in Modern China*, edited by Howard Y. F. Choy, 177–99. Leiden: Brill Press, 2016.

Chang, Hao. "New Confucianism and the Intellectual Crisis of Contemporary China." In *The Limits of Change: Essays on Conservative Alternatives in Republican China*, edited by Charlotte Furth, 276–83. Cambridge, MA: Harvard University Press, 1976.

Chatman, Seymour. *Story and Discourse: Narrative Structure in Fiction and Film*. Ithaca, NY: Cornell University Press, 1978.

Cheek, Timothy. *The Intellectual in Modern Chinese History*. Cambridge: Cambridge University Press, 2015.

Chen Sihe 陈思和. *Zhongguo xinwenxue zhengtiguan* 中国新文学整体观 [Overview of China's new literature]. Shanghai: Shanghai wenyi chubanshe, 2001.

Chen, Thomas. "Ridiculing the Golden Age: Subversive Undertones in Yan Lianke's *Happy*." *Chinese Literature Today* 1, no. 2 (2011): 66–72. https://doi.org/10.1080/21514399.2011.11833936.

– "The Workshop of the World: Censorship and the Internet Novel 'Such Is This World.'" In *China's Contested Internet*, edited by Guobin Yang, 19–43. Copenhagen: NIAS Press, 2015.

Cheng Yumei 程玉梅. "*Lang tuteng* de duozhong jiedu"《狼图腾》多种解读 [Multiple readings of *Wolf Totem*]. *Zhongguo shehui kexue bao* 中国社会科学报, 15 June 2006, 3.

Choy, Howard Y.F. "Review of *Wolf Totem*." MCLC Resource Center, Ohio State University, April 2009. https://u.osu.edu/mclc/book-reviews/wolf -totem.

Ci, Jiwei. *Dialects of the Chinese Revolution: From Utopianism to Hedonism.* Stanford, CA: Stanford University Press, 1994.

– *Moral China in the Age of Reform.* Cambridge: Cambridge University Press, 2014.

Clark, A.E. "Preface." In *Such Is This World@sars.come*, by Hu Fayun 胡发云, translated by A.E. Clark, i–iii. Dobbs Ferry, NY: Ragged Banner Press, 2011.

Cody, Edward. "China's Land Grabs Raise Specter of Popular Unrest." *Washington Post*, 5 October 2004. https://www.washingtonpost.com /wp-dyn/articles/A6968-2004Oct4.html.

Confucius. *The Analects.* Translated by D.C. Lau. London: Penguin Books, 1998.

Connerton, Paul. *How Societies Remember.* Cambridge: Cambridge University Press, 1989.

Creel, Herrlee G. *What Is Taoism? And Other Studies in Cultural History.* Chicago: University of Chicago Press, 1970.

Dai, Qing. *Wang Shiwei and "Wild Lilies": Rectification and Purges in the Chinese Communist Party, 1942–1944.* Armonk, NY: M.E. Sharpe, 1994.

Deng, Chao, and Liza Lin. "In Xi Jinping's China, Nationalism Takes a Dark Turn." *Wall Street Journal*, 22 October 2020. https://www.wsj.com/articles /in-xi-jinpings-china-nationalism-takes-a-dark-turn-11603382993.

Denton, Kirk A. "Literature and Politics: Mao Zedong's 'Yan'an Talks' and Party Rectification." In *The Columbia Companion to Modern Chinese Literature*, edited by Kirk A. Denton, 224–30. New York: Columbia University Press, 2016.

Di Yufei 荻雨菲. "Chan Koonchung: Xiangxiang fei Gongchandang tongzhi de Zhongguo" 陈冠中：想像非共产党统治的中国 [Chan Koonchung: Imagining a China without Communist rule]. *The New York Times* (Chinese edition), 2 November 2015. https://cn.nytimes.com/china/20151102 /c02sino-chan.

Dong Enlin 董恩林. "Dalu 'guoxue re' xianzhuang de fenxi yu pingjia" 大陆 「国学热」现状的分析与评价 [Analysis and assessment of the current situation of the "national studies fever" in mainland China]. *Zhongguo wenzhe yanjiu tongxun* 中国文哲研究通讯 [Newsletter of the Institute of Chinese Literature and Philosophy] 24, no. 1 (2014): 33–54.

Du Ting 杜婷. "Chan Koonchung tan *Luoming*: Zhongguo zuojia de xiangxiang buru xianshi huangdan" 陈冠中谈《裸命》：中国作家的想像不如现实荒诞

[Chan Koonchung talks about *The Unbearable Dreamworld of Champa the Driver*: Chinese writers' imagination is not as absurd as the reality]. *The New York Times* (Chinese edition), 4 March 2013. https://cn.nytimes.com /culture/20130304/cc04chenguanzhong/zh-hant.

Duke, Michael S. *Blooming and Contending: Chinese Literature in the Post-Mao Era*. Bloomington: Indiana University Press, 1985.

– "Introduction." In *Contemporary Chinese Literature: An Anthology of Post-Mao Fiction and Poetry*, edited by Michael S. Duke, 1–5. Armon, NY: M.E. Sharpe, 1985.

– "Reinventing China: Cultural Exploration in Contemporary Chinese Fiction." *Issues and Studies* 25, no. 8 (1989): 9–53.

Eastman, Lloyd E. "The Kuomintang in the 1930s." In *The Limits of Change: Essays on Conservative Alternatives in Republican China*, edited by Charlotte Furth, 193–6. Cambridge, MA: Harvard University Press, 1976.

Eberlein, Xujun. "China 2013." *Foreign Policy*, 30 July 2010. https://foreign policy.com/2010/07/30/china-2013/.

Economy, Elizabeth C. *The Third Revolution: Xi Jinping and the New Chinese State*. New York: Oxford University Press, 2018.

Elegant, Simon. "China's Me Generation." *Time*, 5 November 2007. http:// content.time.com/time/magazine/article/0,9171,1675626,00.html.

Elon, Amos. "Introduction: The Excommunication of Hannah Arendt." In *Eichmann in Jerusalem: A Report on the Banality of Evil*, by Hannah Arendt, vii–xxiii. New York: Penguin Books, 2006.

Fang, Karen. "Rethinking the Orwellian Imaginary through Contemporary Chinese Fiction." *Surveillance & Society* 17, no. 5 (2019): 738–42. https://doi .org/10.24908/ss.v17i5.13458.

Fewsmith, Joseph. *China since Tiananmen: The Politics of Transition*. Cambridge, MA: Harvard University Press, 2001.

Foucault, Michel. *Discipline and Punishment: The Birth of the Prison*. Translated by Alan Sheridan. New York: Vintage Books, 1995.

Gan Yang 甘阳. "Ziyouzhuyi: Guizu de haishi pingmin de?" 自由主义：贵族的还是平民的? [Liberalism: For aristocracy or for populace?]. *Dushu* 读书, no. 1 (1999): 85–94.

Gardels, Nathan. "China vs. America: Which Government Model Will Triumph?" *Christian Science Monitor*, 17 January 2010. https://www.csmonitor.com /Commentary/Global-Viewpoint/2010/0127/China-vs.-America-Which -government-model-will-triumph.

Geertz, Clifford. *The Interpretation of Cultures*. New York: Basic Books, 1973.

Goldblatt, Howard. "Border Crossings: Chinese Writings, in Their World and Ours." In *Chinese Aesthetics and Literature: A Reader*, edited by Corinne H. Dale, 211–28. Albany, NY: SUNY Press, 2004.

– "Translator's Note." In *Wolf Totem*, by Jiang Rong, translated by Howard Goldblatt, vii–ix. New York: Penguin Books, 2008.

Goldman, Merle. *China's Intellectuals: Adviser and Dissident*. Cambridge, MA: Harvard University Press, 1981.

– *Literary Dissident in Communist China*. Cambridge, MA: Harvard University Press, 1967.

– *Sowing the Seeds of Democracy*. Cambridge, MA: Harvard University Press, 1995.

Gong, Haomin. *Uneven Modernity: Literature, Film, and Intellectual Discourses in Postsocialist China*. Honolulu: Hawaii University Press, 2012.

Gramsci, Antonio. "The Formation of the Intellectuals." Translated by Quinton Hoare and Geoffrey Nowell Smith. In *An Anthology of Western Marxism: From Lukács and Gramsci to Socialist-Feminism*, edited by Roger S. Gottlieb, 112–19. New York: Oxford University Press, 1989.

Hamrin, Carol Lee, and Timothy Cheek. *China's Establishment Intellectuals*. Armonk, NY: M.E. Sharpe, 1987.

Han, Dongfang. "From Bloodstained Mine-shafts to Brickyard Slavery, Blind Faith in Deng Xiaoping Theory Is the Real Culprit." *China Labor Bulletin*, 25 July 2007. https://clb.org.hk/content/shanxi-brickyard-scandal-and -child-labour-china.

He Libo 何立波. "The Whole Story of the 'Great Leap Forward' in Xushui County" [Xushui xian "dayuejin" shimo 徐水县"大跃进"始末]. *Communist Party of China News*. http://cpc.people.com.cn/GB/85037/85038/7727231 .html.

Heidegger, Martin. *Kant and the Problem of Metaphysics*. Translated by James Churchill. Bloomington: Indiana University Press, 1962.

Hockx, Michel. *Internet Literature in China*. New York: Columbia University Press, 2015.

Howe, Irving. *Politics and the Novel*. Chicago: Ivan R. Dee, 2002.

Hsia, Tsi-an. *The Gate of Darkness: Studies on the Leftist Literary Movement in China*. Seattle: University of Washington Press, 1968.

Huang Shengbo 黄声波. "Zhengzhi wenhua shiye xia de dangdai guanchang xiaoshuo chuangzuo yu jieshou" 政治文化视野下的当代官场小说创作与接受 [Creation and reception of contemporary officialdom fiction in the context of political culture]. *Lilun yu chuangzuo* 理论与创作, no. 1 (2010): 51–4.

Huang, Yiju. "Ghosts and Their Contemporary Return: The Case of Yu Hua's *The Seventh Day*." *Neohelicon* 43 (2016): 59–71. https://doi.org/10.1007 /S11059-016-0330-4.

Huang Zhaohui 黄兆晖. "*Ruyan@sars.come*: 06 nian zuihuo de xiaoshuo" 如焉@ sars.come: 06 年最火的小说 [*Such Is This World@sars.come*: The most popular novel in 2006]. *Nandu zhoukan* 南都周刊, 10 March, 2006. http://www.hxzq .net/aspshow/showarticle.asp?id=2277.

Hu Fayun 胡发云. *Midong* 迷冬 [Misty winters]. Beijing: Renmin wenxue chubanshe, 2013.

– *Such Is This World@sars.come*. Translated by A.E. Clark. Dobbs Ferry, NY: Ragged Banner Press, 2011.

Huters, T.D. "Critical Ground: The Transformation of the May Fourth Era." In *Popular Chinese Literature and Performing Arts in the People's Republic of China 1949–1979*, edited by Bonnie S. McDougall, 54–80. Berkeley: University of California Press, 1984.

Huxley, Aldous. *Brave New World*. New York: Bantam Books, 1946.

Idema, Wilt, and Lloyd Haft. "The Central Tradition in Traditional Society." In *Chinese Aesthetics and Literature: A Reader*, edited by Corinne H. Dale, 41–54. Albany, NY: SUNY Press, 2004.

Jaivin, Linda. "Review of *Wolf Totem*." *Australian Literary Review*, 7 May 2008. Republished on *China Heritage*. https://chinaheritage.net/journal /1900-2020-an-old-anxiety-in-a-new-era/.

– "Yawning Heights: Chan Koon-chung's Harmonious China." *China Heritage Quarterly*, no. 22 (June 2010). http://www.chinaheritagequarterly.org /articles.php?searchterm=022_golden.inc&issue=022.

Jiang, Min. "Authoritarian Deliberation on Chinese Internet." *Electronic Journal of Communication* 20, no. 3–4 (2010). https://ssrn.com/abstract=1439354.

Jiang Rong 姜戎. *Wolf Totem*. Translated by Howard Goldblatt. New York: Penguin Books, 2008.

Johansson, Perry. *The Libidinal Economy of China: Gender, Nationalism, and Consumer Culture*. Lanham, MD: Lexington Books, 2015.

Johnson, Ian. "On the Party Circuit, and Upsetting the Party." *New York Times*, 29 July 2011. https://www.nytimes.com/2011/07/30/world/asia/30chan .html.

Kahn, Joseph, and Jim Yardley. "As China Roars, Pollution Reaches Deadly Extremes." *New York Times*, 26 August 2007. https://www.nytimes.com /2007/08/26/world/asia/26china.html.

Kinkley, Jeffery. *Chinese Justice, the Fiction: Law and Literature in Modern China*. Stanford, CA: Stanford University Press, 2000.

– *Corruption and Realism in Late Socialist China: The Return of the Political Novel*. Stanford, CA: Stanford University Press, 2007.

– *Visions of Dystopia in China's New Historical Novels*. New York: Columbia University Press, 2015.

Kong, Shuyu. *Consuming Literature: Best Sellers and the Commercialization of Literary Production in Contemporary China*. Stanford, CA: Stanford University Press, 2005.

Kraus, Richard Curt. *The Party and the Arty in China: The New Politics of Culture*. Lanham, MD: Rowman and Littlefield, 2004.

Kren, George A., and Leon Rappoport. *The Holocaust and the Crisis of Human Behavior*. New York: Holmes & Meier, 1980.

Kundera, Milan. *The Book of Laughter and Forgetting*. Translated by Michael Henry Heim. New York: A.A. Knopf, 1980.

– *Unbearable Lightness of Being*. Translated by Michael Henry Heim. New York: Harper & Row, 1984.

Larmer, Brook. "Is China the World's New Colonial Power?" *New York Times*, 2 May 2017. https://www.nytimes.com/2017/05/02/magazine/is-china-the-worlds-new-colonial-power.html.

Lee, Haiyan. "Déjà Vu: Revisiting Hu Fayun's SARS Novel during the 2020 Coronavirus Pandemic." MCLC Resource Center, Ohio State University, May 2020. https://u.osu.edu/mclc/online-series/haiyan-lee.

– "Lord of the Wolves?" *The China Beat*, 19 June 2008. http://thechinabeat.blogspot.com/2008/06/lord-of-wolves.html.

– *The Stranger and the Chinese Moral Imagination*. Stanford, CA: Stanford University Press, 2014.

Lee, Leo Ou-fan. *Voices from the Iron House: A Study of Lu Xun*. Bloomington: Indiana University Press, 1987.

Lei Da 雷达. "*Lang tuteng* zai pingjia yu wenhua fenxi" 狼图腾再评价与文化分析 [Reassessment of *Wolf Totem* and a cultural analysis]. *Guangming ribao* 光明日报, 12 August 2005. https://www.gmw.cn/01gmrb/2005-08/12/content_287926.htm.

Lei Yi 雷颐. "'Guoxue re,' minzuzhuyi zhuanxiang yu sixiangshi yanjiu" 「国学热」、民族主义转向与思想史研究 ["National Studies Fever," turn of nationalism, and studies of intellectual history]. *Ershiyi shiji* 二十一世纪 [Twenty-first century], no. 1 (February 2014): 4–17.

Leung, Laifong. "Yan Lianke: A Writer's Moral Duty." *Chinese Literature Today* 1, no. 2 (2011): 73–9. https://doi.org/10.1080/21514399.2011.11833937.

Levenson, Joseph. *Liang Ch'i-Ch'ao and the Mind of Modern China*. Cambridge, MA: Harvard University Press, 1953.

Li Jianjun 李建军. "Lang shi shuide tuteng (dai xu)" 狼是谁的图腾 (代序) [Preface: Whose totem is the wolf?] In *Lang tuteng pipan* 狼图腾批判 [Critique of *Wolf Totem*], by Long Xingjian 龙行健, 1–8. Shanghai: Xuelin chubanshe, 2007.

Li, Qingxi. "Searching for Roots: Anticultural Return in Mainland Chinese Literature of the 1980s." In *Chinese Literature in the Second Half of a Modern Century: A Critical Survey*, edited by Pang-yuan Chi and David Der-wei Wang, 110–23. Bloomington: Indiana University Press, 2000.

Li, Tuo, and Yan Lianke. "*Enjoyment*: A New Experiment on Surrealistic Writing." In *Debating the Socialist Legacy and Capitalist Globalization in China*, edited by Xueping Zhong and Ban Wang, 151–62. New York: Palgrave Macmillan, 2014.

Li Xuemei 李雪梅. "Dikang yiwang de yizhong fangshi – Lun Hu Fayun de xiaoshuo chuangzuo" 抵抗遗忘的一种方式－论胡发云的小说创作 [A way of resisting forgetting – On Hu Fayun's fiction]. *Dangdai wentan* 当代文坛, no. 3 (2015): 56–61. https://doi.org/10.19290/j.cnki.51-1076/i.2015.03.011.

Li Yunlei 李云雷. "The Rise of 'Subaltern Literature' in the Twenty-first Century: A Speech at the Utopia Forum." In *Debating the Socialist Legacy and Capitalist Globalization in China*, edited by Xueping Zhong and Ban Wang, 165–182. New York: Palgrave Macmillan, 2014.

Li Yunlei 李云雷 and Shi Tianqiang 石天强. "Diceng wenxue: Yizhong xinde wenxue xiangxiang?" 底层文学：一种新的文学想象? [Subaltern literature: A new literary imagination?] *Zhongguo jiyu bao* 中国教育报, 10 October 2008, 4. https://doi.org/10.28102/n.cnki.ncjyb.2008.003299.

Liang Qichao 梁启超. "Yi yin zhengzhi xiaoshuo xu" 译印政治小说序 [Preface to a series of translations of political fiction]. *Qing yi bao* 清议报, 11 November 1898. Reprinted in *Liang Qichao quanji* 梁启超全集 [The complete works of Liang Qichao], edited by Zhang Pinxing 张品兴, 1:172. Beijing: Beijing chubanshe, 1999.

Lin Xi 林希. "'Lang wenhua' yu shikuai zhexue" "狼文化"与市侩哲学 ["Wolf culture" and philistine philosophy]. *Guangming ribao* 光明日报, 15 April 2005, 12.

– "Zai lun lang wenhua yu shikuai zhexue" 再论狼文化与市侩哲学 [Another discussion of wolf culture and philistine philosophy]. *Tianjin ribao* 天津日报, 16 October 2005, 4.

Lin, Yü-sheng. *The Crisis of Chinese Consciousness: Radical Antitraditionalism in the May Fourth Era*. Madison: University of Wisconsin Press, 1979.

Ling Cangzhou 凌沧州. "Nacui youling yu Faxisi bingdu – *Lang tuteng* pipan" 纳粹幽灵与法西斯病毒 – 《狼图腾》批判 [Nazi ghost and fascist virus – Criticism of *Wolf Totem*]. In *Duxuesheng GE yuedu* 大学生GE 阅读 [GE (General Education) readings for college students], edited by Wang Xiaochun 王晓纯 and Wu Wanyun 吴晚云, 5:243–52. Beijing: Communication University of China Press, 2011.

Link, E. Perry. "Introduction to the Revised Edition." In *The Execution of Major Yin and Other Stories from the Great Proletarian Cultural Revolution*, by Chen Ruoxi, edited by Howard Goldblatt, xi–xxxii. Bloomington: Indiana University Press, 2004.

– *Mandarin Ducks and Butterflies: Popular Fiction in Early Twentieth-Century Chinese Cities*. Berkley: University of California Press, 1981.

– *The Uses of Literature: Life in the Socialist Chinese Literary System*. Princeton, NJ: Princeton University Press, 2000.

Link, E. Perry, Richard Madsen, and Paul Pickowicz, eds. *Popular China: Unofficial Culture in a Globalizing Society*. Lanham, MD: Rowman & Littlefield, 2002.

– *Unofficial China: Popular Culture and Thought in the People's Republic of China*. Boulder, CO: Westview Press, 1989.

Liu, Binyan. *People or Monsters? And Other Stories and Reportage from China after Mao*. Bloomington: Indiana University Press, 1983.

Liu, Jianmei. "To Join the Commune or Withdraw from It? A Reading of Yan Lianke's *Shouhuo.*" *Modern Chinese Literature and Culture* 19, no. 2 (2007): 1–33. https://www.jstor.org/stable/41490980.

Long Xingjian 龙行健. *Lang tuteng pipan* 狼图腾批判 [Critique of *Wolf Totem*]. Shanghai: Xuelin chubanshe, 2007.

Lovell, Julia. "Preface." In *The Fat Years*, by Chan Koonchung, translated by Michael S. Duke, 9–21. London: Doubleday, 2011.

– "Translator's Afterword." In *I Love Dollars*, by Zhu Wen, translated by Julia Lovell, 229–40. New York: Penguin Books, 2007.

Lu Xun 鲁迅. *The Real Story of Ah-Q and Other Tales of China: The Complete Fiction of Lu Xun.* Translated by Julia Lovell. New York: Penguin Books, 2009.

Lukács, Georg. *Realism in Our Time: Literature and the Class Struggle.* New York: Harper & Row, 1964.

Luqiu, Luwei Rose. "Why Is China's Younger Generation More Pro-Government than the Previous Generation?" *The Asia Dialogue*, 3 February 2020. https://theasiadialogue.com/2020/02/03/why-is-chinas-younger-generation-more-pro-government-than-the-previous-generation.

MacKinnon, Rebecca. *Consent of the Networked: The Worldwide Struggle for Internet Freedom.* New York: Basic Books, 2012.

Mao Zedong 毛泽东. *Quotations from Mao Tse Tung.* Beijing: Foreign Languages Press, 1966, chapter 5. https://www.marxists.org/reference/archive/mao/works/red-book/epi01.htm.

Meisner, Maurice. *Marxism, Maoism, and Utopianism: Eight Essays.* Madison: University of Wisconsin Press, 1982.

Mooney, Paul. "2013: Them and Us; Koon-chung Chan's 'Shengshi,'" *South China Morning Post*, 7 February 2010. https://www.scmp.com/article/705721/2013-them-and-us.

Moore, Nicole, ed. *Censorship and the Limits of the Literary: A Global View.* New York: Bloomsbury, 2015.

Ng, Lynda. "China's Elusive Truths: Censorship, Value and Literature in the Internet Age." In *Censorship and the Limits of the Literary: A Global View*, edited by Nicole Moore, 234–46. New York: Bloomsbury, 2015.

Oakeshott, Michael. *Rationalism in Politics.* London: Methuen, 1962.

O'Brien, Kevin J., ed. *Popular Protest in China.* Cambridge, MA: Harvard University Press, 2008.

Orwell, George. *Nineteen Eighty-Four.* New York: Penguin, 1949.

Osnos, Evans. "The Age of Complacency?" *The New Yorker*, online edition, 28 July 2010. https://www.newyorker.com/news/evan-osnos/the-age-of-complacency.

Pei, Minxin. "China: From Tiananmen to Neo-Stalinism." *Journal of Democracy* 31, no. 1 (2020): 148–57. https://doi.org/10.1353/jod.2020.0012.

– *China's Crony Capitalism: The Dynamics of Regime Decay*. Cambridge, MA: Harvard University Press, 2016.

– *China's Trapped Transition: The Limits of Developmental Autocracy*. Cambridge, MA: Harvard University Press, 2006.

Perry, Elizabeth J. "Growing Pains: Challenges for a Rising China." *Dædalus: Journal of the American Academy of Arts and Sciences* 143, no. 2 (Spring 2014): 5–13. https://doi.org/10.1162/DAED_a_00268.

Plaks, Andrew, ed. *Chinese Narrative: Critical and Theoretical Essays*. Princeton, NJ: Princeton University Press, 1977.

Pusey, James Reeve. *China and Charles Darwin*. Cambridge, MA: Harvard University Press, 1983.

– *Lu Xun and Evolution*. New York: SUNY, 1998.

Qian Liqun 钱理群. "Xunzhao shiqu de 'daxue jingshen'" 寻找失去的"大学精神" [In search of the lost "university spirit"]. In *Zhi qingnian pengyou: Qian Liqun yanjiang shuxin ji* 致青年朋友：钱理群演讲书信集 [For young friends: A collection of lectures and letters of Qian Liqun], 31–40. Beijing: Zhongguo changan chubanshe, 2008.

Reynolds, Douglas. *China 1891–1912: The Xinzheng Revolution and Japan*. Cambridge, MA: Harvard University Press, 1993.

Roberts, Margaret E. *Censored: Distraction and Diversion inside China's Great Firewall*. Princeton, NJ: Princeton University Press, 2018.

Rojas, Carlos. "Speaking from the Margins: Yan Lianke." In *The Columbia Companion to Modern Chinese Literature*, edited by Kirk A. Denton, 431–5. New York: Columbia University Press, 2016.

– "Time Out of Joint: Commemoration and Commodification of Socialism in Yan Lianke's *Lenin's Kisses*." In *Red Legacies in China: Cultural Afterlives of the Communist Revolution*, edited by Jie Li and Enhua Zhang, 297–317. Cambridge, MA: Harvard University Asia Center, 2016.

– "Translator's Note." In *Lenin's Kisses*, by Yan Lianke, translated by Carlos Rojas, v–ix. New York: Grove, 2012.

Schwartz, Benjamin I. *In Search of Wealth and Power: Yen Fu and the West*. Cambridge, MA: Harvard University Press, 1964.

– *The World of Thought in Ancient China*. Cambridge, MA: Harvard University Press, 1985.

Shao Yanjun 邵燕君. "'Xie shenme' he 'zenme xie' – tan 'diceng wenxue' de kunjing jianji dui 'chun wenxue' de fansi" "写什么" 和 "怎么写" – 谈"底层文学" 的困境兼及对 " 纯文学" 的反思 ["What to write" and "how to write" – A discussion of the predicament of "subaltern literature" and a reflection on "pure literature"]. *Yangzijiang pinglun* 扬子江评论, no. 1 (2006): 1–5.

Shu Chong 舒崇. "Quanru Zhongguo – du Hu Fayun de xiaoshuo *Ruyan@sars.come*" 犬儒中国 – 读胡发云小说 《如焉@sars.come》 [Cynical China – A reading of Hu Fuyun's novel *Such Is This World@sars.come*]. *Beijing zhi chun*

北京之春, February 2008. http://beijingspring.com/bj2/2008/380
/2008128123835.htm.

Solomon, Robert. *The Passions*. Garden City, NY: Anchor Press, 1976.

Song, Weijie. "Yan Lianke's Mythorealist Representation of the Country and
the City." *Modern Fiction Studies* 62, no. 4 (2016): 644–58. https://doi
.org/10.1353/mfs.2016.0057.

Stockmann, Daniela. *Media Commercialization and Authoritarian Rule in China*.
Cambridge: Cambridge University Press, 2013.

Sudworth, John. "Counting the Cost of China's Left-behind Children." *BBC
News*, Beijing, 12 April 2016. https://www.bbc.com/news/world-asia
-china-35994481.

Sun Liping 孙立平. "Quanli shiheng, liangji shehui yu hezuozhuyi xianzheng
tizhi" 权利失衡、两极社会与合作主义宪政体制 [Unbalance of rights, a
polarized society, and cooperative constitutional system]. *Zhanliie yu guanli*
战略与管理, no. 1 (2004): 1–6.

– "Women zai kaishi mianlin yige duanlie de shehui?" 我们在开始面临一个断
裂的社会? [Are we starting to face a society falling apart?]. *Zhanliie yu guanli*
战略与管理, no. 2 (2002): 9–15.

Sun Yu 孙郁. "Cong *shouhuo* dao *rixi* – zai tan Yan Lianke de shenshi zhuyi"
从《受活》到《日熄》– 再谈阎连科的神实主义 [From *Lenin's Kisses* to *The Day
the Sun Died* –Another discussion on Yan Lianke's mythorealism]. *Dangdai
zuojia pinglun* 当代作家评论, no. 2 (2017): 5–11. https://doi.org/10.16551
/j.cnki.1002-1809.2017.02.001.

– "Yan Lianke's 'shenshi zhuyi'" 阎连科的 "神实主义" [Yan Lianke's "mythorealism"]. *Dangdai zuojia pinglun* 当代作家评论, no. 5 (2013): 13–21. https://
doi.org/10.16551/j.cnki.1002-1809.2013.05.008.

Tam, Fiona. "Foxconn Factories Are Labor Camps: Report." *South China
Morning Post*, 11 October 2010. https://www.scmp.com/article/727143
/foxconn-factories-are-labour-camps-report.

Tang Xin 唐欣. *Quanli jingxiang: jin ershinian guanchang xiaoshuo yanjiu* 权力镜
像：近二十年官场小说研究 [Mirror of power: A study of officialdom fiction
in the past two decades]. Beijing: shehui kexue wenxian chubanshe, 2006.

Tao Dongfeng 陶东风. "*Shouhuo*: dangdai Zhongguo zhengzhi yuyan xiaoshuo
de jiezuo" 《受活》：当代中国政治寓言小说的杰作 [*Lenin's Kisses*: A masterpiece of contemporary Chinese novels of political fable]. *Dangdai zuojia
pinglun* 当代作家评论, no. 5 (2013): 31–45. https://doi.org/10.16551
/j.cnki.1002-1809.2013.05.010.

Thornber, Karen. "Chinese Literary Landscapes of SARS and HIV/AIDS: On Hu-
bris and Vulnerability." *Forum for World Literature Studies* 6, no. 3 (2014): 430–42.

Van de Ven, Hans. "The Emergence of the Text-Centered Party." In *New
Perspectives on the Chinese Communist Revolution*, edited by Tony Saich
and Hans van de Ven, 5–32. London: Routledge, 1995.

Wang, Ban. "Geopolitics, Moral Reform, and Poetic Internationalism: Liang Qichao's *The Future of New China*." *Frontiers of Literary Studies in China* 6, no. 1 (2012): 2–18. https://doi.org/10.3868/s010-001-012-0002-1.

Wang, Ban, and Jie Lu. "Introduction: China and New Left Critique." In *China and New Left Visions: Political and Cultural Interventions*, edited by Ban Wang and Jie Lu, ix–xvi. Lanham, MD: Lexington Books, 2012.

Wang, Chaohua. "Dreamers and Nightmares: Political novels by Wang Lixiong and Chan Koonchung." *Chinese Perspectives*, no. 1 (2015): 23–31. https://doi.org/10.4000/chinaperspectives.6636.

Wang, David Der-wei 王德威. *Fin-de-siècle Splendor: Repressed Modernities of Late Qing Fiction, 1849–1911*. Stanford, CA: Stanford University Press, 1997.

– "Geming shidai de ai yu si – lun Yan Lianke de xiaoshuo" 革命时代的爱与死 – 论阎连科的小说 [Love and death in the revolutionary era – On Yan Lianke's fiction]. *Dangdai zuojia pinglun* 当代作家评论 [Contemporary Writers Review], no. 5 (2007): 25–37. https://doi.org/10.16551/j.cnki .1002-1809.2007.05.003.

Wang, Juan. *Merry Laughter and Angry Curses: The Shanghai Tabloid Press 1897–1911*. Vancouver: UBC Press, 2012.

Wang, Zheng. "National Humiliation, History Education, and the Politics of the Historical Memory: Patriotic Education Campaign in China." *International Studies Quarterly* 52, no. 4 (2008): 783–806. https://doi.org/10.1111 /j.1468-2478.2008.00526.x.

Wasserstrom, Jeffrey. "The Fur Is Flying – Or, There's More than One Way to Skin a Wolf." *The China Beat*, 8 May 2008. http://thechinabeat.blogspot .com/2008/05/fur-is-flyingor-theres-more-than-one.html.

Whitehead, Kate. "Author Chan Koonchung Finds Humor in Tibet-China Dynamic." *South China Morning Post*, 25 May 2014. https://www.scmp .com/lifestyle/books/article/1518626/author-chan-koonchung-finds -humour-china-tibet-dynamic.

Wu, Jin. "Rural Woman 'Beaten to Death' in Police Station." *China.org.cn*, 31 December 2014. http://www.china.org.cn/china/2014-12/31/content _34449109.htm.

Wu Xinjun 吴新军. "Xin guanchang xiaoshuo qiuci" 新官场小说求疵 [Criticism of new officialdom fiction]. *Dangdai wentan* 当代文坛, no. 5 (2003): 55–6.

Xie, Haiyan. "An Age without Classics and the Writer's Anxiety: An Interview with Yan Lianke." MCLC Resource Center, Ohio State University, May 2020. https://u.osu.edu/mclc/2020/05/01/interview-with-yan-lianke.

Xu, Ben. "Chinese Populist Nationalism: Its Intellectual Politics and Moral Dilemma." *Representations* 76, no. 1 (Fall 2001): 120–40. https://doi.org /10.1525/rep.2001.76.1.120.

Xu Jilin 许纪霖. "The Fate of an Enlightenment: Twenty Years in the Chinese Intellectual Sphere (1978–98)." In *Chinese Intellectuals between State and*

Market, edited by Edward Gu and Merle Goldman, 183–203. London: Routledge, 2004.

– "Qimeng de ziwo wajie" 启蒙的自我瓦解 [The self-disintegration of an enlightenment]. *Ershiyi shiji* 二十一世纪, no. 4 (2005): 4–16.

Xu Jilin, Liu Qing, Luo Gang, and Xue Yi. "In Search of a 'Third Way': A Conversation regarding 'Liberalism' and the 'New Left Wing.'" Translated by Geremie Barmé. In *Voicing Concerns: Contemporary Chinese Critical Inquiry*, edited by Gloria Davis, 199–226. Lanham, MD: Rowman & Littlefield Publishers, 2001.

Yan Jianbin 阎建滨. "Shengcun zhi lei yu xinyang zhi qing – lun xinxieshi de jingshen jiazhi quxiang" 生存之累与信仰之轻–论新写实的精神价值取向 [Heaviness of existence and lightness of belief – On the spiritual and value orientation of new realism]. *Dangdai wentan* 当代文坛, no. 4 (1992): 41–4. 10. https://doi.org/10.19290/j.cnki.51-1076/i.1992.04.023.

Yan Lianke 阎连科. *Dream of Ding Village*. Translated by Cindy Carter. New York: Grove, 2009.

– *Faxian xiaoshuo* 发现小说 [Discovering fiction]. Tianjin: Nankai University Press, 2011.

– *The Four Books*. Translated by Carlos Rojas. New York: Grove, 2015.

– *Lenin's Kisses*. Translated by Carlos Rojas. New York: Grove, 2012.

– *Serve the People*. Translated by Julia Lovell. New York: Grove, 2007.

Yan, Yunxiang. *The Individualization of Chinese Society*. Oxford: Berg, 2009.

Yang, Guobin. *The Power of the Internet in China: Citizen Activism Online*. New York: Columbia University Press, 2009.

Yang Jisheng. *Tombstone: The Great Chinese Famine 1958–1962*. Translated by Stacy Mosher and Guo Jian. Edited by Edward Friedman, Guo Jian, and Stacy Mosher. New York: Farrar, Straus, and Giroux, 2012. Kindle edition.

Ye Yixiang 叶奕翔. "Changxiaoshu yu minzu zhuyi" 畅销书与民族主义 [Bestsellers and nationalism]. *Zhongguo chuban* 中国出版, no. 10 (2013): 13–16.

Yeh, Catherine Vance. *The Chinese Political Novel: Migration of a World Genre*. Cambridge, MA: Harvard University Press, 2015.

Yu Hua 余华. *Brothers*. Translated by Eileen Cheng-Yin Chow and Carlos Rojas. New York: Anchor Books, 2009.

– "How My Books Have Roamed the World." Translated by Helen Wang. MCLC Resource Center, Ohio State University, 21 September 2017. https://u.osu.edu/mclc/2017/10/18/yu-hua-how-my-books-have-roamed-the-world.

– *The Seventh Day*. Translated by Allan H. Barr. New York: Pantheon Books, 2015.

– *Women shenghuo zai juda de chaju li* 我们生活在巨大的差距里 [We are living in a huge chasm]. Beijing: shiyue wenyi chubanshe, 2015.

– *Yu Hua zuopin ji* 余华作品集 [A collection of Yu Hua's works], vol. 2. Beijing: Zhonggsuo shehui kexue chubanshe, 1994.

Yu, Pauline, and Theodore Huters. "The Imaginative Universe of Chinese Literature." In *Chinese Aesthetics and Literature: A Reader*, edited by Corinne H. Dale, 1–13. Albany, NY: SUNY Press, 2004.

Yu, Zhansui. *Chinese Avant-garde Fiction: Quest for Historicity and Transcendent Truth.* Amherst, NY: Cambria Press, 2017.

– "Questioning the 'Chinese Model of Development': A Critical Reading of *Shengshi: Zhongguo 2013.*" *The China Beat*, 28 August 2010. https://digital commons.unl.edu/chinabeatarchive/721/.

Yuan Weishi 袁伟时. "Xiandaihua yu lishi jiaokeshu" 现代化与历史教科书 [Modernization and historical textbooks]. *Bingdian zhoukan* 冰点周刊, 11 January 2006, 1.

Yun Yetui 云也退. "Gu Bin: *Lang tuteng* rang women xiangqi Hitler shidai" 顾彬:《狼图腾》让我们想起希特勒时代 [Kubin: *Wolf Totem* reminds us of the Hitler era]. http://www.sinologystudy.com/html/yjxl/183.html.

Zarrow, Peter. *Anarchism and Chinese Political Culture.* New York: Columbia University Press, 1990.

Zhang Hong 张闳. "*Lang tuteng*: 'wenhua shifuzhe' de jingshen shengyan" 《狼图腾》:"文化食腐者"的精神盛宴 [*Wolf Totem*: A spiritual feast for "cultural scavengers"]. *Wenhui dushu zhoubao*文汇读书周报, 25 January 2006, 5.

– "Zhongshan lang de zhanyu – Ping *Lang tuteng* ji qita" 中山狼的谵语—评 《狼图腾》及其它 [Delirious talks about the Zhongshan wolf – On *Wolf Totem* and others]. *ai sixiang* 爱思想. http://www.aisixiang.com/data /12347.html.

Zhang, Longxi. "The Utopian Vision: East and West." In *Thinking Utopia: Steps into Other Worlds*, edited by Jörn Rüsen, Michael Fehr, and Thomas W. Rieger, 207–29. New York: Berghahn Books, 2005.

Zhang, Xudong. *Chinese Modernism in the Era of Reforms: Cultural Fever, Avant-garde Fiction, and the New Chinese Cinema.* Durham, NC: Duke University Press, 1997.

Zhang, Yongle. "No Forbidden Zone in Reading? *Dushu* and the Chinese Intelligentsia." *New Left Review*, no. 49 (January–February 2008): 5–26. https:// newleftreview.org/issues/ii49/articles/yongle-zhang-no-forbidden-zone -in-reading.

Zhao Dongmei 赵冬梅. "You diceng wenxue de ji ge guanjianci tanqi" 由底层 文学的几个关键词谈起 [A discussion starting from the keywords in subaltern literature]. *Nandu xuekan*南都学刊, no. 3 (May 2011): 47–51. https://doi .org/10.16700/j.cnki.cn41-1157/c.2011.03.008.

Zhao, Henry. *The Uneasy Narrator: Chinese Fiction from the Traditional to the Modern.* Oxford: Oxford University Press, 1995.

Zhao, Suisheng. *A Nation-State by Construction: Dynamics of Modern Chinese Nationalism*. Stanford, CA: Stanford University Press, 2004.

– "A State-Led Nationalism: The Patriotic Education Campaign in Post-Tiananmen China." *Communist and Post-Communist Studies* 31, no. 3 (1998): 287–302. https://doi.org/10.1016/S0967-067X(98)00009-9.

Zhong, Xueping. "*Internationale* as Specter: *Na'er*, 'Subaltern Literature,' and Contemporary China's 'Left Bank.'" In *China and New Left Visions: Political and Cultural Interventions*, edited by Ban Wang and Jie Lu, 102–20. Lanham, MD: Lexington Books, 2012.

Zhu Xueqin 朱学勤. "Wusi yilai de liangge jingshen 'binzao'" 五四以来的两个精神 "病灶" [Two spiritual "diseases" since the May Fourth onwards]. *Zhanlüe yu guanli* 战略与管理, no. 4 (1999): 62–6.

Zhuangzi. *The Complete Works of Chuang Tzu*. Translated by Burton Watson. New York: Columbia University Press, 1968.

Index